Crimes and Criminals
of 17th Century Britain

Crimes and Criminals of 17th Century Britain

Daniel J. Codd

PEN & SWORD HISTORY

First published in Great Britain in 2018 by
PEN AND SWORD HISTORY
an imprint of
Pen and Sword Books Ltd
47 Church Street
Barnsley
South Yorkshire S70 2AS

ISBN 978 1 52670 608 9

Printed and bound in England
by CPI Group (UK) Ltd, Croydon, CR0 4YY

Typeset in Times New Roman by
CHIC GRAPHICS

Pen & Sword Books Ltd incorporates the imprints of Pen & Sword
Archaeology, Atlas, Aviation, Battleground, Discovery,
Family History, History, Maritime, Military, Naval, Politics, Railways,
Select, Social History, Transport, True Crime, Claymore Press,
Frontline Books, Leo Cooper, Praetorian Press, Remember When,
Seaforth Publishing and Wharncliffe.

For a complete list of Pen and Sword titles please contact
Pen and Sword Books Limited
47 Church Street, Barnsley, South Yorkshire, S70 2AS, England
E-mail: enquiries@pen-and-sword.co.uk
Website: www.pen-and-sword.co.uk

Contents

Acknowledgements

Many thanks must go to the following: Pamela Bromley (Archivist), Warwick Castle, for her help, re the murder of Sir Fulke Greville (the images of King Charles I, the Earl of Strafford and Cromwell's death mask are also used courtesy of Warwick Castle); Val Bush (Collections), Warwick Castle, for her help with Cromwell's death mask; the administrators of St Mary's Church, Horncastle (20 December 2015), for allowing me access and telling me about Sir Ingram Hopton; Michael Ridge, Visitor Services Assistant, Norfolk Museums Service, for help with Sir John Heydon's mummified hand – sadly taken off public display at Norwich Castle Museum at the time of writing, for conservation work; Reverend Kenneth Cross of St Andrew's Church, Old Cleeve, and Jeanne Webb, for their help with the murder of Mr Tratte; A. Cameron (Marketing Executive), Madame Tussauds, London NW1 5LR, for permission to use the images entitled *'The traitors were barbarically executed in public'* and *'A pirate's end at 'Execution Dock'* (see https://www.madametussauds.co.uk/london/en/ for more information on Madame Tussauds and its Chamber of Horrors); Maureen Mathias at Pembroke Castle, for permission to use the images entitled *'A violent street fight between Royalists and revolutionary Parliamentarians'* and *'Poyer was sentenced to death by a perverse lottery'* (see http://pembroke-castle.co.uk/ for more information on the Civil War Exhibition); Alice Marshall, Events Assistant, Doddington Hall, for allowing me to reproduce the image of the 1666 sea battle off the Scillies; Chetham's Library, Long Millgate, Manchester, for permission to use the image of King Charles I, after his head was sewn back on (this portrait, by an unknown artist, is currently on loan to Turton Tower, Lancs); Geoff Stone, for his invaluable help with Glencoe images; Nicola Stone for her help with proof-reading, attention to detail, endless encouragement and limitless enthusiasm; Mr and Mrs Kerton, of Higher Farm, Chilton Cantelo, for allowing me to see and photograph Theophilus Brome's head;

ACKNOWLEDGEMENTS

Owen Teather, for his help with the image of Rochester Cathedral; Josie Mae Skinner, for her help with the image of Marazion, Cornwall.

In particular, I would like to thank Tim Hitchcock, Robert Shoemaker, Clive Emsley, Sharon Howard and Jamie MacLaughlin, et al., The Old Bailey Proceedings Online, 1674-1913 (www.oldbaileyonline.org), for allowing me to cite additional information from the website in the following instances:

Law, Order and Punishment (Kelsey, the Newgate murderer): 13 June 1690, version 7.2, accessed 10 November 2015
Robbers, Bandits and Highwaymen (Golden Farmer): 22 December 1690, Version 7.2, accessed 23 September 2015
Horror Piled upon Horror (Charles Pyne): 11 July 1694, Version 7.2, accessed 19 August 2015
'Why Talk to Me of Heaven?': 10 & 19 December 1679, version 7.2, accessed 10 November 2015
'The Bloody Midwife' (Mary Compton): 23 October 1693, Version 7.2, accessed 23 September 2015

Finally I would like to thank everyone for the kindness and generosity I have been shown at scores of libraries, museums and tourist attractions, large and small, across Britain throughout this journey of exploration, for within such places lie the half-hidden origins of books like this.

All photographs are the copyright of the author, except where otherwise stated above. All other illustrations are in the public domain.

Chapter 1

A Brief Portrait of a Time
Barely Familiar

Anyone wishing to understand what life was like during a particular era would benefit from studying the great criminal cases of the age, for these are among the best indicators as to the social, religious, political and economic doctrines that many ordinary people of the time lived their lives by, day in and day out. Their hopes, fears, beliefs, superstitions, standards of education, past-times, even their levels of compassion; all are laid bare throughout such proceedings. And so a look at crimes and criminals of the seventeenth century forces the reader to consider a curious and revealing version of today's Britain.

On the one hand, the era's populated areas may seem semi-familiar places, through the thousands of yet-existing villages, certain city street-names and a great many landmark buildings nationally, some of which were actually established in the seventeenth century, such as the rebuilt St Paul's Cathedral in London. Despite this, however, virtually all of the taverns, buildings and miscellaneous locations observed herein where heinous crimes were committed no longer exist in the form they did at the time.

This observation even applies to rural locations. Typifying this (natural) advance of history, for our purposes, is Primrose Hill, on the northern side of Regent's Park – site of one of the most infamous acts of the 1680s. This is the place where Sir Edmund Berry Godfrey's garrotted corpse was left in a ditch, with a sword rammed through it; yet one would be hard pushed to realise it these days. In the time we are to consider, Primrose Hill was detached from the City of London by greater than two miles, formerly part of a great chase appropriated by King Henry VIII, and in the late seventeenth century still distant enough to be called the countryside. Nowadays, it has been swallowed up and incorporated into Greater London and while yet impressive, the sense of remoteness it must have presented when Sir Edmund's body was dumped here has gone forever. Its manicured grass slopes are criss-crossed with a network of paths that now accommodate all manner of joggers, kite-flyers, dog-walkers, tourists and so on. One has to leave the paths and walk west into the rougher scrubland along the perimeter of (where is now) the Barrow Hill Reservoir to come anywhere near the approximate site where, almost 350 years ago, a drama occurred that came to both horrify and disgrace London. These days, it is difficult to even sense the echo of Sir Edmund's killing, let alone imagine easily what this place must have been like when his corpse was deposited here.

Over the last four centuries, London has been redeveloped over and over, all the time spreading and growing to such immense proportions that it has now swallowed up every village, pasture and town within a 600-square mile radius. Like other cities, it was still walled at the start of the seventeenth century. Simultaneously, other British towns and villages have risen, fallen or become incorporated; ancestral homes have been rebuilt or fallen into decay; great road complexes and railway lines have opened up formerly-inaccessible parts. In some places the very landscape itself has changed

The approximate site on Primrose Hill where Godfrey's body was dumped, as it is today.

through extensive deforestation, drainage, quarrying or cultivation. The point I am making is this; in most cases, the near-exact locations of the century's horrific crimes can be reliably gauged, lending a strange familiarity to them. But it is important for the reader to consider that we are reaching so far back in history that if one could somehow be transported to the period and the locations then very few places would be immediately recognisable to us.

Equally worth remarking upon are the conspicuously different attitudes of the era. Readers today will no doubt observe a great many generational similarities in evidence, but the fact remains that this was a Britain entirely different socially, economically, religiously and politically to the one we know now. Some motives are all too familiar, it is true, avarice being the most recognisable, as well as sexual jealousy, vengeance and ruthless ambition. But others are not so readily accessible. Murderous purges upon witchcraft occurred, for instance, as well as treasonable assassination attempts, which were not uncommon. And although tyranny among the rulers of the time was recognised and understood as an abhorrent crime, it stopped few in power from practising it.

Throughout the 1600s, many people of position and rank were unjustly manoeuvred to their deaths politically through partisan legal systems that knew no mercy. The seventeenth century was a time when the names of the guilty and the innocent can sometimes appear confusingly blurred, since those with judicial power repeatedly became truly guilty of worse crimes than those they sentenced. This barbarity arose from the fact that to set an example, or undermine a perceived national threat, the authorities in control often felt it necessary to come down all too harshly; this was, after all, a time when domestic politics and personal convictions were worth going to war against your own countrymen for. Therefore, time and again, in obliterating a long-term threat, those in power tyrannically proved themselves willing to commit judicial abuses upon people who were seen to be guilty of heresy, sedition or rebellion.

LAW, ORDER AND PUNISHMENT
Although the highest in the land might be manoeuvred to their deaths through the courts if the political situation demanded it, others of position and rank could be cleared of the most violent of crimes if they pleaded their clergy.

This was one of the more curious loopholes in the law throughout most of the century, owing its origins to an ancient claim to be tried in an ecclesiastical, or church, court under canon law. However, by the seventeenth century this had morphed out of all recognition into a statute allowing partial clemency for first-time offenders accused of certain crimes, including, sometimes, murder and manslaughter. A pardon was often facilitated by a reading test, promises of good conduct in the future, financial compensation, and, no doubt, bribery in certain instances. This, quite naturally, gave the educated and wealthy a certain scope to manoeuvre their freedom, even at the expense of a conviction, while those less privileged generally paid with their necks.

A rare exception to the rule, starkly highlighting the attitudes of the time, was the case of Mervyn Tuchet, 2nd Earl of Castlehaven. On 25 April 1631, the earl was arraigned at the King's Bench Bar and found guilty of rape and sodomy, and after being convicted by a jury of his peers he was executed on Tower Hill the following 14 May. This case is a complicated one. The rape was found to have been committed upon his wife Anne, Countess of Castlehaven, by one of the earl's minions, but abetted by the earl himself. However, the sodomy charges related to (apparently consensual) relations with his page, Lawrence Fitz-Patrick. Castlehaven denied it all, declaring during his trial that he had:

> '*a wife who desires a younger husband, and a son that is gaping after my [Wiltshire] estate, and has the Devil and wicked servants to assist their maliee, in indeavouring to take away my life wrongfully.*'

This was not without foundation, since everyone stood to benefit from the earl's death, and one is left with the feeling that whatever the earl's persuasion, allegations of homosexual behaviour were levelled merely to encourage his conviction. The intolerance of the time is clear: for during the trial it was observed that 'sodomy' – and by association homosexuality – was

> '*of so abominable and vile a nature it is a crime not to be named among Christians; and by the Law of God, as well as the antient laws of England, it was punish'd with death.*'

Fitz-Patrick, the page, and Giles Browning, Countess Anne's rapist, were also executed.

In this case, the earl was accused by his wife, but there is a prevalent suggestion that legal suits against peers were rarely contested successfully by commoners. This is perfectly illustrated by the case of the monstrous Earl of Pembroke during Charles II's reign (1660-1685), whose time is correctly regarded as one when the aristocracy killed almost in contempt of the law, aware that the status quo was likely to see them acquitted. At best, manslaughter convictions were obtained, but unless the crime was proved undeniably premeditated, as opposed to happening in the heat of the moment, acquittals usually still followed. The fact that almost everyone was armed, and murders through loss of control occurred as an inevitable by-product of this, seems to have been something beyond the comprehension of the times.

Such gross leniency for killing a fellow human being appears all the more perverse given the vast array of other offences which were considered prosecutable – many of which today seem Draconian. Throughout the 1600s at York for instance, men and women were arraigned for such crimes as witchcraft; uttering seditious words; defrauding the revenue; sacrilege; libellous words; cattle-stealing; clipping money and melting the clippings into new coins; being an imposter; being a Catholic priest; speaking against the Church of England; spreading false news; not accepting the oath of allegiance; holding a conventicle; publishing unlawful books; scandalous conduct… and so on. As this suggests, commoners generally fared far worse than riotous city gentlemen or the higher landed gentry in the shires. Poorly educated and often desperate, common people frequently felt the full force of the law.

The police forces of the day were often poorly-paid, corrupt, superstitious men appointed by local justices of the peace, or magistrates. Known as parish constables or peace officers, they would be responsible for the administration of justice. Coroners had the power to pronounce someone guilty at an inquest, even before a trial had occurred, whilst paid informers and thief-takers, often with a criminal background themselves, frequently emerged offering their services to catch other criminals.

Assize courts were a feature of the era, occurring periodically in county towns across the land. These were presided over by travelling circuit judges, principally from London, who might spend several days overseeing the trials of various imprisoned suspects before moving on somewhere else. Judges, particularly in Middlesex (that is, London and the wider area), commonly handed out death sentences without pity at mass assizes; multiple executions were not uncommon. In fact, many ordinary trials were mere exercises. One witness became sufficient to convict an accused murderer, burglar, incendiary, highwayman, or a whole gang of 'clippers and coiners' (forgers and coin-debasers) all the way to the gallows. In some cases of high treason, the testimony of a single witness was illegally judged to be enough if the situation dictated that some rebellious gentleman needed to be made an example of.

5

CRIMES AND CRIMINALS OF 17TH CENTURY BRITAIN

Localised civil disorder was quelled by raised militias, or trained bands as they were sometimes called, with shooting melees and force often sufficing as a means of pacification. Simultaneously, huge sections of the regular governmental army were ill-disciplined men, so brutalised by conflicts at home and abroad that they often inflicted great violence on the helpless communities where they were billeted as they moved about the country.

It is well-known that at the start of the seventeenth century, certain medieval tortures were still utilised by the authorities. The average prisoner might expect to be deprived of his reason, starved by desensitised gaolers, beaten or chained, whereas those more stubborn were 'pressed' (crushed) with boards and rocks if they refused to talk, or else stretched on the rack. Corruptly, however, those who had money were allowed many indulgences. The barbaric punishment for treason – infamously hanging, drawing and quartering – was still enforced, although the 'hanging' part began to give way to decapitation by an axeman. Simultaneously, women convicted of murdering their husbands were publicly burnt, the crime being classed as one of petty treason because the law decreed their status was subordinate in the relationship.

Halifax had a guillotine-like contraption for executing felons. It was last used in 1650, on a linen thief called Wilkinson and a horse rustler called Mitchell. Engraving by Wenzel Hollar, reproduced in The Picture Magazine. (Mary Evans Picture Library)

A BRIEF PORTRAIT OF A TIME BARELY FAMILIAR

One of the principal punishments inflicted on the common male murderer however, was 'gibbeting', which is worth briefly observing. By the end of the seventeenth century, many countryside views across the nation in general had become spoiled by the grim and sinister sight of a rotting human carcass encased in a metal cage that hung from a wooden beam, or sturdy oak. This was a practice followed throughout the seventeenth century, occurring post-execution and known as gibbeting, with the gibbet frequently being placed as near as possible to the location of the encased subject's crime. This ghoulish punishment was also known as 'hanging in chains' and afterwards the corpse of the offender might be seen suspended by the roadside for years, perhaps even decades – sometimes until the body presented nothing more than a wind-bleached skeleton and the original circumstances of the crime had become long forgotten. Occasionally, the gibbet post bore its grisly burden until the beam collapsed in strong winds, or the contraption simply fell apart through the ravages of time. If we are to believe certain stories, some murderers were occasionally even gibbeted alive, dooming them to a death by starvation as they languished in the immovable confines of an iron cage on some lonely weather-beaten heath.

At a handful of locations across Britain, battered gibbets (usually replicas) still stand, providing grim testimony to some forgotten atrocity. In fact, in the mid-twentieth century, the remains of what were believed to be a gibbet post were discovered in Potsford Wood, west of Wickham Market, Suffolk. This is likely to have been the site were Jonas Snell's corpse was suspended in 1699, strapped in irons, following his execution for murder. He had used a sledgehammer to kill his employer, John Bullard, as well as the man's father (also John), at Letheringham Mill. The murders were committed during a robbery, and in attempting to get away at three in the morning, Snell, it seems, got hopelessly lost. When he was imprisoned in Bury Gaol, he is said to have composed a gruesome poem in which he admitted the murders, and many years after his execution birds built their nests in his skull, according to an account of the tradition in the *Ipswich Journal* of 18 April 1885. Be that as it may, a cracked plaque is now attached to the crumbling post, declaring:

> *'Remains of Potsford Gibbet. In use at the end of the 17th century. Last known hanging April 14th 1699. (Jonah Snell).'*

Gibbeting does not seem to have had quite the desired effect, despite the greater threat it carried – that of denying the condemned criminal a Christian burial. For when this gruesome post-mortem fate was combined with that of

The corpse of servant George Atkins hung from the Caxton Gibbet, Cambridgeshire; he had murdered three members of the Foster family at Monksfield in 1671. Fleeing after the crime, Atkins remained absent for many years, but was ultimately recognised in a local tavern after returning.

a sure execution, it frequently served only to encourage the criminal to murder his victim in order to avoid being identified in the future. Nor was the threat of being cut to pieces and anatomised on a surgeon's table after hanging enough to stem the surge in banditry that developed as the century drew out.

Those who were not executed faced the living Hell of one of England's disgusting prisons. Of these, perhaps it is Newgate that remains the most infamous; this monstrous fortification loomed on the corner of Newgate Street and Old Bailey, adjacent to the then much smaller criminal court appertaining to the City of London and the wider county of Middlesex. Although Newgate was pulled down in 1904, its reputation as a maelstrom of disease, violence and anarchy has enshrined it in London folklore. In the seventeenth century, libellers, forgers, nonconforming clergymen and gentleman traitors were housed with murderers, pirates, highwaymen and fire-raisers. All levels and types of criminal were imprisoned there and certain snippets of data recorded by the diarist Narcissus Luttrell in the early 1690s provide valuable insights into the Hell-hole it presented to the world by the century's end.

For example, on 22 December 1690 he wrote how a woman had been executed at Newgate for setting the prison on fire; on 8 January 1692, another fire took hold during a foiled breakout by some prisoners. That same night, a highwayman named Robinson died 'of the feaver' as he languished in Newgate – Robinson had been arrested in the Temple by the officers of Newgate on the afternoon of 28 December, having 'killed a porter, and wounded one mortally'. Luttrell also noted the execution in Newgate Street on 13 June 1690 of 'the man who killed the underkeeper at Newgate'. This case concerned a young prisoner named Thomas Kelsey, who on 21 April that year, had taken part in a revolt at the gaol. The mutineers had vowed to raise a 'bloody flag of defiance', and the underkeeper, Henry Goodman, had been stabbed between the ribs during the incident. Kelsey was, naturally, already incarcerated in Newgate when he committed this murder, so his actions were nothing less than suicidal. He was aged just 20 when he was hanged in the road near the gaol.

Site of the Tyburn gallows today.

The terrible conditions of Newgate were hardly unique. James Raine, a Victorian chronicler of the depositions at York Castle, observed:

'It is impossible to speak in terms of too strong reprobation of the state of the Northern prisons in the seventeenth century. They were dens of iniquity and horror, in which men and women herded together indiscriminately. The dungeons of the Inquisition themselves were scarcely worse. Some of them had no light and no ventilation; several of them were partly under water whenever there was a flood! The number of prisoners who died in gaol during this century is positively startling...'

Whenever there was a want of an executioner, a condemned criminal might be reprieved if he accepted the odious office. At York alone it is reckoned that between five and twenty people were executed annually there between 1650 and 1670. At Tyburn, London's great triangular gallows near what is today the junction of Marble Arch and Edgware Road, an equivalent number might be launched to their deaths at a single sitting.

SOCIETY AND VIOLENCE

Behind all the political and economic stresses that agitated the general desperation, it can also be said that something else is observable in the attitudes of the time. Put simply, violence appears to have been astonishingly normal to the people of the seventeenth century. With brutality conspicuous at all levels of everyday society, the threat of lethal punishment by the law was perhaps not the horrifying extremity it might seem nowadays. In fact, most considered the lives of others thoughtlessly cheap. Pity, it may be remarked upon, seems to have been a strange and valuable emotion on all sides and at all levels.

The reasons behind this mind-set could be debated endlessly; they are very complex. During and after the civil wars (1642-1651), it is as though no one knew any different, and the land must have become awash with men who had seen such carnage that they were almost desensitised to it. To the succeeding two generations (who knew their fathers and grandfathers may have killed to achieve a purpose), demanding satisfaction through violence became compulsory following even the most trivial of arguments. Subsequently, in higher circles, as duelling became ever more fashionable, an almost ridiculous blindness to the outcomes of violent actions, especially when in a state of rage or intoxication, seems to have become a point of personal honour in many instances.

Of course, the high murder rate was aggravated by the fact that surgery was much less sophisticated, meaning that some injuries now survivable were then fatal. But without digressing too much, sometimes the levels of violence employed were so mindlessly casual that one can only suppose the people of the time lived in a naturally brutalising, and brutalised, society. Living under barbarous criminal laws that were executed with intentional disregard for the finer sensibilities of human nature, the people of the seventeenth century can be said to have been educated to honour cruel discipline as wholesome discipline; to regard with complacency all suffering from which they were exempt; and to consider benevolence and compassion as sentimental weaknesses. It was a time when gentlemen caned their manservants, ladies beat their maid-servants, fathers horsewhipped their sons, mothers chastised their grown daughters, tradesmen and artisans beat their apprentices and teachers flogged their pupils with repulsive severity.

The worst examples of these excesses make for difficult reading. On 14 September 1699, for example, a schoolmaster called Robert Carmichael was tried before the High Court of Justiciary in Edinburgh for the murder of one of his pupils, John Douglas, son of William Douglas of Dornock. After bolting the door of the school-house in Moffat, Carmichael had ordered two other boys to restrain young Douglas before he thrashed him mercilessly for a prolonged period of time. He also beat the boy violently around the head. Finally, he struck his victim so forcefully between the shoulder-blades with the butt-end of his whip that it caused the child's death. Realising he had committed murder, Carmichael attempted to escape, but was caught; despite the objections of the victim's father, the schoolmaster was convicted only of manslaughter on 13 November. He was sentenced to be whipped in Edinburgh's Lawn-market, as well as at the cross and the Fountain-well, before being imprisoned until he could find security (raise money enough) to leave Scotland, never to return.

What is truly astonishing about this is that Carmichael's actions stemmed from pure revenge; having learned the boy was to be removed from his school, he simply resolved to do the poor child harm.

Everyone lashed out. And when the law was seen to flog lesser convicts through the best streets and most fashionable squares of any town, we can surmise that ordinary people sometimes found themselves compelled to vigorously emulate the example. Even educated people routinely beat their servants. The writing of Samuel Pepys, a Member of Parliament and Chief Secretary to the Admiralty, famous for his diaries and correspondence, reinforces how astonishingly normal violence was, for on 1 December 1660 he observed how he himself had been forced to beat his own maid that morning because certain items had not been prepared adequately. Administering this punishment left the diarist 'vexed'.

The seventeenth century was a truly hazardous time to be a British citizen. But it did at least help shape – albeit violently – the democratic direction the nation was heading in politically and socially. At the very least, in studying the state of society then, we can now see how far we have advanced in our approach to law and order.

REPORTING CRIME

Throughout the 1600s, information on a great many crimes and murders came the way of the London public via media other than newspapers; the famed *London Gazette*, as well as a tiny number of provincial news-sheets, did not begin to emerge until the second half of the century. Much news came in the form of pamphlets, chapbooks and even printed ballads, some of it either alluringly sensationalist or else misreporting rumour as fact. Such pamphlets were usually luridly titled so as to draw the reader's interest. Consider, for example: *Three Inhuman Murthers committed by one Bloudy Person, upon his Father, his Mother and his Wife, at Cank* [Cannock] *in Staffordshire, and the manner how he acted this Bloody Tragedy. Together with his Examination, Confession, Condemnation and Execution, 1675.* We are told the prisoner refused to plead at Stafford Assizes and so was sentenced to be pressed to death by way of a board placed on his chest which was loaded with heavy weights. The pamphlet's frontispiece actually depicted the murderer being crushed in this manner for the titillation of its readership.

Many of the era's chapbooks bear a dubious stamp of unreliability, to researchers today. There can be a journalistic, made-for-the-playhouse feel about them, due in large part to the moralistic lecturing and evidence of crowd-pleasing supernatural intervention they incorporated into the text. Not only that, but some cannot be independently corroborated by even the smallest snippet of data from elsewhere and we are often left guessing to what extent these were based on fact. After all, with large sections of the day's media completely ungoverned, there was plenty of room for speculation to be reported as fact.

But these are not the only sources of information concerning the era that are available to us. In many ways, the most telling data nowadays can be gleaned from contemporary diary entries jotted down by the likes of Samuel Pepys and Narcissus Luttrell.

Personal correspondence shared between the educated gentry also provides valuable insights. For example, the Northamptonshire Record Office retains a letter from a Mr Kent of Brackley to Mr Thomas Chare of Bridgewater House in London, dated 31 March 1626, in which a murder is referenced as having lately occurred near the former town, a place in Northamptonshire. The matter concerned a man called Webb, who had collected various debts due to him in order that he might pay his own rent and have some funds left over for the Brailes Fair. Unfortunately, according to Mr Kent, Webb had been murdered the previous Sunday and his body left at Halse, near Brackley, in a position suggesting his attacker, or attackers, had staged it as though a suicide.

Little more is easily discoverable concerning this matter, so the fact that it was rescued at all from becoming lost entirely, is a circumstance we must be thankful for, despite the frustrating lack of detail. In fact, certain cases are so intriguing precisely because we know so little. Some are snippets of events almost lost to history, and the mind cannot help but speculate upon what other data could have become lost forever were it not for the diligence of local writers compiling folklore, perhaps greater than a century-and-a-half after the event. This circumstance certainly accounts for many seventeenth century crimes having foggy, confused or anecdotal details, like the story of the notorious Doone family.

At the time, to pursue a career in what might loosely be called journalism was sometimes tantamount to declaring one's own political or religious affiliations. This often led to abuse, imprisonment or even murderous assault. The clergyman, pamphleteer and political writer Samuel Johnson is just one example; he was active in promoting the exclusion of King James II from the throne and became marked for persecution as soon as that prince came to power in 1685. The pretext for his punishment was his publication of a rallying cry to all Protestants in the army (James being a Catholic), for which he was sentenced to be degraded from the priesthood, fined, pilloried and whipped from Newgate to Tyburn. King James allegedly declared that, since Johnson had the spirit of a martyr, it was only fit he suffer like one. Following his publication of *The Abrogation [removal] of King James* in 1692, Johnson suffered an attempted assassination. Seven men broke into his London house in Bond Street, Mayfair, where they found him in bed with his wife. Setting about him with swords and clubs, they raged against him for the book he had written. Johnson was badly wounded in a number of places and fortunate not to have been killed; however, he recovered and lived until 1703.

In many ways, this illustrates the seventeenth century perfectly – any viewpoint, be it a political one, a libellous one, a religious one, a drunken one, or simply an unguarded one brought with it the threat of violent attack from some quarter if expressed warmly enough.

Prior to 1752, when Britain did away with the Julian Calendar, the New Year officially started on 25 March. For the purposes of this work, the years certain events occurred have been standardised accordingly so as to conform to our current Gregorian Calendar. When the calendars changed in 1752, eleven days were lost, however, and therefore many of the day dates cited in this work conform to the old style Julian Calendar. In fact, most day dates can be considered old style, as much of this work has been drawn from the contemporary literature of the era, with the specific dates not being adjusted in the retelling. It is also important to consider that this book has been written from an English perspective; although the state of law and order in Scotland and Wales is also frequently referenced; the politics of the century have made such inclusion a necessity, since one cannot fully understand England in these times without considering what was happening with regards its immediate British neighbours.

Such was the revolutionary nature of the British people throughout the seventeenth century that certain spectacular crimes of the day are still celebrated now. Numerous crimes transcended the sphere of mere *cause celebres* to become national scandals, even national emergencies – the massacre of Glen Fruin, the Gunpowder Plot, the assassination of Archbishop Sharp, Colonel Blood's attempt on the Crown Jewels, the murder of Sir Thomas Overbury, the murder of Sir Edmund Berry Godfrey, the abuses of Matthew Hopkins and the Glencoe Massacre among them. Overshadowing it all mid-century was the execution of a king, Charles I, considered in some quarters a crime so monstrous as to be barely comprehensible, as the title of Richard Perrinchief's 1676 biography *The Royal Martyr* implies.

Plots and tumult reigned during the first part of the seventeenth century, whilst the 1640s and 1650s were set against a backdrop of uncontrollable civil war and counter-insurgency. This then, is British history as seen through the great criminal cases of the period: a 100-year story evidencing the most appalling crimes, unjust massacres, and violent excesses imaginable.

In the words of John Evelyn, the writer and diarist, remarking upon the complete degeneration of law and order as the century drew out: 'Such horrible robberies and murders were committed, as had not been known in all the nation.'

Chapter 2

Royals and Rulers

When the British Isles entered the seventeenth century, few could have foreseen the calamitous detour the nation would take upon its road to the democratic process. At the beginning of the 1600s, English society very much retained distinct Tudor echoes: Queen Elizabeth I was yet the reigning monarch and William Shakespeare was still alive. Meanwhile, Scotland, under King James VI, was a wholly independent nation.

However, change was imminent. Queen Elizabeth was by this time an old woman, a relic from another dynastic era, and – since she had no children – destined to be the last of her line; while in Scotland, James was fated to be the final king of that northern nation alone and become the first ruler of 'Great Brittaine', as he would style himself. This was due to the nearness of his relationship to Elizabeth; his mother, Mary, Queen of Scots, had been Elizabeth's first cousin once removed.

However, both royal houses – Tudor in England, and Stuart in Scotland – were yet threatened by conspiracy, intrigue and drama. In fact, in the immediate years of the new century there were still dangerous incidents that illustrate just how unpredictably volatile the politics of the day could be for the reigning monarch.

In Scotland, there occurred the famous Gowrie Conspiracy, the circumstances of which were never wholly explained to everyone's satisfaction. Briefly, in the autumn of 1600 news spread throughout Scotland that John Ruthven, 3rd Earl of Gowrie, and his younger brother Alexander had been slain at Gowrie House, Perth, by King James's attendants during an attempt to murder, or seize, the visiting monarch. Many circumstances were afterwards related by the king that appeared so strange and improbable that for a long time the whole story was discredited, and the stabbing of the two young men attributed to the personal or political animosity of the royal house. But eight years later (after a form of celebration had been observed on each 5 August for his majesty's providential escape) certain discoveries were made in the repositories of a humble participator in the plot, Robert Logan of Restalrig, which allegedly confirmed James's version in many respects – without, however, providing any particular clarity on the intentions of Ruthven.

In England, there occurred a threat to Queen Elizabeth of an entirely different character. This was a failed coup attempt headed by Robert Devereux, 2nd Earl of Essex, a politically-ambitious former Lord Lieutenant of Ireland who knew he was falling out of the queen's favour dramatically. The seeds of his destruction had been sown in 1599 when the earl was aged around 34, after he was charged by the Palace of Westminster's Star Chamber court with maladministration and abandoning his command in Ireland against the express orders of the queen. That March, Essex had failed to crush a rebellion by the Earl of Tyrone, reaching such conciliatory terms with Tyrone that government spies began to suspect the two had accommodated their differences by discussing the possibility of taking an army back to England to seize the throne. Essex had panicked and hastily returned to England, bursting into the queen's chamber at Nonsuch Palace, near Ewell in Surrey, while she was undressed, where he attempted to better explain his position.

After this disgraceful invasion of the queen's privacy, Essex was placed under house arrest while his conduct was examined. However, it was decided not to try him, and subsequently he was granted his freedom, against the desires of Elizabeth's chief minister, Sir Robert Cecil.

By October 1600, Essex had been manoeuvred close to financial ruination when his monopoly on imports of sweet wines was removed. This is generally considered to be the significant aggravating factor that forced Essex's subsequent actions. According to a 1666 chronology of remarkable British events, *The Faithful Annalist: Or the Epitome of the English History*:

'Sunday the eighth of February [1601], about ten of the clock in the fore-noon Robert Deveraux Earl of Essex assisted by divers noble men and gentlemen in warlick [warlike] manner, entered the City of London at the Temple Bar, crying for the queen, till they came to Fanchurch-street, and there entered the house of Master Thomas Smith, one of the sheriffs of London, who finding himself not master of his own house, by means of the strength the earl brought with him, conveighed himself out of a back door to the lord mayor of the city; whereupon the earl and his troop turned into Grace-street, and there perceiving himself and his assistants to be proclaimed traytors, also the citizens to be raised in arms against him, he with his followers wandring up and down the City, towards Ludgate would have passed through, which was closed against him.'

Essex had gambled on many Londoners swarming to his cause, but the streets remained quiet and support for his coup began to melt away. At Ludgate, the rebels' way was barred by a party of troops under Sir John Leveson. Despite his waning circumstances, Essex ordered a charge, and there occurred a brief, violent collision during which a shot was fired through the earl's hat. A relative of his, Sir Christopher Blount, was badly wounded in the face and apprehended; and a young gentleman named Tracey – said to be a favourite of the earl – was fatally wounded. Two or three London citizens were also killed in the skirmish.

Then:

'He was forced to return to Queen Hith, and from thence by water to his own house in the Strand, which he fortified; but understanding that great ordnance were brought to beat down his house, he yielded and was conveyed to the Tower about midnight.'

On 19 February, Essex and his principal co-conspirator Henry Wriothesley, 3rd Earl of Southampton, were arraigned at Westminster and convicted of treason. Thanks to the intervention of Sir Robert Cecil, Southampton's death sentence was commuted to one of imprisonment, but the Earl of Essex was beheaded in the Tower of London on the morning of 25 February. It is reported that the executioner was brutally beaten by supporters of the earl, forcing the sheriffs of London to rescue him from being murdered. The following month, Sir Gelly Merrick and Henry Cuffe were hanged and quartered at Tyburn for 'being actors with the Earl of Essex', while Sir Charles Danvers and Sir Christopher Blount were beheaded on a scaffold on Tower Hill that had been erected especially for their decapitation.

Before his death, Essex remarked to Cecil, 'I must confess to you that I am the greatest, the most vilest, and the most unthankful traitor that ever has been in the land.' But this violent episode was just one threat among many that the royals and rulers of the seventeenth century faced. From open insurrection to treasonous plots and revolution, none escaped the times unscathed; some may even have been quietly assassinated.

THE PLOT THAT ENTERED LEGEND

When Elizabeth I died childless, there was something of a grim irony in the succession. Elizabeth was succeeded by King James VI of Scotland, who thus also claimed the thrones of Ireland and England by her death. In 1587, Elizabeth had had James's mother, Mary, Queen of Scots, beheaded at

There is a tradition that the Gunpowder Plot was first discussed in this tiny upper room atop the tower of Stoke Dry's church, Rutland.

Fotheringhay in Northamptonshire for plotting against her life and conspiring to seize the English throne – the irony being that the House of Stuart replaced the House of Tudor by default anyway following Elizabeth's passing in 1603.

Although England and Scotland yet remained separate nations, their union was greatly strengthened by James's accession. Dubbed 'the wisest fool in Christendom', his reign was memorable for many reasons, not least his judicial murder of Sir Walter Raleigh to appease Spain (see Chapter 12). However, one incident above all has endured through history to this day thanks to its spectacular aspirations. This was, of course, the famous Gunpowder Plot. It is an event so familiar that there is little need to go too deeply into its details, much having already been written on the matter.

At its heart the Gunpowder Plot was a treasonable conspiracy, which came within sight of its accomplishment, among certain provincial Catholic gentlemen to assassinate the newly-enthroned King James I. Simultaneously, they planned to raise an armed rebellion in the English Midlands and install

18

Princess Elizabeth, James's daughter, as a replacement Catholic monarch; James's own affiliation was to the Church of Scotland, and later the Church of England.

The plot was devised by Robert Catesby, an Oxford-educated Catholic who had taken part in Essex's abortive rebellion but been captured and fined. However, after months of preparation the conspiracy was betrayed when a Catholic peer, William Parker, Lord Monteagle, received an anonymous warning, possibly sent by Francis Tresham, his brother-in-law and one of the plotters. He in turn told Sir Robert Cecil, 1st Earl of Salisbury and Secretary of State, following which an urgent hunt began for the traitors. These included Guy 'Guido' Fawkes, the 35-year-old son of a Yorkshire notary and a Catholic convert – whose name has come to symbolise the plot. This is because of the manner in which he was caught. Fawkes was apprehended in the early hours of 5 November 1605 in the very act of preparing to blow up Westminster Palace during the opening of the next Parliamentary session using barrels of gunpowder smuggled underneath the House of Lords.

A number of other principal conspirators were subsequently besieged in Holbeche, the house of a supporter in Staffordshire between Stourbridge and Wombourne. On the morning of 8 November 1605, the house was stormed by the men of Richard Walsh, the Sheriff of Worcestershire, whereupon four conspirators – including Catesby – died in a lethal skirmish.

Francis Tresham, the plot's likely betrayer, died in the Tower of London on 23 December 1605, prior to his trial, of a urinary infection. The surviving conspirators were ordered by Sir Edward Coke, the Attorney General, to suffer the punishment of hanging, drawing and quartering, on 30 and 31 January 1606.

The executions occurred at two locations – near St Paul's Cathedral and at the Old Palace Yard, Westminster. As is well known, the guilty men were drawn upon hurdles to the places of execution and hanged until they were barely conscious. Next, they were taken down, castrated and disembowelled while still alive, before their bodies were chopped into four pieces – 'quartered'. Many family members of the condemned men are supposed to have been present among the multitude that turned out to watch this brutal spectacle, and afterwards the heads and other body parts of the cadavers were displayed publicly throughout the kingdom. Guy Fawkes thwarted the more gruesome part of his punishment by ascending the ladder to the noose too high, meaning that the rope was adjusted round his throat incorrectly. This miscalculation allowed him to throw himself bodily off the ladder and break his neck. Nonetheless, his corpse was still mutilated post-mortem so that his

The traitors were barbarically executed in public. (Courtesy of Madame Tussauds, London)

quarters could be displayed in a public manner as a warning to other potential traitors.

There is little doubt that the explosion, had it occurred, would have massacred the assembled bishops, peers and dignitaries, as well as killing the monarch himself and obliterating the Palace of Westminster. Executions of other conspirators peripheral to the plot followed. But very soon the government repression began to resemble something approaching judicial slaughter; a matter addressed when the Gunpowder Plot is revisited in Chapter 12.

'THERE NEVER WAS KNOWN... SO MANY GREAT MEN DIE WITH SUSPICION OF POISON'

Less well known than the Gunpowder Plot are the accusations that there was a system of secret poisoning said to have plagued King James's government.

During James's reign, the nation was beset by an event considered a national tragedy, the death on 6 November 1612 of the monarch's son and successor, Henry Frederick Stuart, Prince of Wales. Henry was aged 19 when he died following a short illness that began immediately after a dinner at

Whitehall with his father on 25 October. The young man had been extremely popular; the Earl of Dorset wrote somewhat prophetically to a fellow nobleman, 'Our rising sun is set ere scarce he had shone, and all our glory lies buried.' Prince Henry had entertained an entirely different class of men at his court to his father, and relations between the two had become strained. King James was heard to exclaim, 'Will he bury me alive?' while Henry, who formed a friendship with the imprisoned Sir Walter Raleigh, reportedly said only a monarch such as his father would 'keep such a bird in such a cage'.

Prince Henry and the king's then-favourite – the courtier Robert Carr – also regarded each other with barely-concealed enmity. Therefore, when the popular, athletic and handsome young prince died there were immediate rumours that he had been poisoned. On 12 December, it was announced the prince's death was brought about not by poison but 'the pestilential fever of the season'. Sir Simon d'Ewes, a near-contemporary antiquary and politician, nonetheless recorded the belief that Prince Henry was commonly suspected to have been poisoned by contaminated grapes he partook of during a game of tennis. If we are to believe Bishop Gilbert Burnet, whose *History of My Own Time* references the matter, Henry's younger brother Charles, later King Charles I, certainly believed these rumours. Burnet observed:

> *'Colonel Titus assured me that he had [heard] from King Charles the first's own mouth, that he was well assured that he [Henry] was poisoned by the Earl of Somerset's means.'*

Carr was later made 1st Earl of Somerset. However, a credible motive for engineering the young prince's death remains somewhat vague, although Burnet suggested the youth's open reluctance to enter into an arranged marriage to a European Catholic princess may have been an aggravating factor.

Rumours of foul play stubbornly refused to abate, resurfacing three years later when an infamous scandal rocked King James's court.

Robert Carr was a former equerry to Lord Hay, one of James's bosom companions. An accident introduced him to the king, who taught him Latin, played familiar tricks with him, gave him large grants of land and created him Earl of Rochester. Being uneducated, Carr made Sir Thomas Overbury, an able and accomplished scholar, his secretary. He then fell in love with Frances Howard, the daughter of the Earl of Suffolk. But since she was already the wife of the 3rd Earl of Essex, Carr proposed she should sue for a divorce so that they could be married. Sir Thomas Overbury violently opposed their union, upon which the Howard faction manipulated the king into jailing him in the Tower of London; the lady, in her fury, offered a gentleman £1,000 if he would take Overbury's life in a duel. This was refused, but Frances's animosity continued to simmer.

When Frances's divorce was brought to court, the king personally interfered on behalf of Carr to help settle the matter for his favourite. The separation was granted and the parties were afterwards married in the royal chapel, Carr having first been created Earl of Somerset.

In the meantime, an event had happened that considerably aggravated the king's unpopularity and ultimately left an indelible stain on his character and his reign. On the day before the divorce, 15 September 1613, Sir Thomas Overbury died in the Tower at about five o'clock in the morning, aged around 32. When found, he was laid in his bed and Sir John Lidcott, his brother-in-law, begged to be granted the body to give it a decent burial, but this was refused. Officially, the cause of Overbury's death was an infectious disease and according to the register of the Chapel in the Tower he was hastily – and secretly – buried. There were immediate suspicions he had been poisoned to death, but the matter was passed over with little investigation. A Coroner's Inquest observed how his body 'was worn to skin and bone' and 'many yellow blisters' were found upon him. He was interred between three and four in the afternoon on the day he died.

The circumstances were so suspicious a public inquiry was instituted two years later when Carr's influence was on the decline. The result of this was that the earl and his heavily-pregnant countess were committed to the Tower on a charge of having poisoned Overbury. He was aged around 28 at this time, she 25.

Four people who they had enlisted in their plot were first tried, condemned and executed in 1615. The following year the countess was arraigned before a court of peers, whereupon she pleaded guilty and was sentenced to death; the following day, Carr received the same sentence. Within a few days, James – who had called upon God to curse him if he pardoned anyone involved – pardoned both of the criminals. It is said that the earl reacted so indignantly at the proceedings that it became self-evident he was master of some secret which would have highly prejudiced the king's honour were it to be divulged. Whatever the secret was, the conduct of James in these dark transactions implied he was terribly afraid of any exposure that Carr might make (or fabricate); and after commuting the sentence of death imposed on the earl and his wife, he privately renewed his correspondence with the former.

It appears that Overbury's primary opposition to Carr marrying Frances Howard was the benefits the union would bring to the pro-Catholic Howard faction. A rare near-contemporary book, Fulke Greville's *The Five Years of King James*, explained that the imprisoned Overbury was gradually poisoned with a gut-destroying combination of aqua-fortis, white arsenic, mercury, powder of diamonds, *lapis cortilus*, great spiders and cantharides – these latter bugs and beetles believed to be the most deadly, and 'to be sure to hit his complexion.' The poisoning was perpetrated with fiendish perseverance and it was suggested in evidence that arsenic had always been mixed with Overbury's salt. The plot almost claimed a second life, when the wife of Langton, a warder, having partaken of some broth left by Overbury, suddenly fell very ill.

The four other people convicted of the murder were: Sir Gervase Elwes, the Lieutenant of the Tower at the time; Richard Weston, a warder who had been entrusted with the immediate custody of Overbury; James Franklin, an apothecary of Tower Hill; and Mrs Anne Turner, Frances's confidante. Dr Franklin's professional reputation as an apothecary was thoroughly destroyed during the trial. Apart from his involvement in the Overbury affair, to which he confessed, he was also accused of blasphemy, conjuring, the poisoning of his own wife and the murder of the nurse-maid who tended her during the last days of her sickness. Franklin denied to the end he was responsible for his wife's murder, but admitted culpability in the death of the sick-nurse, who died after taking a powder at his direction.

Although history has largely forgotten her, one of the most interesting people in this cast of characters was Mrs Turner. This lady acted as Frances's waiting-woman, living with her both as a companion and a dependant. She was the widow of a physician, but his death had left her in much straightened circumstances, owing to their extravagant and riotous lifestyle; therefore, she was only too eager to assist her mistress in wicked scheming that might secure both their futures. Mrs Turner was executed on 15 November 1615 at Tyburn, her death exciting immense interest among the London populace. She was reportedly a woman of great beauty, who had much affected the fashion of her time. Her sentence was to be 'hang'd at Tiburn in her yellow Tiffiny Ruff and Cuff, she being the first inventor and wearer of that horrid garb'. The 'Ruff and Cuff' was a fashion item stiffened with yellow starch, and in passing sentence upon her Lord Chief Justice Coke told her that she had been guilty of all the seven deadly sins. Mrs Turner reportedly dressed herself with deliberate flair for her execution; her face was highly rouged, and she wore a 'cobweb-lawn ruff', yellow starched.

Her hands were bound with a black silk ribbon, as she desired, and immediately before her death the executioners pulled a black veil over her face. The cart in which she stood was then driven away, and Mrs Turner was left hanging from a noose. After a short while she stopped struggling, and no motion was perceived in her. On account of her penitent death she was allowed a burial in St Martin's Church-yard.

The case is interesting since it indelibly tarnished King James's court with a reputation for debauchery, conspiracy and self promotion that failed to stop at assassination. Indeed, the matter of Prince Henry's strange death was resurrected during the Earl of Somerset's trial, for Coke commented, 'God knows what went with the good prince, Henry, but I have heard something.' It is also noteworthy that these were just two among several suspicious deaths among the upper echelons of society during King James's reign. Fulke Greville's *The Five Years of King James* elaborated:

'There never was known, in so short a time, so many great men die with suspicion of poison and witchcraft; for first there was my Lord Treasurer, [then] the Prince, the Lord Harrington and his son, Sir Thomas Overbury, Northampton… which are no less than six, within three years-and-a-half.'

'My Lord Treasurer' is a reference to Sir Robert Cecil. His health failing, Cecil had died in the house of a Mr Daniell in St Margaret's, Marlborough, during a journey from Bath to the capital in 1612.

At the conclusion of King James's reign, rumours like this still circulated, as in the case of James Hamilton, 2nd Marquess of Hamilton, who died at Whitehall on 2 March 1625. A letter from John Chamberlain of London to Reverend Joseph Mead of Christ's College two days later reported:

'On Thursday, between one and two in the morning, died the Lord Marquis of Hamilton, not without suspicion of poison, as is said, because after death his whole body, with neck, face, and head, swelled exceedingly, and was strangely spotted.'

Some have suggested that the prime agent behind the alleged state poisonings in the English capital was Dr Theodore Mayerne, King James's physician and former physician to Henry IV of France. Mayerne came to England in 1606 and despite his high reputation he was observed at the time to have made mistakes so elementary in the care of some upper-class patients that it seemed as if he was almost deliberately mismanaging their health. He had been present during the fatal decline of both Prince Henry and Sir Thomas Overbury, among others. His remedies, far from being progressive, often mirrored something more akin to a witch's cauldron and when he died in Chelsea on 15 March 1655, aged 82, his end was in itself not without suspicion of poisoning. He had apparently foretold as much whilst drinking moderately at a tavern in the Strand with friends not long before a fatal cup of bad wine was allegedly delivered to him. He was buried in the church of St Martin-in-the-Fields.

THE DEATHS OF JAMES AND HIS SON, CHARLES

When King James I died aged 58 at Theobalds House, two miles west of Cheshunt in Hertfordshire, on 27 March 1625, poisoning was also suspected. The king's physician, Dr Eglisham, was forced to exile himself overseas for some opinions he passed about the manner of his majesty's death and thereafter forced to live in Brussels for many years. Whilst in exile, he published a book alleging James had been poisoned, giving a particular account of the king's sickness and laying his death upon George Villiers, 1st Duke of Buckingham, the monarch's new favourite, as well as implicating the duke's mother. Buckingham had been at the king's bedside during his final decline, and Eglisham cited as Buckingham's motive the desire to consolidate his family's power under the next-in-line to the throne, Charles, over whom he also exerted considerable influence.

The king had initially developed a fever following a hunt in Theobalds Park on 5 March and, according to Dr Eglisham, this presented Buckingham with an unexpected opportunity to manoeuvre the king out of the picture. Eglisham alleged that the duke had ordered a servant, Baker, to travel to the home of a Dr Remington in Essex, to procure a famed plaister (medicinal treatment). This treatment was subsequently applied, together with a posset, or spiced alcoholic milk beverage, to the ailing king at Theobalds – although in fact it made the royal patient's downturn that much greater. When Eglisham had cause to be in Essex himself a week after the king's death, he arranged a meeting with Dr Remington – whereupon it became abundantly clear that the medicines the latter had supplied were of a different type to that actually used on the king at Theobalds. In short, Eglisham suggested that Buckingham had taken receipt of the doctor's plaister and posset, but either replaced or contaminated them. When they were applied, they served only to accelerate the king's pre-existing sickness, rather than aid his recovery.

As with the death of Prince Henry thirteen years earlier, the crime remains unproven and generally considered unlikely, but interesting nonetheless in that accusations of regicide should be so publicly voiced at the time.

King James's accomplishments as monarch – such as his attempt to harmonise the national church through a new translation of the Bible, his attempts to supress tobacco smoking and his reputation as a peacemaker – were counterbalanced by many negatives. Vulgar, slovenly, emotional and addicted to hunting, he also relied on the advice of inefficient favourites, mainly young men, at the expense of forming a working relationship with the House of Commons, the lower house of the Parliament of England. The last of these were traits regretfully inherited by his son and heir, King Charles I.

Charles's reign was overshadowed by the descent of England into civil war. The implosion of the nation, which also drew in Scotland, Ireland and Wales, is without doubt a story more suited to other works concerning the seventeenth century; suffice to say that a great portion of Charles's reign was set against a backdrop of general discontent, political schisms, power struggles, and, finally, all-out warfare between Royalist forces and Parliament. His execution in 1649 marks the last time an English king was premeditatedly put to death by his subjects (see Chapter 12 for more on this).

THE USURPATION OF THE THRONE

The period that immediately followed Charles I's death has become known as the Interregnum. The front-runner to rule England may have been the commander-in-chief of the Parliamentary army, Sir Thomas Fairfax. But his abhorrence over King Charles's execution, and his refusal to go to war in Scotland – where the powerful Presbyterian Covenanters were helping Charles's son, also Charles, consolidate his position – elevated Fairfax's theoretical subordinate Oliver Cromwell to power.

Cromwell was aged 49 and the latent MP for Cambridge when he helped organise the king's death. A public servant, radical politician and God-fearing Puritan, he was moreover a brilliant military strategist who had streamlined his army and was not afraid to fight as well as command. He created the famous New Model Army and his military prowess, when combined with his great skill as an orator in Parliament, made him the front-runner to rule England – a land he had helped make kingless by his ruthlessness. In 1653 Cromwell – assisted by a file of musketeers – dissolved the 'Rump' Parliament at Westminster during a dramatic coup; in December, he was further elevated to the dictatorial position of Lord Protector. By this time, he

Portrait of King Charles I. (after an original by Sir Anthony van Dyck, courtesy of Warwick Castle)

had also forced the would-be King Charles II (Charles I's son) to flee for his life into exile after the Battle of Worcester in 1651.

Oliver Cromwell could be considered extremely lucky, given the number of times he escaped a violent death. For example, on 11 October 1643,

The Winceby Boulder, on Slash Lane, marks the perimeter of a field where Cromwell was nearly killed during the Battle of Winceby.

Colonel Cromwell, as he was then, narrowly avoided being killed by the battle-axe of Sir Ingram Hopton during a lethal fight with Royalists at Winceby, on the southern edge of the Lincolnshire Wolds. According to a Horncastle tradition, Sir Ingram's head was struck clean off in the melee, whereupon his horse bolted the field of conflict and carried the headless cadaver of its master all the way back to the town.

Then, on 12 July 1645, during the siege of Bridgwater in Somerset, Cromwell – by now a lieutenant general – escaped death again. The attempt occurred when he approached the walls of the town in order to view it for storming purposes. Mrs Christabel Wyndham – the wife of the Royalist commander there, and reputedly a very beautiful woman – fired a musket at Cromwell from a distance in an attempt to assassinate him, although she in fact killed an officer standing by his side. Afterwards, tradition says she sent a messenger to Cromwell and outraged him further by asking if he had received her love token. Fairfax chivalrously allowed her and other ladies to leave the castle before the bombardment began. Whether this is true or not is uncertain, although a contemporary news pamphlet, *Mercurius Civicus*, implies that there was an early instance of shooting at the besiegers.

Following the Battle of Dunbar on 3 September 1650, during which Parliamentary forces annihilated the Royalists under the Covenanter General

David Leslie, Cromwell marched directly to Edinburgh, and then onwards to Glasgow, where he escaped another attempt on his life. Glaswegian citizens had calculated on his entering the town by the Townhead Road, past the old castle of Glasgow, a place which had formerly served as the palace of the archbishops. By 1650, this building (upon the site of the current Glasgow Royal Infirmary) had fallen into disuse, and therefore its vaults were hastily filled with gunpowder and other destructive materials. A trail of gunpowder was carefully laid and it was resolved to ignite it at the precise moment Cromwell's entourage passed by – in the hope of enveloping them all in one common ruin which may very well have severely damaged Glasgow Cathedral as well. However, Cromwell is believed to have been forewarned that some act of sabotage was likely. At the last moment, he diverted his course, approaching the town from a different direction – avoiding both the castle and the explosion that would have consumed him.

The abatement of the civil wars, and Cromwell's elevation, brought no respite from direct attacks on his person. In 1654, several gentlemen were apprehended and charged with a conspiracy to assassinate the Lord Protector as he was travelling to Hampton Court on 13 May, before seizing the guards, the Tower of London and the magazines in support of the exiled Charles II. The plot was discovered in advance by government agents and Cromwell's entourage frustrated the attack by travelling to Hampton Court on the river. The plotters were arrested eight days later prior to a second attempt that was to involve a surprise assault upon Whitehall Chapel. The chief plotters were Mr Somerset Fox, Mr John Gerard and Mr Peter Vowel; these were tried by a High Court of Justice, with Fox confessing much of what he was charged with and earning the benefit of a reprieve. However, Gerard was beheaded on Tower Hill, and Vowel was hanged at Charing Cross, both of them denying they were part of a counter-revolutionary plot to murder Cromwell. They died with great magnanimity and resolution, and afterwards others among the conspirators were sentenced to transportation.

In 1657 a former Parliamentarian, Quarter-master Miles Sindercombe, after several aborted attempts at assassination, attempted to set fire to Whitehall with a view to murdering the Protector in the ensuing panic. He was betrayed by his co-conspirators and apprehended, but eluded punishment by dying in confinement on 13 February. Parliament subsequently convened in order to offer its congratulations to Cromwell upon his escape. Although a coroner's jury, at the direction of the Lord Chief Justice, decided that Sindercombe had committed suicide by taking poisoned powder he had somehow procured, it was put about by Royalists and the Levellers alike that

Cromwell had ordered him to be smothered to death whilst he laid in his bed.

Sindercombe had lately become a supporter of the Levellers, broadly a tolerance movement that emerged during the civil wars and was opposed to an absolute dictatorship. He was reportedly hired by a Royalist colonel named Edward Sexby, who readily confessed to numerous intrigues after being followed and arrested by Cromwell's agents. Whilst imprisoned in the Tower and apparently feigning madness, Sexby admitted plotting with the Spanish court and supplying Sindercombe with money. Moreover, he confessed to being the author of an infamous pamphlet then in circulation called *Killing No Murder*, which justified and advocated the assassination of the Protector on the grounds it was a legitimate and necessary homicide. Whether Sexby was the author of this tract is questionable, but his overall guilt in counter-revolutionary plots appeared plain. However, like Sindercombe, he never saw trial: he died on 13 January 1658 during the sixth month of his imprisonment, probably by violence.

There were other assaults. A tall man aborted an attempt to stab Cromwell as his coach passed through a narrow street between Westminster and Whitehall, escaping when challenged by the dictator's entourage; and a plot to kidnap Cromwell at Whitehall and convey him along the Thames was uncovered by Colonel John Hutchinson. In one incident during the war, a Gloucestershire Royalist called Sir Zachary Howard, reduced to highway robbery by the extremities of the fighting, is said to have gained access to Cromwell's chambers at an inn in Chester. He violently beat him, tied him up and robbed him before escaping – refraining from shooting him only because he knew the noise would rouse Cromwell's attendants downstairs. In 1654, Letitia Greenville of Cambridgeshire allegedly fired at Cromwell from a balcony as he passed by on his way to a banquet in the City. A horse was the only casualty, struck by a brace of pistol balls. These last two instances, however, are very likely examples of later Royalist story-telling.

Be that as it may, terror of assassination is said to have perpetually haunted Cromwell's innermost thoughts. He never stirred from his palace without a personally appointed bodyguard; he wore a shirt of chain mail; carried loaded pistols about his person; changed his bedchamber almost nightly; and conducted every journey with as much secrecy and circumspection as would befit a military manoeuvre. Rumoured and actual attempts on his life notwithstanding, the Protector passed away at Whitehall on 3 September 1658, aged 59, following a fatal decline after six months of ill health. So great was England's dependency upon him that even to his final breath many refused to believe that God would allow him to die. In his last hours he was heard to cry out, 'Truly God is great!' from his deathbed, leading some to expect his salvation at the last moment.

Oliver Cromwell fell ill due to – it is believed – a combination of malaria (possibly caught while campaigning in Ireland) and urinary infections. His downturn is reputed to have been further aggravated by a broken heart, for he had previously been forced to sit at the bedside of his beloved daughter Elizabeth whilst she died from a painful illness the very month before. There has been a persistent allegation, however, that Cromwell's physician – Dr George Bates – was at the time mismanaging his health. Bates had formerly been King Charles I's physician when at Oxford, and in later years would serve King Charles II following the Restoration. According to the contemporary writing of

Death mask of Oliver Cromwell. (courtesy of Warwick Castle)

Oxford antiquary Anthony Wood, shortly before Bates himself died *c.*2 June 1668 in London of the French pox, he made an extraordinary deathbed confession. This was to the effect that he had poisoned Oliver Cromwell to death at the behest 'of two that are now bishops… and his majestie was privi to it.'

'UNEASY LIES THE HEAD THAT WEARS THE CROWN'
'His majesty' was King Charles II.

Cromwell's son Richard – a politically inexperienced country gentleman – succeeded his father as Protector, but was overthrown the year following his father's death during an army coup. The so-called Rump Parliament, contemptuously dismissed by Cromwell in 1653, was recalled by the army leaders, but nonetheless the nation began to slide once more into civil conflict. A Royalist counter-insurrection was crushed at Winnington Bridge near Northwich on 19 August 1659, and civil war next threatened between the army and the recalled Rump. In the end, George Monck, the commander of the army in Scotland, returned to London in triumph, dissolving the Rump and establishing a free Parliament – one that admitted many members with Royalist sympathies. Although Monck was a Rump supporter, the clamour from all sides at every level for some form of settled constitution forced his hand.

Among the first acts of the new Parliament, other than to make Monck commander-in-chief of all forces, was a vote for the restoration of the monarchy. Charles II was invited to return to the country and take the thrones of England, Ireland and Scotland. Thus, nine years after his defeat at the Battle of Worcester, following which engagement the monarch-in-waiting had famously hidden in the Boscobel Oak to escape detection, Charles II re-entered London from his European exile. The Restoration caused wild celebrations; the famous diarist Samuel Pepys became so drunk he toppled over.

Charles II's court earned a legendary reputation for sophistication, ostentation and licentiousness. Despite his undoubted charm, however, the new king would not hesitate to judicially eliminate his enemies where the situation demanded it (see Chapter 12). Towards the end of his reign a clamour among Whig politicians over the succession of his brother James, the Catholic Duke of York (Charles II had no legitimate offspring), led to the monarch turning dictator. Donning full regalia, he formally dissolved the House of Commons during a ceremony at Oxford in March 1681.

These were religiously intolerant times. Charles's move precipitated a conspiracy among extremist Whig politicians to assassinate the king and his heir, and place James Scott, 1st Duke of Monmouth – Charles's eldest illegitimate son – on the throne to ensure a Protestant monarchy. The plot was hatched at the Green Ribbon Club in Chancery Lane. To the conspirators' minds the most practical method was to ambush Charles as he travelled with his brother James from Newmarket to London on 1 April 1683 along the road near Rye House in Hoddesdon, Hertfordshire. A cart would be overturned in the road by two men dressed as labourers, halting the king's coach, whereupon a group of men would appear and open fire from the hedges at his majesty, killing him as well as his heir James and the party of Life Guards that accompanied them. Plans were made for the assassins to escape through by-lanes and across nearby fields.

The scheme was thwarted by pure good fortune because the king chose to leave Newmarket eight days sooner than anticipated, thanks to an accidental fire there. A great many men were involved in the attempt, and following the aborted regicide those with less courage or conviction began to betray their comrades, or otherwise emerge as informants. Popular opinion turned against the Whigs and, amid a fever of intrigue, numerous politicians, gentlemen and noblemen were executed, jailed, exiled or otherwise implicated. These included the Duke of Monmouth, who escaped to the Low Countries, and Arthur Capell, 1st Earl of Essex, whose mysterious and violent death is noted in Chapter 12.

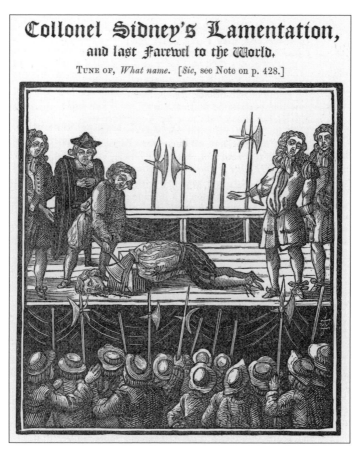

A Rye House plotter, Algernon Sidney, is brutally executed: a woodcut illustration to the Roxburghe Ballads volume 5 part 2. (Mary Evans Picture Library)

Charles II died aged 54 on 6 February 1685 at Whitehall Palace, four days after suffering an apparent stroke. There were immediate suspicions, however, that he had been poisoned. According to the contemporary chronicler of events, Bishop Gilbert Burnet, these sinister concerns were raised by a famous physician named Needham, who was present at the autopsy and observed three mysterious blue spots on the outside of the king's stomach lining. Needham twice requested that the stomach be opened, a request which the appointed surgeons ignored. Furthermore, another eminent physician present, named Lower, was heard to whisper to one surgeon, 'Needham will undo us, calling thus for the stomach to be opened, for he may see they will not do it.' After this, the king's stomach was removed from his body by surgeons using scalpels, denying Dr Needham an opportunity to examine its contents more closely.

The situation around the autopsy seems to have been somewhat chaotic. Two other physicians present entertained their own suspicions that the king's death had been engineered. These were a Frenchman – who observed an injury, mysteriously mortified, upon the shoulder – and a Catholic named Short. Both chose to vocally express their belief that the king had met with foul play.

Short died not long after the autopsy, having partaken of a 'large draught of wormwood wine' at the house of a Catholic patient near the Tower. The latter had specifically sent for him, and before he died, Short told a number of brother physicians he believed he had been poisoned for talking too freely about the king's death.

As to the motive for engineering the monarch's death, Catholic supporters of his brother James, the Duke of York, were held responsible. According to a later deposition from the lips of the Catholic Duchess of Portsmouth, she had been privy to the knowledge that Charles II was within a day of exiling his brother via an Act of Parliament. The duchess had been sworn to secrecy at the time, but nonetheless let this information slip to her Confessor, who – she supposed – had sent the news urgently to pro-James sympathisers eager to see the Duke of York upon the throne. This came to light in 1699, when the duchess told it to Mr Henly of Hampshire, who in turn passed it to Bishop Burnet in November 1709. Burnet then recorded it for posterity in his posthumously-published memoirs, *History of My Own Time*.

That Charles II was poisoned on this basis seems unlikely, given that he apparently converted to Catholicism the evening before he died. However, it is unclear whether this was at his own direction, given his fatal decline.

Charles was succeeded as king by his brother James, the Duke of York, whose reign was as short as it was unpopular. He had barely been on the throne four months before he faced a violent insurrection by his nephew, Monmouth, who had been encouraged by advocates of the Bill of Exclusion during his father's reign, to believe that one day he might be king in his own right. The rebellion was unsuccessful and brutally supressed by James II's regime. Subsequent perceived oppression of Protestants nationwide engineered a revolution against the new king. This was also precipitated by news that on 10 June 1688, the queen had given birth to a son, also James, at St James's Palace, who was immediately baptised a Catholic, ensuring a Catholic succession.

The frantic celebrations that followed the release of seven gaoled Anglican bishops who had been held on charges of seditious libel persuaded a group of Tory and Whig nobles, more usually political opponents, to enter into a treasonous plot. James's daughter Mary and her Dutch husband Prince William of Orange were urged to invade England with an army to oust the king and ensure the Protestant future of the British nation. That September, the Prince of Orange accepted the call to arms and produced a *Declaration of Reasons* that justified a Protestant revolt. This suggested the birth of the infant prince was a hoax and James II was a tyrant. England's so-called 'Glorious Revolution' forced James from his throne in the winter of 1688 and into exile.

Ruling jointly, William and Mary unfortunately inherited a land riddled with social problems, and in places ripe for rebellion. Highland armies supporting the exiled James II, known as 'Jacobites', quickly engaged government forces at various dramatic locations in parts of Scotland, notably at Killiecrankie on 27 July 1689. And while one element of the Jacobites proceeded against King William in the usual way of exciting an insurrection, another group formed a cabal to assassinate the Protestant monarch. At the head of one scheme was Sir George Barclay, a Scottish army officer and Catholic agitator who had served under James II. Following various consultations, his group resolved to attack the king as he returned from hunting in Richmond Park on 15 February 1696. The scene of the intended ambush was a miry and narrow lane between Brentford and Turnham Green and it was decided that an army of forty horsemen would be required to engage the guards that attended the king's coach. During the fighting, Barclay would lead a troop of eight men who shot the king's horses and then fired directly into the coach itself with their pistols. Informants betrayed the murderous plot and ultimately nine Jacobite rebels were executed by the state. Others were gaoled for life, although Barclay slipped through the net and managed to escape to France.

Those arraigned as a result of this counter-revolutionary plot included Sir John Fenwick, 3rd Baronet, whose travesty of a trial illustrates that, as the seventeenth century drew out, judicial murder was still utilised if the government felt it justifiable or necessary (see Chapter 12). However, this condensed history of murderous attempts upon the rulers of the day highlights one thing above all; if the very highest in the land could not consider themselves safe, then what chance did the average person have of avoiding violent confrontation at some point in their life?

Chapter 3

Murder and Crime in London

It was in the early seventeenth century that London began to assume its present form. For centuries, it had represented a medieval walled city, almost wholly contained within defensive fortifications, but by Queen Elizabeth's reign it was developing rapidly beyond these walls and encroaching upon the many villages situated on the outskirts. The rage of building continued at a frightening pace during the reign of her successor, James I, and these places, formerly separated from the capital by fields and open spaces, were brought into contact with the city. James did not entirely approve of the expansion, but proclamations against building in the environs of London were in vain. The capital was too small for its daily-increasing population; wealthy citizens, requiring larger buildings in the immediate vicinity than they could conveniently erect within the walls, easily found means to avoid the penalties, or simply paid them. Over the course of a few years, London increased to almost double its original extent. The walls, however, remained, marking the ancient limits of the city.

London in these times is not an easy city to understand. It might be expected that it was more progressive than the other smaller cities and county towns dotted across the land, but this was not the case. In the final four years of Queen Elizabeth's reign, Catholic seminary priests were publicly hanged and quartered with appalling regularity for what was termed 'coming into the realm contrary to the Statute'. This lethal intolerance extended to citizens convicted of harbouring said priests, as well as those 'libelling against the queen's proclamation' and printing books considered offensive to the queen and state. Common criminals were also brutally mutilated prior to their deaths. According to one account of an incident in 1600, told in the *Faithful Annalist*, written by an 'Impartial Hand' in 1666:

> *'Two men were set on the pillory in Fleet Street, whipped with gags in their mouths, and their ears cut off, for attempting to have robbed a gentlewoman in Fetter-lane, putting gags into the mouths of the*

36

Whereas pillories forced prisoners to stand upright, stocks – such as this example in Oakham – immobilised their feet, at least allowing them to sit down.

servants of the house because they should not cry out; one of these thieves was then hanged and quartered at Saint Thomas Watrings [Old Kent Road].'

The pillory was a wooden framework with holes for the head and hands, where convicted prisoners were forced to endure public abuse and attack whilst held immobile in the structure.

What passed for entertainment was often barbaric and sometimes of a strange nature. On 13 June 1609, for instance, lions from the Tower of London's menagerie were pitted against a bear in the full expectation of bloody combat; however, the animals only edged warily around each other, even when a stallion was introduced to the proceedings to agitate the lions. Eventually, several dogs were added to the group, but they attacked the stallion, which had to be rescued by 'bear-wardens'. This disturbing spectacle was witnessed by King James, Queen Anne, Prince Henry and various assorted dignitaries. The bear had formerly mauled a child to death, and we learn, again from the 'Impartial Hand':

'On the fifth of July this bear according to the king's commandment was baited to death by dogs upon a stage, and the mother of the murdered child had £20 given her out of the money given by the people to see the death of the bear.'

Whilst executions of seminary priests still occurred occasionally in London during the first years of James's reign, he nonetheless gave his support to efforts aimed at controlling prostitution in the capital and, by association, the alcoholism, begging, crime and gambling that went on in the vicinity of brothels. His ordinance *Touching on Disorderly Houses in Saffron Hille*, issued in 1622, evidences a certain alarm that was developing over a perceived moral decline in London: but although a series of raids resulted in hundreds of prostitutes being gaoled, in the long run the purge had little effect.

The murder in 1628 of Dr John Lambe at the hands of a crowd of Londoners illustrates vividly the political power the mob held when roused. Lambe was an infamous quack doctor and conjurer who had nonetheless earned the patronage of the Duke of Buckingham, acting as the nobleman's confidential physician and personal advisor. He had formerly been convicted of diabolical practices at Worcester Assizes and of rape at the Old Bailey in London. On Friday 13 June 1628, Dr Lambe went to see a play at the Fortune Theatre near Whitecross Street in St Luke's. Whilst walking alone he was recognised by some boys, who shouted at him, 'Down with the conjurer! Down with the Devil!' A hostile crowd developed quickly, pursuing the doctor along Coleman Street to the Old Jewry, where he hammered upon doors as he went, pleading for assistance. No-one came to his aid. Once these events had been set in motion, Lambe's octogenarian frailty did not save him; stones were aimed at his head, and after being dragged into the open space at Paul's Cross he was beaten all over with cudgels and other weapons. One or more of the blows dashed his skull in before some constables were able to wrestle him from the melee and conduct him to the Counter in the Poultry, a small gaol in Cheapside.

Dr Lambe spoke not another word after his ordeal and died the following morning. It is said that Charles I, accompanied by his bodyguards, witnessed the crowd at Paul's Cross dragging the doctor along the road by his hair, violently striking him as they went. Seeing it as an attack on the Duke of Buckingham by proxy, Charles later levelled all manner of dictatorial threats against the lord mayor and magistrates of London in an effort to get them to identify the riot's ringleaders. He blamed the city itself for the murder, but although a few youths were rounded up, a lack of enthusiasm on behalf of the city authorities left the matter in abeyance. Charles ultimately failed to enforce his threats to abolish London's charters – his climb-down hinting that he dare not antagonise the city and its people too much.

On the day of Lambe's death, placards containing the following words were displayed on the walls of London:

> 'Who rules the kingdom? The king! Who rules the king? The duke! Who rules the duke? The Devil! Let the duke look to it, or he will be served as his doctor was served.'

George Villiers, 1st Duke of Buckingham, was perhaps the most despised man in England by this time, a boastful, vainglorious courtier who threw away men's lives pursuing his dreams of glory during naval campaigns in France. According to a 1728 history of this period:

> 'Another expedition was resolved on with a greater navy, and the Duke of Buckingham designed admiral, who going to Portsmouth to hasten business, one John Felton, a lieutenant, stabbed him in the heart with a knife; which the murderer flying left sticking in his body till the duke himself dragged it out, and died. Felton was apprehended and laden with irons; and being asked what inclined him to commit so horrid an act, he boldly answered, "He killed him for the cause of God and his country". He [Felton] fastened a paper in the crown of his hat, which intimated, "That his only motive to this fact was the late remonstrance of the Commons against the duke and that he could not sacrifice his life in a nobler cause than by delivering his country from so great an enemy".'

Buckingham's assassination, which occurred on the morning of 23 August 1628 as he was passing through a doorway to the Greyhound Inn on Portsmouth's High Street, caused a sensation. Felton's passage to London for interrogation produced extraordinary scenes; pitied, blessed and toasted in equal measure, mothers actually held up their children to see the man many believed was the saviour of the nation through his violent act. One old woman is said to have exclaimed as Felton passed her, 'God bless thee, little David!' in reference to David and Goliath. In fact, the assassin was all but sainted by the time he arrived in the capital, illustrating just how much King Charles's policy of reliance on ineffectual favourites was detested.

John Felton, the duke's assassin: after a portrait reproduced in the Gentleman's Magazine *in 1845.*

John Felton was hanged at Tyburn on 19 November 1628. His body was afterwards transported to Portsmouth, where it was encased in chains and hung from a gibbet post just outside the town. As for George Villiers, his own inherent ignorance and disdainful arrogance may, in fact, have contributed to his death. According to the contemporary commentator Sir Simon d'Ewes:

> *'Some of his friends had advised how generally he was hated in England, and how needful it would be for his greater safety to wear some coat of mail, or some other secret defensive armour: which the duke slighting said, "It needs not, there are no Roman spirits left".'*

In 1665 London's population was almost decimated by a ferocious outbreak of plague and the following year an apocalyptic fire destroyed 400 streets, 13,200 dwelling houses, almost 100 churches, four of the city gates, St Paul's Cathedral and many other public edifices. A new, improved city slowly emerged from the ashes; streets were widened, brick and stone houses replaced clustered wooden ones and landmark buildings were rebuilt.

During the reign of King Charles II, London appears nonetheless to have become more hazardous than it had been during the Interregnum and Cromwell. When evening closed in, the difficulty and danger of walking about the capital became serious indeed. Garret windows were opened and pails emptied out, with little consideration for anyone passing by below; falls, accidents and broken bones were a constant occurrence; whilst thieves and robbers operated with impunity. The old salutary terror of the Tudor Star Chamber court had become lost following its abolition in 1641 and many common people of the time began to despise the ordinary administration of justice, or else in their passion paid little heed to any consequence their violent actions might bring upon themselves. Policing in the capital during this time can be considered somewhat shambolic. An Act of Common Council had dictated in 1663 that over 1,000 night watchmen were needed on the streets, every day from sunset to sunrise, to help enforce law and order during the almost-total darkness and that every inhabitant should take his turn on duty. But the Act was negligently executed, with few of those summoned leaving their homes, while those who obeyed were apt to spend their 'watch' drinking in the alehouses. Certain districts such as Whitefriars became virtual sanctuaries for all manner of insolvents, false witnesses, forgers and highwaymen; they were places where peace officers feared to tread lest the cry of 'Rescue!' swept the mob and they launched an assault. In such districts, even the warrants of the Chief Justice of England could not be executed without the help of a company of musketeers. London became a prey to daring thieves, hired assassins and loutish young rakes who went about armed and looking for trouble.

The truly dire state of order around this time can be gleaned by two entries in Narcissus Luttrell's diary. In January 1686, he wrote:

'Jack Ketch, the hangman, for affronting the Sheriffs of London, was committed to Bridewell, and is turned out of his place, and one Rose, a butcher, put in.'

Four months later, Luttrell observed:

'Five men of those condemned at the sessions were executed at Tyburn, one of them was one Pasha Rose, the new hangman, so that now Ketch is restored to his place.'

Rose had been convicted of a house robbery. But for the grim picture it suggests, the fact that London hangmen might themselves be hanged may seem ironically comical.

The population at large was itself a hardened one by today's standards. City-dwellers walked past bodies lying by the roadside with as little comment as if they were passing a dead animal, preferring not to concern themselves with the question of whether the person was dead drunk, or actually dead. Quite frequently, a passing jest, a warmly expressed difference of opinion or an accidental push could only be atoned for by drawn swords or an all-out melee. Ladies of position and fortune were sometimes abducted and carried forcibly to a wedding ceremony against their will that tied them to a stranger.

Common executions were carnival occasions worthy of family entertainment, particularly if the criminal was a notorious one. Psalms, speeches, repentance and wit from a criminal on the point of death delighted the multitudes, whereas cowardice, denial and arrogance earned them a poor reputation in the folk-memory of Londoners. Fighting frequently broke out over the rights to the best views of the execution: and it can realistically be said of these times that the sight in which the English most delighted was a hanging.

The following cases are representative of London throughout the seventeenth century.

GUN LAW

The pistol was still an unfamiliar weapon for a criminal to wield in the very early seventeenth century. This we can glean from an entry among the Middlesex Sessions Rolls dated 22 May 1602, when the case against a man named Kimber ('late of London, gentleman') was heard. He was accused of assaulting William Peverell with 'a certain instrument called a pistol.' During the incident, which occurred on the highway at Hounslow, Kimber had clapped the weapon to Peverell's breast, threatening to shoot him dead and 'putting him in great fear and terror.' Kimber was imprisoned in Newgate Gaol for this transgression.

It is also evident that people were apt to use this new weapon, for the same records tell us that Mr Rowland Pottell was fatally wounded during an altercation on the highway at Mile-end in Stepney near midnight on 25 May 1602. Pottell had been assaulted by three men, one of whom was Roger Some, a London gentleman who produced a pistol loaded with gunpowder and 'dropshott', which he fired into the victim's left thigh, killing him immediately. All three were arraigned at the Middlesex Assizes, Mr Some being accused of murder whilst the two others, a haberdasher named White and a yeoman named Gerling, were accused of complicity in the shooting.

In the end, Roger Some admitted manslaughter, and all three were sentenced to be branded with the letter 'T' upon their hand after pleading their clergy and showing the court they could read. The standing of the accused thus proven, and simultaneously the seriousness of their offence becoming reduced, the three were 'delivered according to the Statute.'

One is merely left wondering to what extent other riotous gentlemen of the time were encouraged in their rakish ways by such leniency.

'DOTH THE MAN YET LIVE?': MURDER DEFERRED

Robert Crichton, 6th Lord Sanquhar, was a Scottish nobleman who committed an infamous crime and met an ignoble end. His fall from grace was singularly spectacular, as he boasted an exceptionally distinguished background; in fact, he was the lineal descendant and representative of one of Scotland's most influential families, whose historical predecessors had accumulated many accolades in serving the advancement of the royal Stuart line.

Around 1605, the young peer was a guest at Lord Norrey's manor-house at Rycote, west of Thame in Oxfordshire. There, he engaged in an ill-advised fencing match with John Turner, a master of the sport. Taking up the foils, Lord Sanquhar remarked to his opponent that he played merely as a scholar, and not as one who could contend with a master in his own profession. Therefore, he requested Turner fence with him as such and in particular, spare his face. Sanquhar's concern was legitimate: Turner had killed an adversary named Dunn in 1602 by piercing his brain through the eye.

Notwithstanding this precaution, Turner struck out one of his lordship's eyes, by accident it would seem. He wounded him so badly that for several days afterwards Sanquhar's life was in danger. Following this, Lord Sanquhar took to wearing a glass eye to disguise his injury.

After a lapse of seven years, the peer took the decision to have John Turner assassinated. Although a natural enmity had been seething beneath the surface, it seems the aggravating factor that turned Lord Sanquhar's mind conclusively to thoughts of murder occurred when he visited the court of France. There, the king, Henry the Great, casually asked him how he came to lose his eye. 'By the thrust of a sword,' replied his lordship, not caring to enter into the particulars. The king, supposing his accident to be the result of a duel, immediately enquired, 'Does the man yet live?' These words merely added to the peer's desire for vengeance on Turner, who, he was now persuaded, had struck out his eyeball on purpose. Sanquhar had by this point resided in France for some time: he now decided to return to England immediately, his rage increasingly inflamed over the matter.

Sanquhar appears to have convinced himself that in killing Turner he was merely acting within traditional laws of honour and for several days he tracked his potential victim up and down London in vain, with the intention of accosting him. Following some thinking-time in Scotland, however, he returned to the capital with a more devious scheme in mind. He had learned that Turner's fencing school was to be found in White-friars, an area of London between Fleet Street and the Thames. However, he was only too aware that if he went and killed Turner there, he would be recognised; after all, Sanquhar's damaged face was very distinctive. He therefore entered into a conspiracy with two fellow Scotsmen, hiring them to act as assassins in his place, before taking himself back to France in a mood of satisfaction that the deed – when perpetrated – would not be connected with him.

For some time, he waited for correspondence from England that his enemy had been killed but it never came, either because the two hired ruffians never intended to execute the plan or because their nerve failed them.

Sanquhar returned to London to find Turner still alive and well as normal. He next employed two of his trusted servants, Robert Carlyle and a man named Gray, also Scotsmen, to commit the deed. Gray's heart failed him at the last minute and he immediately fled for Sweden to avoid the wrath of his master; Carlyle, however, was more than eager for the crime to go ahead and he assured Sanquhar that a friend of his, James Irving (or Irwin) would accompany him in Gray's stead.

On 11 May 1612, the two men called at Turner's lodgings in White-friars. Here, whilst the master swordsman was completely off his guard, and offering his two guests his hospitality, Carlyle surprised him by suddenly pointing a pistol at his chest and firing it directly into his heart.

It seems curious that Sanquhar ever thought he could deflect suspicion for instigating this crime, despite his reliance upon an alibi. Such a killing, premeditated and in cold blood, quite naturally pointed towards a personal motive and since Lord Sanquhar's hatred of the victim was hardly a secret, it was quite clear that he might have conceived the murder, despite having been nowhere near the vicinity when it was committed.

Robert Carlyle immediately escaped to Scotland but Irving was arrested in the capital and interrogated on what he knew of the killing. Irving, who seems to have been the weakest of the conspirators, gave the examiners reason to believe that Lord Sanquhar was implicated and the nobleman himself fed this suspicion. He became conspicuous by his absence, keeping himself fully out of sight for three or four days. Therefore, descriptions of Sanquhar's distinctive appearance were posted as far north as Carlisle and Dumfries, in the event that he had escaped north with his principle accomplice.

King James followed the investigation keenly and put up a reward of £500 for the capture of Lord Sanquhar, alive or dead. A reward of £300 was similarly offered for the taking of Carlyle, also alive or dead.

However, Lord Sanquhar very quickly surrendered himself to George Abbot, the Archbishop of Canterbury, after appearing at Lambeth Palace. The peer initially declared his innocence in the strongest terms, it being his belief that nothing tied him directly to Irving. He was also reassured by the fact that both Carlyle and Gray were as yet nowhere to be found.

Unfortunately for Sanquhar, Gray, in his flight to Sweden, had only made it as far as Harwich in Essex, where he was arrested as he boarded a ship. Under interrogation, Gray made it clear that Sanquhar was the driving force behind the plot. Back in London, the peer, once informed of Gray's words, ceased his continual denial and admitted that Turner's murder was due to his scheming.

Carlyle, a Scottish borderer, was shortly thereafter caught in his native country and returned to the capital, where he and Irving were convicted of murder with little difficulty. Both were hanged at Tyburn on 25 June. Gray, having become a witness for the prosecution, appears to have escaped the noose.

Lord Sanquhar was arraigned before the Court of King's Bench, Westminster Hall, on 27 June 1612, accused of ordering the murder. It is an interesting fact that since his was a Scottish title, his status was not recognised at the hearing. He was arraigned and tried under the name of Robert Crichton, Esquire, only.

His trial took place on the same day as his arraignment and he removed all doubt as to his complicity by making an eloquent speech confessing the crime. He was immediately afterwards capitally convicted upon his own evidence. Part of his confession spoke volumes, for the peer stated at one point he was 'never willing to pardon where I had power of revenge'. However, he did acknowledge a degree of culpability, ending his speech with a plea that mercy might be shown unto him. Sir Francis Bacon, the Solicitor-General, who was present during the proceedings, stated:

'Certainly the circumstance of time is heavy unto you; it is now five years since this unfortunate man, Turner, be it upon accident or despight, gave the provocation which was the seed of your malice.'

In his role as prosecutor, Bacon also further observed the singular lapse in time between insult and deed, commenting:

> *'All passions are assuaged with time: love, hatred, grief, and all fire burns out with time, if no fuel be put to it; for you to have been in the gall of bitterness so long, and to have been in a restless case for his blood, is a strange example...'*

Sincere attempts were made to procure a pardon for the nobleman by a number of influential people, among them the Archbishop of Canterbury, but to no avail. On 29 June, Lord Sanquhar was hanged on a specially-erected gibbet placed in 'Great Palace yard, before the gate of Westminster Hall'. He died penitently, professing the Catholic faith, and it is a curious fact that the vast crowd who gathered to watch him die were up until this point largely sympathetic to his predicament. However, this visibly abated following the nobleman's public declaration that he died in the faith of the Roman Catholic Church.

Lord Sanquhar had formerly been married in 1608, to Anne, daughter of Sir George Farmer of Easton, Northamptonshire. However, by the time of his execution the couple had separated. Nonetheless, he left an heir in the shape of his son, also Robert Crichton, who inherited his father's title and estate in 1619. After the peer's execution, correspondence dated 2 July 1612 between John Chamberlain, Esquire and Sir Dudley Carleton hints at what became of the murderer's corpse:

> *'His body was taken down presently after he was dead, and carried away by the Lord Roxburgh, the Lord Dingwall, and two or three Scottish lords more, who took order to embalm it and send it to Scotland.'*

The king had formerly ordered that the victim's body be privately buried 'to avoid concourse of people, that might breed inconvenience.'

'THE UNPOPULARITY OF HIS OFFICE'

Sir John Tyndall was an exceptionally prestigious fellow. He practiced in Chancery, and was appointed one of the Masters of the Court on 17 April 1598. Married in 1586 to Anne, widow of William Deane, Esquire, he was also a doctor of civil law who was knighted at Whitehall on 23 July 1603. Zealously Protestant, his wife persuaded him to purchase Chelmshoe House near Halstead in Essex with an additional 249 acres.

Sir John was also for many years the steward of Queen's College, Cambridge. But despite his impressive portfolio his administration in Chancery, a court of equity handling matters such as lawsuits, was not without suspicion of corruption. By the early seventeenth century, the Court of Chancery was not particularly renowned for its integrity, and had fallen into disrepute; this lack of faith in his office among the population in general appears to have been the driving force behind a remarkable incident that occurred in 1616.

On the afternoon of 12 November, as Sir John was entering his Lincoln's Inn chambers, on his return from Westminster Hall, he was approached by an elderly gentleman who simply walked up to him, put a pistol to his back and fired into it. Sir John's body was thrown forward by the impact, and according to most reports he was dead by the time he hit the ground, the pistol having been loaded with three bullets, all of which were lodged in his spine. There is some suggestion that prior to this, the armed man had attempted to harangue the old knight when he alighted from his carriage, but Sir John rebuffed him and turned his back on him to enter his door. The judge was above 70 years of age at the time of his murder, and up to that point in good health both bodily and mentally. His last word was 'only a deep-fetched groan'.

When the shooting was carried out, the streets were crowded. The assassin was apprehended immediately, which was unsurprising, given the fact that he was almost 80 years old himself. He initially showed no remorse, saying he had done his country a good service. His name, it turned out, was John Bertram, of Westminster; Sir John had angered him by adversely reporting against him in a case then pending at the Court of Chancery. The sum at stake, which Bertram stood to lose thanks to Sir John's recommendation, had been in the region of £300, a significant amount in those days and Bertram's whole fortune. Sir John had previously advocated in favour of Bertram's antagonist, Sir George Symeon.

Two days after the crime, Bertram was sent for by the judges to be examined. When he was called to the bar, he pleaded 'not guilty'. At his passing along the streets, great emotion was elicited among the common people, who prayed for him and cursed the authorities. He appeared 'so full of age, and his face so full of sorrowes, together with the rumour of his wrongfull undoing' that many are held to have openly wept as he passed them. According to one account, Bertram moved at a 'slow and dulle pace, fitting to his yeeres', and seemed in his cell rather confused. A contemporary woodcut depicting the crime displays Bertram as a bald-headed old man with a long white beard and stooping shoulders.

Bertram is said to have described his act as 'no worse than killing a thief or robber upon the highway' and the circumstances of the crime raised such a clamour among the mob that King James himself resolved to examine Bertram personally and assess whether his grievance against the justice system was legitimate. The Court of Chancery was subsequently attacked verbally from all sides by statesmen, with Sir William Walter of Wimbledon, a noted wit, commenting, 'The fellow mistook his mark, and should have shot hailshot at the whole court.'

Although Bertram's actions threatened to open the lid on a network of alleged corruption, it never happened. – An inquiry by the law-officers of the Crown, and the attorney-general, Bacon, predictably vindicated Sir John's character, even going so far as to call him 'a kind of martyr'.

As for Bertram, he was subsequently seized with remorse over what he had done, and became alarmed at the thought he might be tortured. In particular, he was greatly worried that he would be gibbeted whilst still alive and left to starve to death whilst strapped in irons and hung from a gallows post. Without waiting for the outcome of the inquiry into his legal grievances, he contrived to hang himself from a nail fastened high upon his cell wall in the King's Bench Prison, Southwark, on Sunday, 17 November 1616.

THE SERVANT'S OFFENSIVE REWARD

Fulke Greville was another notable figure of the era whose life was cut short through violence. Greville, later 1st Baron Brooke of Beauchamp Court, stood high in the court of King James I. He was a statesman, scholar, poet, dramatist and author, and exceptionally well-educated. He wrote several works, among them *A Treatise of Human Learning* (in verse); *The Life of Sir Philip Sydney*; and *An Inquisition upon Fame and Honour* (in 86 stanzas).

King James was so impressed with the baron's capability that in 1604 he granted him Warwick Castle, a landmark medieval structure built on the western banks of the Avon. By 1628, however, Greville was in old age and he made the mistake of offending his elderly valet, Ralph Hayward, by writing into his will that the latter was to receive just £20 annually. Hayward had spent the greater part of his life in Greville's employment and when he discovered this he was outraged at what he considered a meagre sum for so many years of service. There is some suggestion that Hayward's animosity had been simmering for several weeks, ever since he had been present, along with others, at the execution of the baron's will on 18 February 1628. On that occasion, Hayward had witnessed most of his master's estate willed to a cousin. It is also perhaps the case that Hayward was historically affronted,

Greville's final resting place in St Mary's Collegiate Church, Warwick.

because according to a later writer, John Aubrey, Greville had earlier adopted a one-eyed park keeper's son as his heir, although he apparently changed his mind over this.

On 1 September 1628, whilst Greville was in residence at another of his properties, Brooke House (near Brooke Street, Holborn), his valet began confronting him over the matter of the annuity; Greville, outraged by Hayward's impertinence, rebuked him sharply. Finding himself alone with his master in the bed-chamber of Brooke House, Hayward drew a sword, or a knife, and plunged it into Greville's back, mortally wounding him. According to Aubrey, Greville was attacked 'coming from stoole', and Hayward was actually in the act of helping his master to dress when his rage

49

overtook him. The assassin immediately withdrew into another room, locked the door, and committed suicide with the same weapon.

According to information available at Warwick Castle, Greville might have survived were it not for the fact that his incompetent physicians treated his wounds with pig fat, which, being rancid, infected his blood and saw to it that he died some four weeks later on 30 September, writhing in agony. Despite his negligent treatment Greville apparently made a last-minute alteration to his will in which handsome legacies were left to his surgeons. He was aged about 74 when he died and was later buried – embalmed and wrapped in lead – in St Mary's Church, Warwick. Over his remains was placed a magnificent monument of black and white marble.

MURDER IN THE EXETER CHANGE: A DIPLOMATIC AFFAIR
One of the most sensational murders that took place in the capital during Cromwell's post-war governance of the nation occurred in 1653. The culpable party in this case was an eminent European nobleman, Don Pantaleon Sa, the Portuguese ambassador's brother and a Knight of Malta. Out of a curiosity to see England, he had accompanied his brother the ambassador when the latter travelled to London.

On 21 November 1653, Don Pantaleon was walking among the crowds in the New Exchange – an arcade-type complex sited in the vicinity of the Strand – when he happened to collide with a young colonel named John Gerard. Don Pantaleon, it appears, had been passing comment upon late developments in France with two of his friends, when Gerard casually informed him his politics were incorrect. A quarrel developed between them with both men drawing their rapiers and entering into a contest, during which the Portuguese nobleman was bested. One account claims Gerard received a dagger wound to his shoulder but was saved by a man called Anthuser who came to his rescue.

To avenge his injured pride, Don Pantaleon made his way to the Portuguese

Don Pantaleon Sa: after an illustration from The Book of Days. *(W R Chambers, 1870)*

Embassy where he raised a small army of some twenty servants, fitting them with breastplates and headpieces before arming them with swords and pistols. The group returned quickly to the Strand in search of Gerard, roaming the upper and lower parts of the New Exchange.

However, they were unable to locate either Gerard or Anthuser and so Don Pantaleon returned to the Exeter Exchange the following day with an even greater number of Portuguese comrades. On this occasion, there were perhaps fifty or more of them in total, all breast-plated and armed. Some accounts allege that their coaches were filled with gunpowder so that – in the event they could not obtain entry – they might blow up the arcade.

There, someone called Thomas Howard challenged their behaviour, and the shopkeepers, aware that trouble was imminent, began shutting up their establishments. The sequence of events is unclear, but a prolonged pitched battle followed in which a man named Greenaway (evidently mistaken for Gerard by one among the Portuguese) was fatally wounded.

Greenaway, of Gray's Inn, appears to have been entirely innocent and only in the vicinity by chance; he was in fact, due to be married and at the time was merely shopping in the company of his sister and his fiancée. Conscious of a hubbub, he pushed the two women into a shop for their safety and went to see what the matter was. His enquiry into the Portuguese group's business probably sparked the entire episode, but at any rate one of the affronted Portuguese beat him and then fired a pistol directly into his head, killing Greenaway instantly.

Witnesses were forced to run for cover as a bloody collision erupted between the armed Portuguese and numerous outraged Englishmen who had waded in with drawn swords. At one point, a certain Colonel Mayo fought against twelve of the Portuguese before his hand was cut and he dropped his sword; he was stabbed a number of times and lucky not to have been killed – the colonel may have been drawn in because someone mistook him for the aforementioned Anthuser. Howard was also wounded, as was a man named Carter and several passers-by. The fighting ended when a pistol fired by somebody in the west-end of the Exchange sent everyone, including Don Pantaleon, scattering.

When word of this incident spread, widespread tumult gripped London and great mobs of people surged to the Portuguese ambassador's house where it was believed the gang had sought refuge. Cromwell himself was informed of the matter and he ordered an officer, together with a party of soldiers, to go to the ambassador's residence so as to take the suspects into custody.

It seems the ambassador attempted to argue some form of diplomatic immunity on behalf of his hot-tempered brother but he was bluntly informed that if Don Pantaleon was not handed over, then the troops would force their way into the building and turn the place upside down until he was found. Cromwell himself, the officer argued, had declared that, 'a gentleman had been murdered, and others wounded, and… justice must be satisfied'. Meeting further resistance, the officer stated that if the guilty parties were not handed over then he would withdraw his troops and leave the matter in the hands of the highly-agitated mob, who by now were screaming they would pull down the house; the ambassador found it in vain to protest any further. To his great grief, he was forced to deliver over his brother and four others, who were subsequently all lodged in Newgate on 23 November following an examination by Lord Chief Justice Rolles. Don Pantaleon managed to escape the notorious gaol on 13 December, but he was quickly retaken.

The ambassador continued to solicit Cromwell directly in a bid to earn his brother's freedom, all the while seemingly unconcerned as to the fate of the others. The only response he received was that 'justice must be done', and in the end, it was.

Don Pantaleon and the four other prisoners were tried before two commissioners at the King's Bench on 6 July 1654, the jury being comprised of half-English and half-foreign citizens. All the accused were convicted of murder and felony, much to Don Pantaleon's astonishment. He had argued that he was Portuguese ambassador in his brother's absence and therefore felt entitled to a special diplomatic consideration under the 'Law of Nations'.

According to some accounts, all those convicted were hanged at Tyburn. However, the majority of reports suggest the convicted men earned a reprieve – that is, with the exception of Don Pantaleon, whose cry for vengeance had precipitated the entire disturbance. State Trial records imply the truth is somewhere in-between; one of those convicted was an English boy (Pantaleon's servant), who was executed by hanging, while the rest of the nobleman's co-accused may have been reprieved for reasons somewhat unclear.

Don Pantaleon himself made another attempt to escape on the very day of his execution, but he was detected in the act. On 10 July 1654, the Portuguese nobleman was conveyed from Newgate to Tower Hill in a mourning coach drawn by six horses. His journey was attended by a retinue of his distraught brother's employees.

He continued to deny any guilt in Greenaway's murder, blaming English troublemakers. His last minutes were spent in private conversation with his

Catholic Confessor, then, on a scaffold, he was beheaded by the executioner, evidently displaying in his final moments much terror and dejection of spirit. It took two blows to sever his head.

This display of justice greatly raised the Protector's standing in the opinion of Londoners, particularly in view of the fact that, on the very same day his brother was executed, the Portuguese ambassador was made to sign the articles of peace between Britain and Portugal. Afterwards, the ambassador immediately went out of the city and returned to his home country via Gravesend, Kent.

Interestingly, John Gerard is the same man mentioned earlier who was executed for plotting against Cromwell's life. Ironically, he met his death on the same day as the Portuguese nobleman.

THE MORIARTY OF BRITISH CRIMINALS
The self-styled 'Colonel' Thomas Blood is a man who has come to define the times. This extraordinary adventurer appears to have been born of respectable Anglo-Irish parentage in Ireland; he took the side of Cromwell during the civil wars, and married a Lancashire woman, Mary Holcroft, in England. An Act of Settlement in 1662, which overturned many of Cromwell's laws in Ireland, seriously affected his fortunes after he had returned home, leading him to attempt an insurrection in Dublin in 1663. His hunted status thereafter led Blood to attempt the assassination of his inveterate enemy, James Butler, the Anglo-Irish 1st Duke of Ormond and Lord Lieutenant of Ireland. Whilst living in London under an alias, Blood and five others brazenly abducted Ormond from his carriage in St James's Street, before – it is reputedly said – conveying their captive to Tyburn with the intention of lynching him from the great triangular gallows. Luckily, the duke managed to free himself from his captors and escape in the vicinity of Knightsbridge.

Six months later, as is well known, Blood artfully attempted to steal the Crown Jewels from a room called the Jewel House in the Martin Tower of the Tower of London. The details of the theft, which occurred on the morning of 9 May 1671, have entered London folklore and there are numerous historical biographies on Blood which elaborate on the matter. Suffice to say that the colonel (disguised as a parson) and several of his cronies managed to make off with the jewels after beating, stabbing and incapacitating the elderly guardian, Talbot Edwards. Blood fired randomly at his pursuers during his escape, and was shortly after wrestled under control by Captain Beckman. When the fight went out of him, Blood said resignedly, 'It was a gallant attempt, however unsuccessful, for it was for a crown!'

The Byward Tower, where Blood shot at sentries during the escape.

This story is a comparatively well-known one and has been liberally written about. What may not be so familiar, are the means by which Blood managed to keep his liberty. He was aged about 53 at the time of his arrest. When news was conveyed to King Charles II of the robbery, an examination of the culprits was conducted before the monarch himself at the Palace of Whitehall. The colonel admitted his guilt in everything, including his attempt upon the life of Ormond, but refused to implicate anyone other than himself in these crimes.

Blood's testimony, however, also began to reveal sinister intrigues hitherto unsuspected. He admitted that, on one occasion, he had concealed himself in the reeds above Battersea, in order to shoot his majesty whilst he bathed in the Thames, over against Chelsea Reach. The king often went to swim among the tame swans that inhabited that then-lonely bank. However, even as he took aim with a loaded carbine, Blood claimed to have aborted this assassination because 'his heart was checked by an awe of Majesty'.

Blood also claimed that he had hundreds of followers, similarly disaffected and hinted that any leniency shown to him would reflect itself in their general attitude towards the monarch and perhaps prevent an uprising.

There was some evidence that Blood's argument was not entirely bluff. This plot to shoot the king had occurred after Blood's attempt to seize Dublin Castle in 1663, around the time that a series of dissenters' conspiracies against the government was occurring in England, which became known as the Northern Rising, or the Yorkshire Plot. These dissenters, northern English Presbyterians and Anabaptists, had hoped to seize Wales (under an exiled regicide, Edmund Ludlow) and then take Whitehall, forcing the king to adhere to certain religious and political demands.

Four years after said rising, when captured rebel Colonel John Mason was being conducted to York, the convoy had been ambushed by a mounted party of about six men in a narrow lane near Darrington, West Yorkshire, on the evening of 25 August 1667. During a brutal shooting, in which the attackers killed a York barber called Scot and fatally wounded at least two troopers, Colonel Mason was set free. A government spy had recognised Thomas Blood among the attackers, as well as a man named Lockyer and others, but none was captured at the time. Blood apparently sustained a number of injuries in this skirmish, and was lucky not to have been killed outright.

The Northern Rising had collapsed in October 1663, but Blood's admission of involvement in that plot's aftermath had the desired effect upon the king, who perhaps saw Blood as a man who controlled an as-yet unknown, shadowy network of malcontents. Somehow, the villainous colonel managed to both awe the monarch and captivate his interest, Charles not only pardoning him but giving him a grant in land of £500 a year in Ireland. Colonel Blood subsequently found favour in polite society, whilst the Edwards family were negligently compensated for their actions in attempting to protect the Crown Jewels. Old Edwards survived his injuries until 30 September 1674, when he died aged 80. Meanwhile, the Duke of Ormond was officially informed that no-one would be prosecuted for attempting to assassinate him. The mystery remained and Colonel Blood afterwards lived in a house on the corner of Great Peter Street and Tufton Street, Westminster. He died on 24 August 1680, apparently exhausted and ruined by a term of imprisonment for libelling his former friend the Duke of Buckingham. He was quietly interred in New Chapel Yard, Broadway, two days later.

The diarist John Evelyn, who met Blood, described him unflatteringly as having a 'villainous, unmerciful look; a false countenance, but very well spoken, and dangerously insinuating.' Following his death there was a sudden realisation that Blood might have faked his own end to avoid his libel case, and substituted a corpse. But, to the general satisfaction of most, the cadaver was proved that of the colonel because of a difficult-to-fake thumb deformity he suffered.

MURDERED BY THE KING'S OWN SON

Nothing illustrates the Restoration period better than the killing of one particular beadle – parish officer – in London. The incident occurred very early on the morning of Sunday, 26 February 1671 when the beadle, Peter Vernell, responded to a disturbance at a brothel in Whetstone Park, Holborn. When he and his colleagues attempted to gain admittance, they were attacked by a party of intoxicated gentlemen in masquerade costumes, and Vernell was murdered in cold blood while praying for his life upon his knees.

Whetstone Park was at the time a narrow lane between the north side of Lincoln's Inn Fields and Holborn, and it entertained a reputation as a notorious district for courtesans. Among the party who attacked Vernell was James Scott, the 21-year-old Duke of Monmouth, eldest of the king's illegitimate sons. In fact, it may even have been the case that Monmouth physically contributed to the murder with his sword, because, according to a contemporary writer, Andrew Marvell, the beadle died of 'many wounds'.

A later poem blamed the attack on 'three bastard dukes', suggesting it was common knowledge Monmouth and his cronies had gone to the brothel with the intention of assaulting a specific prostitute, whose cries of 'Murder!' brought the beadles running. The furore caused by the killing had the effect of cancelling an important ball at the palace that evening, and King Charles II professed to be outraged by the crime.

The contemporary letters of Lady Mary Bertie to a relative suggest that moves were made to try and prosecute someone for the murder:

> *'I doubt not but that you have heard of the watchman that was killed. They say the gentlemen that were in it are fled, and 'tis believed the two dukes will also be tried by their peers. They say the king has put out a proclamation to forbid masquerades and to command those who were concerned in killing the man to come to their trial.'*

The two dukes were Monmouth and Monck, the teenage Duke of Albemarle, but there was never really any risk they would suffer for their actions. Pardons were granted to both of these men, as well as another present, Edward Griffin. Similar pardons for three more who had been indicted – Robert Constable, Peter Savage and John Fennicke – were also requested. A third duke, Somerset, was also present but appears to have been above suspicion.

Robert Constable was the 20-year-old 3rd Viscount Dunbar. The *Middlesex County Records* suggest he was primarily culpable, having struck Vernell on the right side of the head with a rapier. He allegedly even admitted as much while being held in gaol; nonetheless, the writer Marvell later observed, 'They have all got their pardon for Monmouth's sake, but it is an act of great scandal.'

This was not the first time that Monmouth had been implicated in something of this nature. When Sir John Coventry insulted his majesty's honour during a debate in the House of Commons, Monmouth ordered a group of men, led by a lieutenant of his troop of guards, to punish the politician. Coventry was ambushed by these men on 21 December 1670 in Suffolk Street and although he defended himself gallantly, wounding some of his attackers, he was in the end disarmed before being kicked and beaten senseless. His nose was brutally cut to the bone to teach him respect for the king and he was afterwards left for dead, although he did recover.

It is entirely possible that this attempted murder was perpetrated with the connivance of the king.

THE MURDER OF SIR RICHARD SANDFORD

On the evening of 8 September 1675, Sir Richard Sandford, of Howgill Castle, and a friend, Captain George Hilton, had the misfortune to encounter Henry Symbal and William Jones at the George Inn, Whitefriars. The latter were a pair of professional criminals who lived via threats, extortion and the receipt of protection money. Jones approached Captain Hilton, insisting the latter's brother owed him 48 shillings. When Hilton refused to pay the money in his brother's stead, a violent brawl ensued which only ended when a parish constable intervened.

When Sir Richard and Captain Hilton left the George, their two antagonists pursued them, ambushing them on the corner of a dark alleyway not far from the inn. Symbal rammed his sword into Sir Richard's left side with such force he struggled to withdraw the weapon; he then stabbed his victim twice more, before he and Jones turned upon Captain Hilton. Hilton had already been struck on the head with a sword and he now found himself battling his attackers alone.

Hilton's luck ran out when two more men joined Symbal and Jones in the attack. Once he was disarmed, Symbal stabbed him viciously in the left side. All four attackers immediately ran off; it was around ten o'clock in the evening.

Sir Richard died of his wounds the next morning at ten o'clock, the same hour his son and heir was being born. However, Captain Hilton miraculously survived.

Symbal and Jones were arrested in Wallingford, Oxfordshire, on 16 September, their notoriety in Whitefriars having made them despised in the community even before they murdered Sir Richard. The pair were pursued and caught thanks to the endeavours of a prosecutor, who managed to follow their trail through a combination of bribery and confrontation with their known acquaintances. In fact, a 1680 account of the affair, *God's Revenge Against Murther*, explains that the perseverance and bravery of the unnamed prosecutor was quite astonishing.

When trapped, Symbal was identified by a wound known to be on his body; both murderers were lodged in Reading Gaol before being escorted to Newgate, London.

They were tried at the Old Bailey the following month, the nature of their crime proving so abhorrent that, in this instance, there was no question of an escape from the noose. Both Symbal and Jones were convicted of murder and hanged on 22 October 1675 in Fleet Street, their corpses afterwards being hung in chains from gibbet posts at Stamford Hill and on Finchley Common respectively.

THE AGE OF PERJURY

Another notable event of the era, as worthy of remembrance as the Gunpowder treason of 1605, was the Popish Plot.

This uncomfortable episode in London's history developed in 1678 when 'Doctor' Titus Oates and Dr Israel Tongue presented themselves before the king, the Privy Council and Parliament to pass on fabricated intelligence concerning a dire threat to the kingdom. Oates was a former Anglican chaplain to the Duke of Norfolk; however, it might be more accurate to describe him by 1678 as a clergyman of low repute who lived on Jesuit charity while feigning conversion to Catholicism. Tongue, a fanatical visionary, had encountered Oates in 1677 and later they collaborated on a number of anti-Catholic manifestos.

When Oates and Tongue stood before the Privy Council in September 1678, the former claimed to have learned – while on the Continent – of a wide-ranging Catholic plot to assassinate the king, massacre all Protestants, burn London to the ground and raise a Catholic army under James, the Duke of York. Among the first to be implicated was Edward Coleman, secretary to the Duchess of York, a man well known at Westminster as a Catholic lobbyist.

When Coleman was placed under arrest, along with a number of 'Jesuits and Papists', he was interviewed by Sir Edmund Berry Godfrey, an eminent justice of the peace who happened to be a good friend of his.

On Saturday, 12 October 1678, Sir Edmund was found to be missing from his house in Green's Lane in the Strand, near Hungerford Market, where he was a wood merchant. Exhaustive enquiries established that the magistrate had left his home at nine in the morning, and had next been spotted near St Clement Danes Church in the Strand. Later on, he had been seen in Marylebone, whilst the last positive sighting of him was around noon, when he attended a business interview with one of the churchwardens of St Martin-in-the-Fields.

Five days later, at six o'clock on the evening of 17 October, two men were crossing a field on the south side of Primrose Hill which was then a rural expanse providing a spectacular panoramic of London to the south. They were mildly puzzled to discover a sword-belt, a cane and a pair of gloves scattered beside a hedge that ran alongside the muddy track they followed. They later returned with a third man to retrieve the garments.

One of them, stooping down, looked into an adjoining ditch and saw the body of a man lying on his face. The corpse proved to be that of Sir Edmund Berry Godfrey. He was impaled upon his own short sword, which stuck out through his back. It was subsequently established that he had also suffered other injuries consistent with murderous violence; his breast was bruised and his neck broken. It was further apparent he had been garrotted. This was suggested by the fact that a laced neckerchief he had worn on the morning he went out was missing, whilst an ugly inch-thick dark mark all around his neck was visible. However, there were no bloodstains on his clothes or person, and his shoes were likewise clean – suggesting he may have been killed elsewhere and brought to Primrose Hill.

Sir Edmund was 56 years old at the time he was killed. His body was carried to a place called the White House on Primrose Hill, and thence home. Ever since his disappearance the coffee-houses of London had throbbed with speculation that Sir Edmund had come to possess explosive information on Catholic plotting and so had been assassinated; a jury impanelled to assess his death decided that this indeed appeared to be the case. Following its embalming, and after two days of lying in state at Bridewell Hospital, the magistrate's body was carried with great solemnity to St Martin's Church, where it was interred. Meanwhile, anti-Catholic hysteria engulfed the nation. Sir Edmund was mourned as the first victim of a 'Popish Plot', and rumours swept London of an imminent French invasion, leading to the positioning of cannons around Whitehall Palace. Warrants were also signed for the arrest of twenty-six people implicated by Titus Oates. These surrendered themselves in an atmosphere of terror and were committed to the Tower.

On 20 October, a reward of £500 was offered for information on Sir Edmund's murder. This tempted William Bedloe in Bristol to emerge as a new informant; this witness was a former valet to Lord Bellasis and afterwards a standard-bearer in the Low Countries. Bedloe claimed that, after returning to London, he had seen the magistrate – already dead – in Somerset House, on the south side of the Strand. He also stated he had been offered a large sum of money to help dispose of the body. Somerset House was at the time an occasional residence of Catherine of Braganza, King Charles II's Catholic wife.

Bedloe may simply have been a man on the fringes with cunning enough to tell a plausible tale but his testimony pointed the finger at Miles Prance, a goldsmith who had previously plied his trade in the Queen's Chapel, St James's Palace. Prance was severely interrogated and chained to the floor in Newgate and appears to have been all but forced into becoming a prosecution witness.

He claimed that Sir Edmund's murder was committed by six people, three of whom held subordinate positions at Somerset House. They were called Robert Green, Henry Berry and Lawrence Hill. They had allegedly been acting in conjunction with three other 'Papists, and maintainers of the Romish superstitions', called Mr Gerald, Dominick Kelly and Philbert Vernatt – although these latter had all absconded and could not be found. The gist of Prance's story was that the victim was 'a very busie man, and would be very troublesome'; therefore, during several meetings at the Plough alehouse, a conspiracy had been formed to assassinate him. At 9 o'clock on the evening of 12 October, the magistrate had been waylaid at the gate of Somerset House and decoyed onto the premises by the suggestion that he could intercede in a non-existent fight. Whilst the others restrained the magistrate, Robert Green garrotted him using a linen handkerchief, and 'with all his force, wrung his neck almost round'. On the fourth night after, the conspirators conveyed the body to Primrose Hill in a sedan, where one of the Jesuits rammed the sword into it and threw it in the ditch.

Green, Berry and Hill were placed under arrest and imprisoned in Newgate around Christmas-time 1678. They were aware of Prance's accusations against them, yet appear to have made no attempt to escape. Following a trial in the Court of King's Bench, Westminster Hall, they were found guilty of murder and sentenced to be 'severally hang'd by the neck till they were dead'. Green and Hill were hanged on 21 February 1679 at Tyburn,

This depiction of Godfrey's murderers being hanged may be incorrect, since it appears they were not executed in one go. (INTERFOTO/ Sammlung Rauch/Mary Evans)

The Execution of the mur: : therers of Sr E.B.Godfree

declaring their innocence to the last; Berry, who also declared himself innocent, was executed on 28 February following a temporary reprieve. The downward slope of Primrose Hill where the men afterwards hung in chains, became known for a time as 'Green-berry Hill' after their names. The diarist Luttrell states with authority that, remarkably, 'old leases' proved this site had been called Green Bury Hill before any of these events took place.

By this time, the unfortunate Coleman had also been executed following a trial at the King's Bench Bar on 27 November 1678, during which 'Dr' Oates had appeared as a prosecution witness. Nor was he the last. Dozens, largely comprising 'Priests and Jesuits', died languishing in gaol or were executed following show trials; including William Howard, 1st Viscount

Stafford. The king, although aware of Howard's innocence in any plot, did not have the strength of character or moral conviction to save him and Howard was beheaded on Tower Hill on 29 December 1680. Stafford declared his innocence before his death and cries of 'We believe you, my lord! God bless you, my lord!' swept through the ranks of the crowd. The affair culminated with the execution of Oliver Plunket, the Roman Catholic Archbishop of Armagh (see Chapter 12).

There is little doubt that the most culpable person in the entire episode is Titus Oates. At the very least, he had the blood of all those he falsely accused to the gallows on his hands, and his very name subsequently became synonymous with perjury. On 16 May 1685, justice finally caught up with him when he was convicted of that offence at the King's Bench, Westminster. Witnesses were procured who discredited his testimony and an infamously ruthless judge, Sir George Jeffries, condemned him to have his priestly habit taken from him, before sentencing him to life imprisonment. Jeffries also sentenced him to ever after be publicly set on the pillory four times a year and whipped by the common hangman from Aldgate to Newgate and Newgate to Tyburn alternately. This last part was executed with so much vigour that 'his back seemed to be all over flead [flayed]'. It is possible that Jeffries – frustrated by the fact that Oates could not be sentenced to death – hoped his harsh punishment would kill him off in its stead, although the perjurer was in fact released in 1689.

Still, Oates fared better than one of his contemporaries, Thomas Dangerfield, an Essex farmer's son of poor reputation who emerged from the woodwork as a secondary witness and accomplice to perjury during those treacherous times. After being convicted of publishing a libel which alleged he had been hired by the Duke of York to assassinate Charles II, Dangerfield was being conducted in a coach through St Andrew's, Holborn, following a whipping at Tyburn, when he was attacked. A Gray's Inn barrister named Robert Frances ran alongside the coach, throwing insults before stabbing Dangerfield in the eye with a small bamboo cane when he insulted him back. Dangerfield languished in agony for two days before expiring on 24 June 1685 aged in his mid-thirties. The attacker was apprehended whilst hiding in St Thavie's-Inn in Holborn and afterwards hanged for murder at Tyburn on 24 July 1685, aged around 40 years old.

The famous nineteenth century pamphleteer, politician and journalist William Cobbett concluded of the Popish Plot, simply and correctly, 'The affair was never examined with tranquillity or even with common sense…'

THE FRENCH MIDWIFE'S TRAGEDY

That convicted women criminals were sentenced to execution by public burning nowadays presents us with perhaps the cruellest indictment upon the times, illustrating vividly that 'mercy' was a strange, incomprehensible emotion to most, particularly so when it becomes known that crimes other than murder – like clipping and diminishing coins in circulation, for example – were also punishable by this method for women.

Unfortunately, it would be possible to list many examples of female prisoners being burnt throughout the century and across the country. In some cases, no doubt, the punishment was deemed fit enough for cold-blooded murderesses; but not all cases were so clear-cut.

A French midwife, Marie Hobry, of St Martin-in-the-Fields, was married to Denis Hobry, but their union was not a happy one. Her husband was a drinker, and frequent quarrels over her independent income led him to beat – and rape – her. After around four years of this domestic torture, during which she became consumed with the urge to kill her husband, Marie finally committed murder on the night of 27 January 1688.

Marie waited until her drunk husband came home. When he passed out on the bed at five o'clock in the morning she strangled him with a strong length of twine whilst he slept. The next day she awoke in dread when the realisation of her actions hit her and for at least a day the corpse remained in the house undisturbed. Marie had the presence of mind to collect her son, a servant, and bring him home, admitting what she had done and showing him his father's corpse. A jury would later decide he played no part in her subsequent actions.

After this revelation, Marie set to work on the body, dismembering it and furtively scattering the pieces across London. The arms, legs and thighs were thrown into a communal privy in the Savoy, while Mr Hobry's torso was deposited in Parker Street, between Drury Lane and Kingsway. The head was wrapped in a cloth and thrown in another 'house-of-office', in the expectation it would disappear into the Thames along with the excrement.

These parts did not remain hidden for long, however. By 30 January, most of the pieces had been recovered, some having been washed into the Thames and then deposited on the shoreline near an inn. Furthermore, one of the arms bore a distinctive mark upon its hand which very quickly identified it infallibly as Denis Hobry's.

When she was questioned by parish officers, Marie made a half-hearted attempt to persuade them her husband had gone to the Indies to collect diamonds; before caving in completely and admitting the murder. She went on trial at the Old Bailey, admitting her crime through an interpreter. On 22 February 1688, she was convicted of murder and petty treason. Her son was acquitted of any involvement, as were a fellow French couple, against whom it was alleged they had concealed knowledge of Mrs Hobry's actions. On 2 March, she was drawn to Leicester-Fields, where she was publicly burnt to ashes.

There were a number of news pamphlets produced on Marie's case. Some displayed a degree of sympathy – such as *An Epilogue to the French Midwife's Tragedy* – while others were more scathing, perhaps on account of the murderess's Catholicism. What is sad is that Marie accepted her life was over almost from the moment she was first questioned. One wonders, though, whether she had in fact accepted such a miserable fate long before. The implication is that she opted to kill her husband before he killed her, and therefore dying by the law was perhaps a risk worth taking, since dying by her husband she viewed as an unequivocal certainty.

CARRIAGE ASSASSINATIONS

In 1682, there occurred one of the most sensational killings of Restoration London, that of 35-year-old Thomas Thynne, of Longleat, Wiltshire, otherwise known as 'Tom of Ten Thousand' because of his large income.

Thynne, who also sat in the House of Commons as MP for Wiltshire, had formerly been a friend of the Duke of York (later to become James II) but, having quarrelled with his royal highness, he attached himself with great zeal to the Whig, or opposition, party, and subsequently their figurehead, the Duke of Monmouth. Thynne was also a womaniser. Shortly before his death he had succeeded in marrying Elizabeth, the youthful widow of Henry Cavendish, Lord Ogle, against her will. Her detestation of the union is implied by her immediate flight to Holland thereafter.

Between seven and eight o'clock on the night of Sunday, 12 February 1682, Thynne's coach was passing along Pall Mall when three men on horseback rode up alongside it. All were armed and, after waylaying the coach with a shout of 'Hold!', one of them pointed at Thynne in the carriage, as if to identify him. Another of them then poked a short-barrelled musket through the window and fired four or five bullets directly into the politician's stomach and body. Smoke filled the carriage and Thynne cried out that he was murdered. The three attackers then immediately galloped off in the direction of the Haymarket.

Thynne survived his injuries by only a few hours. An immediate investigation was launched under Monmouth and Sir John Reresby, a justice

Thynne is held up and assassinated: drawn by I Nicholls and engraved by James Basire in Hayward, Lives of the most remarkable criminals, *1735.* (Mary Evans Picture Library/GROSVENOR PRINTS)

of the peace for Westminster and Middlesex. Lady Ogle's unwanted seduction by Thynne had long been a common topic for upper-class coffee-house gossips, as was the fact that she had entertained another suitor in the form of a Swedish count called Carolus Joannes von Koningsmark, a nobleman of rank and fortune from Saxony. Koningsmark, a former soldier, had moved in societal circles after coming to London, making himself popular by winning considerable sums at the gaming tables whilst attempting to woo Lady Ogle.

Three European followers and servants of the count – Captain Christopher de Vratz, Lieutenant John Sterne and a Polish man called George Boroski – were arrested the next day, speedily confessing that they had been recruited on the Continent by Koningsmark before being brought over to England specifically to target Thynne. Boroski had been the man who physically shot him, whilst the other two, both Swedes, appeared very remorseful, implying their intention had been to assault Thynne and not murder him. Boroski, who spoke no other languages than Polish and High Dutch, had misunderstood their orders, however.

It is perhaps the case that the count sincerely believed Elizabeth was genuinely unhappy with Thynne and would be relieved by his removal. Koningsmark, a handsome man in his early twenties, was arrested in mid-February 1682 by one of Monmouth's attendants called Gibbons, who seized him as he was boarding a ship bound from England at Gravesend. It appears his location was betrayed by his landlord in Rotherhithe.

The four were tried at Hicks Hall later that month. Unfortunately, nothing connected the count directly to the murder other than the testimony of his co-accused; this produced a legal stalemate in his case that saw him acquitted, whilst de Vratz, Sterne and Boroski were convicted of murder. His acquittal was also greatly helped by a summing-up in his favour by the trial judge, Chief Justice Pemberton, who seemed determined to have him cleared.

Sir John Reresby wrote in his *Memoirs* that an attempt had been made to bribe him during the investigation; and, more suspiciously, that, 'Being at the king's couchee [reception] on the 21st, I perceived by his majesty's discourse that he was willing the count should get off.'

On 10 March 1682, the three convicted men were hanged in Pall Mall, at the scene of the crime and Boroski's corpse was afterwards hung in chains a little beyond Mile-End Town. Having paid his court fees, Count Koningsmark left England as quickly as possible, avoiding a challenge to a duel put to him by one of Thynne's friends, the Earl of Devonshire.

Another murder committed inside a London carriage is less well known;

but it was if anything even more cold-blooded. The incident began on the night of 4 January 1692, when two men hired an enclosed carriage at the corner of Fetter Lane and Fleet Street. They ordered the coachman, who sat outside upon a seat and whipped the horses, to drive them to the home of Andrew Clenche, a 'doctor of physic', in Brownlow Street, Holborn. When they arrived, the coachman was ordered to go and wake the doctor and tell him his urgent medical assistance was required. By this means Dr Clenche (at the time in his nightgown) was encouraged to get dressed and enter the vehicle, despite the unsociability of the hour.

The coach thus trundled off with its three passengers through London's unlit streets. The coachman's movements were directed by the two original fares from within the carriage. The journey was somewhat meandering – backwards and forwards, but in a generally-eastern direction towards Leadenhall. It was finally brought to a halt in the vicinity of Lime Street.

Here, the innocent – and somewhat bemused – coachman found himself unexpectedly dismissed by orders from within the carriage to buy a couple of fowls for supper. When he returned with the birds, however, the coachman found the vehicle eerily quiet. The two original passengers had absconded and the only thing that occupied the carriage interior now was the corpse of Dr Clenche.

The physician had been garrotted in the most cold-blooded and callous fashion. A pocket handkerchief had been wrung round his neck; the material had had a hard piece of coal wrapped in its folds, which had been clapped against his windpipe to better strangle him and crush his larynx.

This mysterious crime shocked and baffled Londoners. However, a suspect very quickly emerged in the form of a former soldier and lawyer's clerk, Henry Harrison, against whom numerous witnesses came forward with incriminating testimony. These included the coachman, of course, who provided a description of the man who had hired his carriage; a woman in Brownlow Street who had heedlessly peered into the carriage as it waited and seen a man of Harrison's description sitting within, draped in a cloak; a seamstress who recalled selling the distinctive handkerchief to Harrison; and the daughter of Harrison's landlord, who had seen the tell-tale garment in the suspect's Threadneedle Street lodgings. When he was apprehended in Whitefriars, Harrison could present no convincing account of where he had been between nine and eleven o'clock on the night of the murder.

Harrison was tried at the Old Bailey on 6 April 1692, pleading 'Not guilty in thought, word, nor deed'. During the trial, however, it became apparent that he despised the murdered doctor, whose finances, properties and investments had become hopelessly entangled with those of a widow called Mrs Vanwicke. Harrison was greatly attached to this woman and had acted as her financial administrator; in the end, it appears, matters financial had turned extremely acrimonious and therefore, Harrison opted to remove Dr Clenche altogether.

Harrison was convicted of murder and sentenced to death, still denying he had been one of the assassins in the carriage. He remained obstinate even on the point of execution. Nonetheless he was hanged from a specially-erected beam at Brook-street end in Holborn on 15 April 1692, with his last breath denying any guilt whatsoever.

The identity of the second murderer in the carriage was never satisfactorily ascertained. For a while, an Irishman named Rowe was thrown into Newgate upon suspicion, since he too was heavily entangled in Mrs Vanwicke's financial quagmire and also stood to gain by Clenche's murder. However, the case against him collapsed.

THE LAW AND ORDER CRISIS

By the end of the seventeenth century, it can safely be said that London, much like the rest of the country, was in the grip of a law and order crisis.

The shambolic state of policing inherited from Charles II's reign became exacerbated by a number of factors largely beyond the control of any government. At sea, for instance, hostile European vessels disrupted trade. And a catastrophic earthquake in Jamaica in 1692 severely affected the great mercantile houses of London and Bristol, while that same year the harvest failed calamitously at home. No fruit ripened and the price of wheat doubled. Old men in 1692 remembered no such year like it since 1648. The evil was aggravated by the state of the silver coin, which had been clipped to such an extent that the words 'pound' and 'shilling' ceased to have a fixed meaning. The necessity of retrenchment was felt by families of every rank in society and in some counties mobs of peasants began attacking granaries. Smuggling on the coast, to sidestep the law, and ambushes by highway robbers inland began to reach epidemic proportions.

It can be no coincidence that during the autumn and winter of 1692, the capital was kept in a constant state of alarm thanks to a surge in house-breaking. One gang, thirteen strong, entered the mansion of the Duke of Ormond in St James's Square and all but succeeded in carrying off his magnificent plate and jewels. According to the diarist Narcissus Luttrell, writing in November 1692, another gang made an attempt upon Lambeth Palace. When stately abodes guarded by numerous servants, were in such danger, it may easily be surmised that no shopkeeper's stock nor the contents of more humble dwellings could be considered safe. From Bow to Hyde Park, from Thames Street to Bloomsbury, there was no parish in which some quiet dwelling had not been sacked by burglars.

This situation often forced civilians to use extreme violence in defence of their property. Luttrell recorded in September 1693 how a servant had discharged a blunderbuss at a burglar who had broken into the house of his employer, Mr Vanderbendy, in Pall Mall at three in the morning. The wounded man was dragged off by his comrades; a great trail of blood that was followed all the way to Leicester Fields (Leicester Square) suggested his injury had been mortal.

The government's reaction to the problem was utterly predictable. Ruthless punishment was imposed for all manner of crimes, regardless of their severity; one statute enacted as of May 1699 made burglary, housebreaking, and the theft of goods worth more than five shillings from shops, warehouses, coach houses and stables a hanging offence. Lethal punishment was also directed at those who ordered such crimes or assisted in them.

Chapter 4

Lawless Noblemen and Duelling Gentlemen

Sir John Townsend was one of the leading politicians of the late Tudor era, having behind him a distinguished military career before becoming an MP for Castle Rising, Norfolk. He later became a leading member in King James I's first Parliament in 1603, entrusted with many important responsibilities. It was during the sitting of this Parliament that he had the misfortune to fall into an argument with Sir Matthew Brown, of Betchworth Castle in Surrey, which ended in a duel fought between them on horseback on Hounslow Heath. Both men mortally wounded each other; Sir Matthew was killed on the spot aged about 40 and Sir John died not long afterwards on 2 August, aged about 35.

It is not clear what the duel concerned; but Sir John Townsend had previously been involved in another duel, when he had been the second of Sir John Heydon. During this encounter, which happened at Rackheath, Norfolk, in 1600, Heydon's left hand was lopped off by Sir Robert Mansel and ever after he went by the name of 'Heydon with the one hand'. This hand, now blackened and shrivelled but still with its nails visible, is held by Norwich Castle's Museum, mummified in a posture that suggests it remains as it did when clutching the sword's hilt.

Although duels fought on horseback were somewhat unusual, combat in which both participants died, or were critically wounded, was less so. In London, two Scottish courtiers, Sir George Wharton (son to Lord Wharton), and Sir James Stewart, eldest son to the Treasurer Lord Blantyre, fought a private combat with rapiers and daggers, after passing scathing letters between each other. After searching each other's person for hidden armour, they fought at three o'clock in the afternoon, in a field 'at ye farther end of Islington' - whereupon they killed each other. According to one account, each fatally wounded the other at the first thrust and they died collapsing in each other's arms. The sad accident made King James extremely unhappy – since

Stewart had been his godson – and he ordered the dead men to be buried in the same grave. Islington's parish register confirms both were interred on 10 November 1609.

The senseless and suicidal nature of duelling is shown by an incident in 1625. According to correspondence received by Joseph Mead of Christ's College, dated 4 March, a Kentish gentleman called Sir Humphrey Tufton and a Scotsman called Murray (of the Prince's bed-chamber) squared up in St George's Fields after falling out at a stage play. However, by mutual consent the combat did not occur, because although Sir Humphrey had called for a private duel, Murray accidentally turned up with a second. This was another Scot called Gibson, one of the king's servants. After the two participants went their separate ways, Gibson apparently began lambasting Murray, calling him a coward and a disgrace to Scotland. He then secretly drew his sword and thrust Murray through both cheeks. In the melee that followed, both Gibson and Murray stabbed each other fatally.

Despite this, during these times there was something approaching legitimacy, and perhaps even a perceived nobility, to duelling. Sir Humphrey Tufton had requested that his duel with Murray be deferred because 'they might do it privately, and none might see them'. Had Murray not been slain by Gibson, his quarrelsome second, there is no question but that combat would have occurred; matters like these were ones of honour, or private warfare, in which the participants knew that execution was unlikely in the event of their survival.

Mid-century, during the Interregnum, the number of duels dropped. Carrying weapons became prohibited by Cromwell's government, and to kill someone when duelling was equated with murder. Whilst not exactly ensuring a death sentence, a parliamentary ordinance against duels in 1654 threatened much harsher punishment than had gone before.

This situation reversed itself for the worse following the Restoration in 1660. Rapiers and other weapons became symbols of liberty, openly worn in the streets. The inevitable by-product was, of course, that they were frequently used. By the time Charles II issued a proclamation against duels on 11 March 1679, it was almost too late: for law and order had degenerated in London greatly and violent, drunken brawls across the capital were virtually endemic. Duelling was so common around this time that in many cases it was barely noteworthy. Young men frequenting the pits of the theatres in the capital, often ended up adjourning to the duelling ground; the death of one whose uproarious conduct had interrupted the early scenes of a play seldom produced any marked sensation later on.

It is important to consider the backdrop against which this was all set. Until the last year of Charles II, most of London's streets were left in profound darkness, allowing gangs of dissolute young gentlemen to swagger about the town by night, smashing windows, overturning sedans, assaulting women and attacking other men. Throughout the Restoration, certain gangs assumed varying slang denominations: the Muns; the Tityre Tus, who attacked the poet John Milton's house and broke his windows; the Hectors; the Scourers; and later the Nickers and the Hawkubites. Luttrell recorded on 3 January 1683 that 'three hectors' randomly smashing windows in Holborn after a drinking session had lately stabbed a watchman who confronted them. For good measure, they killed the watchman's dog before running off. The implication is that these gangs were comprised of groups of young men with too much money to waste and not enough responsibility.

The behaviour of those who moved in the sphere of gentlemen around this time was appalling. Typical was the case of Sir Thomas Halford. During a violent tavern argument in Bishopsgate, London, Sir Thomas hit Edmund Temple on the skull with a wine bottle so violently that he died a few weeks later, on 23 February 1668. According to the *Middlesex County Records*, Sir Thomas put himself on trial and was acquitted of murder, although he was convicted of manslaughter. He pleaded his clergy, and avoided being branded with a hot iron thanks to the special order of the king. Furthermore, Charles II dictated that Sir Thomas 'be no further molested in respect to the said felony.' For the most part, no modish person thought any the worse of perpetrators like Sir Thomas. Many were young men – and their violent acts were seen only in the context of festive brawls, committed without premeditation.

Of particular note is Charles Mohun, 4th Baron Mohun, a turbulent man in turbulent times, who has perhaps come to epitomise the era. He very likely grew up with the notion that violence was the natural way to obtain satisfaction in a disagreement. His father, the 3rd baron, had died in 1677 after being badly wounded in a duel, when Charles was around two years old. This was how Mohun inherited his father's estate and before he was twenty he had fallen into the gambling, squandering, duelling lifestyle that the capital by then encouraged so easily.

On the evening of 9 December 1692, he was present when a friend of his, Captain Richard Hill (of Colonel Earle's regiment), attempted to abduct the celebrated actress Anne Bracegirdle after she left a tavern in Prince's Street and set off along Drury Lane. The kidnap was thwarted thanks to the clamour it caused and an irate Hill later confronted one of Ms Bracegirdle's fellow players, William Mountfort, in 'that part of Howard Street which lies between Norfolk Street and Surrey Street'. Hill was under the impression that Mountfort was his rival for the actress's affections and in a confusing melee, of which there were several versions, Mountfort was fatally wounded. According to witness Ann Jones, a servant at Miss Bracegirdle's house, Captain Hill had simply walked up to Mountfort whilst Lord Mohun embraced him and punched him in the side of the head; after a short scuffle, he then stabbed Mountfort in the stomach underneath his ribcage.

Mountfort died the following afternoon, aged about 33. The suggestion that Mohun may have been distracting the victim deliberately led to his arrest and on 28 January 1693 he was tried before a jury of his peers at Westminster Hall. In the end the jury found him 'Not Guilty' by a majority verdict; Mohun was then allowed to symbolically break a staff, signifying his innocence, before he left the court.

What became of Captain Hill is not known for certain. There is a belief that he fled to Moon's Moat, a medieval moated house south of Beoley in Worcestershire, where Mohun had humble relatives. It may be that, whilst there, he caused the death of the daughter of the house, Mariolle Mohun, who disappeared around this time. For this killing, he was subsequently murdered after leaving the Angel Inn, Alcester, in February 1693, his body being secretly disposed of.

Back in London, Lord Mohun could not stay out of trouble. On 29 October 1698, aged around 23, he facilitated a duel between Captain Richard Coote and Captain Richard French behind the Cross Keys tavern at the corner of Green Street, by 'the lower corner of the paved stones going up to Leicester House'. Coote was killed after being stabbed in his left side under the ribs and through the lungs. Coote's chairmen went to collect him as he lay dying, but struggled to carry the sedan over some railings; farcically, when they saw how blood poured from Coote's wounds, they refused to allow him to enter it anyway, declaring his blood would spoil the chair's interior.

The confusing circumstances surrounding Coote's death led to Mohun and a friend of his, Edward Rich, 6th Earl of Warwick and Holland, who had also encouraged the duel, standing trial before the House of Lords in Westminster Hall on 28 March 1699. Warwick was convicted of manslaughter, despite not having been the man who killed Coote, but set free after pleading the benefit of clergy and paying the usual fees. Lord Mohun

Charles Mohun's behaviour symbolises the era. (Mary Evans Picture Library)

was cleared altogether, the jury unable to decide what his level of participation had been. Captain French – the actual killer of Coote – was tried at the Old Bailey and found guilty of manslaughter, but allowed his clergy, which let him off with his life.

Mohun's second trial seems to have affected him greatly, for he made a determined effort to give up the excessive drinking that was the cause of his many fights. He gave himself over to study, distinguishing himself as a speaker on behalf of the Whig party in the House of Lords, having also become the colonel of a regiment in the meantime. In 1701, he accompanied the Earl of Macclesfield to Germany to negotiate the Act of Settlement, paving the way for the House of Hanover to take the British throne.

Mohun's notoriety largely stems from his brutal duel with the Earl of Hamilton in 1712, when both parties fought like enraged tigers and both lost their lives.

What is disturbing is that the 4th Baron Mohun's conduct was not exceptional for the times; in London and across the country in general, there were a great many gentlemen, peers and noblemen whose behaviour was worse.

'PRINCE GRIFFIN', THE MISSING MURDERER

John Aubrey's *Miscellanies* (1696) tells us that the son and heir of Warwick, 2nd Lord Mohun, was murdered *c*.1647. This young man – 'a gallant gentleman' – had quarrelled with a Prince Griffin. There was a challenge, and they agreed to fight upon the following morning, on horseback, in Chelsea fields. Whilst young Mohun was on his way to meet his enemy, he was accosted by some men near Ebury Farm (Ebury Square) who attacked him and 'pistolled him' (shot him). Young Mohun's injuries proved fatal and it was subsequently speculated that Griffin had ordered Mohun killed when he realised he was much the better horseman, and would have won their duel.

'Prince Griffin' was probably the nickname of John Griffiths, a Welsh politician and MP for Caernarvonshire who was expelled from the House of Commons in 1642 for raping Lady Elizabeth Sedley. He would appear to be the same Prince Griffin reported to have been in Cheshire around February 1647, who attempted to woo Lady Causley, wife of Sir Hugh Causley of Saighton, south of Chester. At first, Griffin tried sending silk stockings, ribbons, gloves, etc. to the Causley's house. When he learned that Lady Causley was throwing these gifts on the hearth, however, he sent a parcel with 'crackers, squibs and wild-fire' in the wrapping, which when tossed on the fire exploded and flew about the room.

Next, he surrounded himself with a group of friends and tried to forcibly accost Lady Causley at the house in Saighton in a 'rash and incivill' fashion. When a servant tried to defend his mistress, Griffin stabbed him in the body with a sword before one of his comrades shot the man dead with a pistol.

Correspondence dated 4 March 1647 suggested Griffin had thereafter escaped to Edinburgh, but what became of him after this seems to be missing from the record. It is possible he left the country for Paris, where he died. The lack of data is not surprising, given that Griffin's abuses occurred during the confusion of the civil wars.

A COMPLICATION OF DUELS

In August 1662, Mr Henry Jermyn, nephew to the Earl of St Albans, was challenged to a duel by Captain Thomas Howard, although Howard refused to be forthcoming in what his quarrel with Jermyn was about. When they met on 18 August at the Old Pall Mall at St James's, Howard and his second turned up wearing hidden body armour, which was only discovered when the fighting started and Jermyn's sword thrusts had no impact. Inevitably, Jermyn was critically wounded and his own second, Colonel Giles Rawlins, was killed; after which, Howard and his man escaped the battlefield on horses they had positioned nearby. Although Jermyn did not die, it was clear he had been effectively ambushed – apparently following a warm-up game of tennis between all concerned, no less. The murderous nature of the affair caused great disquiet, and Pepys wrote:

> 'The Court is much concerned in this fray, and I am glad of it; hoping that it will cause some good laws against it.'

This affair was even more complicated than Pepys suggests. It transpired the duel was over the hand of a woman, Lady Anna Maria Brudenell, who entertained the affections of both Captain Howard, the challenger, and Jermyn, the injured man, who, it should be noted, survived despite suffering three wounds at Howard's hand.

Colonel Rawlins, who died in the melee, had several years previously killed William Ashburnham in a duel under such questionable circumstances that a coroner's jury on 29 August 1656 declared the case amounted to murder. Following his victim's burial in East Sussex two days later, the charge against Rawlins appears to have collapsed. Therefore, it is entirely possible that Howard, the challenger, was aware of Colonel Rawlins's historical reputation for being underhand in such matters and so chose to wear body-armour to thwart him.

Howard's second, who escaped with him after the combat, turned out to be Colonel Cary Dillon, later 5th Earl of Roscommon; after about a quarter of a year, both returned to England to take their trial for Rawlins's murder, but were acquitted.

It is said of Howard that he was also involved in a separate killing, that of a horse-courier in St Giles, but the circumstances surrounding this incident are not clear. He later married the Duchess of Richmond.

THE SILLY QUARREL

1667 saw the killing of Sir Henry Bellasis, knight and politician, who was stabbed with a rapier in the right breast during a duel with his friend, the dramatist Thomas Porter. Sir Henry was wounded near St Paul's 'the Actor's Church', Covent Garden, on 28 July 1667. The knight languished for several days before expiring on 11 August and when an inquest was held, it was established that Porter had escaped; in fact, he was still missing on 20 May 1668 when he was outlawed. Pepys wrote of 'the silliness of the quarrel', for it seems the pair were the best of friends, until the day of their argument, when Porter drunkenly declared that no man in England would dare to strike him a blow. Following this comment, Sir Henry punched him in the face and their fight escalated until Porter stabbed him. As the knight sagged, clutching his wound, he kissed Porter and then said, 'Tom, thou hast hurt me; but I will make shift to stand upon my legs till thou mayst withdraw, for I would not have thee troubled for what thou hast done.' Sir Henry was at the time MP for Grimsby, Lincolnshire, and aged in his late twenties.

Porter, the killer, had formerly been a groom of the royal bed-chamber as well as a playwright. Subsequently he escaped to France, thus avoiding punishment. He had other blood on his hands too; in 1655, his sword had mortally wounded a soldier called Thomas Salkeld during a disagreement in Covent Garden. This occurred around the time that Porter had abducted Ann Blount, daughter of the Earl of Newport, and forced her to marry him – therefore it is perhaps the case he killed Salkeld over this affair. Although he denied murder, Porter admitted the soldier's manslaughter and, having 'read his verse and pleaded his clergy', he avoided execution on that occasion and was merely burnt upon his hand at the time.

BUCKINGHAM, SHREWSBURY AND THE 'INFAMOUS STRUMPET'

Undoubtedly the most infamous duel that occurred during Charles II's reign was the contest between George Villiers, 2nd Duke of Buckingham, and Francis Talbot, the Earl of Shrewsbury.

Buckingham, the son of the duke who had been assassinated four decades earlier, led a life of intrigues, affairs and other deeds of profligacy. He had lately seduced Anna Maria Talbot, Shrewsbury's wife; as a result of which the earl made the challenge. Word of the proposed combat reached the ears of the king, who attempted to arrange for Buckingham, his friend and comrade-in-arms, to be confined and so miss the engagement. However, the Duke of Albemarle, to whom this task was entrusted, misunderstood the responsibility asked of him and the duel went ahead.

On 16 or 17 January 1668, the combatants arrived at the designated place, a close near Barn Elms, not far from the Thames at Barnes. The duke, who was almost 40 years old, was accompanied by two seconds, Captain Holmes and Sir Jones Jenkins. The seconds of the Earl of Shrewsbury were Sir John Talbot, a gentleman of the privy chamber, and Bernard Howard, son of the Earl of Arundel.

According to the fashion of the age, all four of the seconds took up swords against each other. Buckingham and Shrewsbury also fought like wild animals and the duel developed into a deadly three-a-side melee from which no-one escaped unscathed. Shrewsbury, the challenger, was run through the body from the right breast to the shoulder, and so badly wounded that he died on 16 March after lingering for around two months. Jenkins, one of Buckingham's seconds, was killed in the field, whilst Talbot was severely wounded in both his arms. Buckingham and the other seconds escaped with slight wounds.

Perhaps the most well-known detail of this bloody skirmish concerns Lady Shrewsbury, who is said to have watched the duel dressed as a page and holding her paramour's horse in a thicket nearby. The poet Alexander Pope understood the duel to have been arranged by her and Buckingham, so that she might rid herself of her husband, although it is unclear whether this was the case. However, Pope's assertion that Buckingham slept with Lady Shrewsbury on the night following his victory while still wearing his bloodied shirt is generally considered to be a historical truism. This is said to have occurred at Buckingham's own house, he having the affront to take his mistress home, introduce her to the duchess, and then take Lady Shrewsbury to bed!

Following his death, the Earl of Shrewsbury was buried in the parish of Albrighton, Shropshire.

The Earl of Westmoreland attempted to get Buckingham charged with murder, in the interests of Shrewsbury's eldest son, declaring that Buckingham had also made Lady Shrewsbury a whore and was 'keeping her as an infamous strumpet'. Buckingham, in his defence, claimed that

Shrewsbury had threatened to shoot him on numerous occasions and because of this he had been in constant fear of his life.

In the end, Buckingham was preserved from prosecution thanks to the intervention of Lady Castlemaine, the monarch's mistress. And although King Charles II pardoned all concerned on 5 February – before Shrewsbury's death – he nonetheless appears to have recognised the outrage the affair had caused; the deed of pardon also contained a clause stating that, in future, his mercy would not extend to others in such a situation.

Amazingly, the Countess of Shrewsbury was the same Anna Maria over whom Jermyn and Howard had fought in 1662. Interestingly, the Countess later lost one of her own sons to a duel. John Talbot, younger brother to the subsequent Earl of Shrewsbury, was fatally wounded by Henry Fitzroy, Duke of Grafton, on the morning of 2 February 1686 in Chelsea Fields. Grafton was, in fact, one of King Charles II's illegitimate sons by his mistress the Countess of Castlemaine.

THE SOCIOPATHIC EARL

By 1678 Philip Herbert, 7th Earl of Pembroke and 4th of Montgomery, was an accident waiting to happen. His pedigree was impressive – he was the representative of a distinguished line, the son of a Wiltshire MP and married to Henrietta de Querouaille, a sister of the Duchess of Portsmouth, one of the king's favourite mistresses. But he seems by the age of 25 to have developed into what can only be described as a homicidal maniac. In November 1677, he nearly killed a man in a duel but his conduct had yet to become much worse.

John Aubrey tells us of Pembroke's character that he 'espoused not learning, but was addicted to field-sports and hospitality'. On 28 January 1678, the earl was committed to the Tower of London 'for uttering such horrid and blasphemous words, and other actions proved upon oath, as are not fit to be repeated in any Christian assembly'. The House of Lords petitioned the king on Pembroke's behalf and as a result the earl did not spend long imprisoned.

However, inside of a week he had violently assaulted a man named Philip Ricaut in the Strand one evening, nearly knocking his eye out of his head with a tremendous blow from his fist. He then further attacked his victim like a raging maniac and was in the act of drawing his sword when Ricaut managed to scramble away through a doorway. On 5 February, the injured man petitioned the House of Lords to 'be an asylum to him' in the event that Pembroke tried to finish what he had started. The Lords ordered the earl to 'give security by recognizance of £2,000 to keep the peace towards the said Philip Ricaut, and all others of his majesty's subjects.'

The Earl of Pembroke seems to have been possessed of an uncontrollable rage, particularly when in drink. Around the same time as his attack on Ricaut, Pembroke had assaulted another man. On 4 February, he simply walked up to Nathaniel Cony in a tavern called Long's in the Haymarket and punched him in the left side of the head. When Cony crashed to the floor, Pembroke continued kicking him so viciously that the injured man died five days later.

What triggered the incident is unclear, since it had been late and most of those present were in drink but it seems to have begun when Pembroke threw a glass of wine in the face of one of Cony's associates, a man named Goring. Swords were drunkenly drawn, but a friend of the latter named Captain Savage took Goring's weapon from him, snapping it and leading him off to bed in an effort to end the argument. However, under somewhat uncertain circumstances the disagreement resurrected itself – with Nathaniel Cony suffering the vicious assault that led to his death. On 6 February, as he lingered, he weakly told Goring that 'my lord of Pembroke' had done him the initial injury, and although the brutal kicking he next received might have been dealt him by Pembroke and others, 'My lord should answer for it.' It is possible Cony had been attacked for trying to retrieve Goring's periwig and broken sword, which had been stolen during the initial arguing earlier on.

On 11 February 1678, the Middlesex coroner brought in a verdict of 'Wilful Murder' on the body of Nathaniel Cony, the Earl of Pembroke being named as his murderer. Pembroke arrogantly denied any culpability in the killing, but was nonetheless imprisoned in the Tower prior to facing his trial in the Court of Westminster Hall.

This began on 4 April 1678 and the nobleman was tried by a jury of his peers. The prisoner was brought from the Tower accompanied by guards who ceremonially carried an axe before them; however, when the trial started it was reasonably clear what was going to happen. The Lord High Steward, the Earl of Nottingham, referred in his opening remarks to the murder charge as 'no more than a bare accusation'. Nonetheless, Pembroke's trial proceeded before 'the whole House of Peers, who are met together to make inquisition for this blood'.

Goring and Savage were among the witnesses for the prosecution, the latter claiming to have seen the deceased physically attacked by the accused, whilst a male nurse named Hemes declared he had observed a great deal of internal bleeding in the victim's stomach when he was autopsied. In fact, the autopsy suggested Cony had been dealt a shocking deal of violence.

Throughout the proceedings, the Earl of Pembroke said little, and following two hours of private debate in the House of Lords, six among his inquisitors found him 'Guilty' of murder; eighteen found him 'Not Guilty' and forty convicted him of manslaughter only. Following this, Pembroke claimed 'the privilege of the statute' and was set free following the payment of certain fines. The Lord High Steward dismissed the earl with a caution that he would be allowed such leniency but once.

Thus, on account of his noble status, the Earl of Pembroke – a man with a proven history of violence – did not even suffer the indignity of being burnt upon his hand, the inadequate-enough punishment imposed on common people who had proved they could read and thus successfully pleaded their clergy.

On 28 November, the earl was arraigned before his peers again, for challenging the Earl of Dorset to a fight, following a quarrel whilst under the roof of Mr Lloyd. During this altercation, Pembroke 'laid violent hands upon' Dorset, in so threatening a fashion that one of the latter's footmen thought it prudent to swipe the Earl of Pembroke's sword away in fear of what might follow. For this transgression, Pembroke was requested to 'retire himself to his house at Wilton' (Wilton House, Wiltshire).

Around this time, Pembroke is said by John Aubrey to have kept an astonishing menagerie at the stately home, which included fifty-two mastiffs, thirty greyhounds, 'some beares, and a lyon', as well as entertaining a retinue of sixty fellows as unpredictable and degenerate as himself.

The earl was not only uncontrollable but also by now a liability, and on 18 August 1680 he and his friends ran into more trouble. This occurred when their coach was stopped near a tavern as it trundled homeward across Turnham Green following a heavy drinking bout. A Chiswick watchman and a constable demanded to know where the vehicle was heading. While the questioning continued, Pembroke – who was sitting on the far side of the coach – opened his door and ran round to meet the men who had inconvenienced him. Without ado, he rammed his sword into the gut of William Smeethe, a gentleman belonging to the Court, who happened to be present, the blade passing entirely through his body. He then wheeled around and stabbed a constable named Halfpenny a number of times. A third person was less seriously wounded by the earl's sword. Remarkably, Smeethe, though dangerously wounded, cried out, 'I will not be thus killed like a dog!' before knocking the nobleman over with a staff. A general melee next followed between Pembroke's friends, who numbered about six, and the watchmen; but the louts were beaten into submission, probably on account of them being so drunk they were almost incapable.

The Earl of Pembroke was dragged into a chamber at the nearby Cock and Half Moon tavern and there kept imprisoned. It so happened that a coach following the earl's contained a 'person of quality', who recognised what had happened and immediately interfered, corruptly influencing the prisoner's release. Quite how is unclear, but it is implied that the watchman assigned to the earl's chamber was bribed or threatened. It was around one in the morning when Pembroke managed to slip away in the direction of London.

Despite the attention of surgeons, Mr Smeethe died from his injuries. He is said to have been a stout, worthy man of considerable estate, and had he not been stabbed unexpectedly, he would have beaten his cowardly attacker hands down. Halfpenny, the constable, is also suggested to have been so critically injured that he could neither be operated upon nor saved.

Predictably, a contemporary pamphlet observed, 'On Fryday the Crowner [coroner] and his Jury *sate* upon the deceased; but could not agree in giving in their Verdict.'

According to Narcissus Luttrell, Pembroke did eventually stand trial for this murder (or murders). But, as before, on 22 June 1681 he came into court, pleaded the king's pardon and was discharged – despite all the warnings he had received following his first conviction. It is entirely possible that the earl's sister-in-law, the Duchess of Portsmouth, who had the king's ear, used a certain amount of her influence to prevent Pembroke's deserved incarceration upon this occasion.

In addition to his homicidal tendencies, Pembroke is also held to have mismanaged his Wiltshire estate, and bullied his wife Henrietta. When he died abroad aged just 30 on 29 August 1683, he was heavily in debt. Fittingly, he died through the effects of his intemperance. The Earl of Pembroke was buried at Salisbury, Wiltshire, and one cannot help wondering whether most of his contemporaries were pleased to see the back of him, despite his youth.

KILLER PEERS

As incredible as it may seem, the case of Pembroke was hardly unique. For example, on 14 April 1666 a warrant had been issued by the Lord Chancellor ordering Thomas, Lord Morley and Monteagle, of St Giles-in-the-Field, to appear at Westminster in two weeks' time on a charge of murder. It was alleged that Morley had become embroiled in an argument with Henry Hastings over half-a-crown at the Fleece Tavern, Covent Garden. The two may have held a former grudge, for two witnesses declared that the peer had rammed his sword into Hastings's head and yelled, 'God damn, I promised

This effigy in St Michael's Church, Rudbaxton, is of Thomas Hayward, MP for Haverfordwest. The red mark on his torso signifies his death in a duel fought on 7 July 1682 atop a nearby hillfort, the Rath. His opponent, who may have been a man called Scotton, appears to have been hanged.

thee this, and now I have given it thee.' The victim was fatally wounded, and when Morley appeared at Westminster Hall as ordered he was tried in a specially-erected court before the House of Lords. His argument was that he had killed Hastings in self-defence and evidence was presented that the victim had been guilty of killing a man not long before. Hastings had also previously been imprisoned in the Tower for threatening Lord Morley in the street.

On 30 April, all but two of the noble jury found Morley 'Not Guilty' of murder, and so the Lord Steward convicted him of manslaughter only. After pleading his clergy and benefit of the statute, Morley was typically allowed to go free following the payment of certain fees. On 11 May, one of Morley's friends, Captain Francis Bromwich, was convicted as an accessory in the death of Hastings and sentenced to 11 months imprisonment, which appears to have been overturned in July on condition he 'serve his Majesty in the wars' abroad.

Then there was the case of Charles Cornwallis, 3rd Baron Cornwallis. In the small hours of 18 May 1678, he entered into an argument with a Whitehall sentinel guarding the foot of the stairs at his lodgings after the latter merely enquired 'who goes there?' Cornwallis was with a friend called Gerrard and both were utterly drunk; in fact, they began arguing with each other for the privilege of stabbing the watchman with their swords for his impertinence. Two young men, who lodged elsewhere in the same building, suffered the misfortune of blundering into this threatening situation and Cornwallis next turned his inebriated rage upon them, threatening one of the youths he would 'kick his arse to Hell'. The arguing between the respective parties continued up the stairs until someone – either Lord Cornwallis or Gerrard, it is not clear who – descended half-way back down and struck one of the youths, Robert Clerk, so forcefully that it knocked him off his feet. Clerk broke his neck in a catastrophic fall down the stairs and died almost instantly.

When Cornwallis appeared at Westminster for his murder trial, his peers found him 'Not Guilty'. This was mainly on account of the fact that a deliberate intention to kill Clerk could not be proven. The youth's death Cornwallis termed an accident, adding that it had taught him a lesson about his rakish lifestyle. Most of the evidence also suggested that Gerrard had killed the youth, although he had escaped and was not yet caught.

MURDER IN THE GLOBE TAVERN
A brutal, drunken fracas in London's Globe Tavern ended the life of a distinguished gentleman Sir William Estcourt, 3rd Baronet of Long Newnton. In November 1684, the knight and politician sat as a juror at the trial of Edward Noseworthy in the Court of King's Bench. Noseworthy was at the time being tried for treasonable utterances in support of Edward Fitzharris, an Irish Catholic agitator who had been convicted and executed in London under questionable circumstances; Noseworthy's comment that he hoped the judges who had hanged Fitzharris would themselves be hanged, had brought him before a jury that included Sir William. Due to a farcical misunderstanding about which county Noseworthy had been in when he uttered this treasonable sentence, he was acquitted.

It was after the trial, on 14 November 1684, that Sir William made his way to the Globe in Fleet Street with his fellow jurymen and some friends from the country. Here, he entered into a drink-fuelled argument with Sir Henry St John, a Whig politician, and Colonel Edmund Richmond-Webb, a Tory, following an initial confrontation with another Tory present, Francis Stonehouse. The breath-taking suggestion is that the argument was not even about Noseworthy's trial, which might possibly have been a natural focus for political disagreement. It appears in fact to have been over horseracing. The end result was an attack on Sir William Estcourt by St John and Richmond-Webb, who stabbed him five times in the hand, stomach and groin, killing him. The knight was aged 30 at the time and unarmed; since he was without heirs the title became extinct.

Later that month, both murderers were taken from Newgate to the Old Bailey for their trial. They were found guilty and condemned to death, but predictably on 16 January 1685 they 'severally pleaded his Majesty's pardon' and were discharged. Bishop Burnet adds that St John initially pleaded guilty on the promise of a pardon, but found royal mercy would not be granted until £1,600 had been delivered over – of which the king took half before giving the rest to two ladies. As for Richmond-Webb, his pardon is said to have been abetted thanks to his loyalty to the crown during 'turbulent and staggering times'.

Certain taverns, like the Globe, earned a reputation for murder. Of the Fleece Tavern, York Street, Covent Garden, Pepys wrote, 'there had been a great many formerly killed there.' His contemporary, John Aubrey, knew of 'three in my time' who had died through violence at the inn.

THE MURDER OF THE MYSTERIOUS 'BEAU' WILSON

One of the great intrigues of William and Mary's reign concerned the killing of Edward 'Beau' Wilson. It was not so much his killing, but the man himself that was the subject of much coffee-house gossip.

This very mysterious person, the younger son of a respectable Leicestershire family, was so broke after a short stint in the army in Flanders that he was forced to borrow 40 shillings simply to return to London. However, not long after his arrival in the capital, Wilson's circumstances somehow changed dramatically. His coaches, saddle, racehorses and wardrobe were the admiration of London society, and he quickly became something of a celebrity. Wilson kept his family in great splendour and no-one complained of his being their debtor, yet how Wilson maintained his equipage was a mystery to all, since he had no visible means of support. He barely gambled, so could not have won at the tables. Furthermore, he was so conspicuous that any missed time he spent earning his income, by whatever means, would have been noticed by his contemporaries.

Whilst he hinted that he was assured of an income for the rest of his life, 'Beau' Wilson could not be tricked or persuaded to reveal how he had come by his fortune, remaining tight-lipped even when in drink. This naturally generated rumours; for instance, that while in Europe he had robbed a Holland mail of a huge quantity of diamonds, letting another man hang for it. Other stories circulated that a third party was maintaining him for mysterious reasons, and that he may have even accidentally discovered the secret of converting base metals into gold.

Spending money freely, Wilson lived every day as though it was his last. In fact, his last day came on 9 April 1694, thanks to a long-running feud with a young Scotsman called Captain John Lawes, of St-Giles-in-the-Fields. What their difference concerned was never made clear. It may have had something to do with Mrs Lawrence, an acquaintance of Lawes's who Wilson insulted. At any rate, it seems to have involved a woman, but not to have been a romantic affair – since Wilson was not known to be an admirer of ladies.

Things finally came to a head in the Fountain tavern. The two men left to fight a much-anticipated duel and squared off in front of a number of

Wilson is fatally wounded: a later imagining.

witnesses in Bloomsbury Square. There, Wilson was fatally wounded when Lawes stabbed him in the stomach with a sword.

On 18 April 1694 Lawes was convicted of Wilson's murder by an Old Bailey jury and sentenced to death. However, this was later changed to a manslaughter conviction and a fine. By October 1694, Wilson's brother had challenged this decision and Lawes was re-incarcerated in the King's Bench Prison. Luttrell recorded how later that month Lawes attempted to escape his captivity by filing down four bars in his cell. This endeavour, or another like it, was successful, because the killer was next heard of being apprehended in Leicestershire, during a flight to Scotland. However, he avoided the law entirely and escaped to Europe, notwithstanding a reward put on his head. He ultimately received a pardon in 1719.

'Beau' Wilson lived in unaccountable splendour until the day of his death. The mystery of his income rather augmented than diminished afterwards, for he was found to be in possession of very little money, leaving Londoners to guess where the funds came from that had supported his extravagant lifestyle.

Luttrell also recorded in January 1693 how 'one Wilson' had proposed to the king a means of making a vestment more likely to defend a soldier from sharp weapons, which would not be heavy or costly. The Earl of Galloway and other officers approved the idea; so perhaps this is where his income came from.

THE CIVILITIES OF DUELLING

Although some duels were the result of drunken posturing, or even deliberate ambushes, the case of Sir Henry Hobart illustrates the strange formalities that semi-legitimised this murderous past-time.

Sir Henry, of Blickling Hall, Norfolk, was an MP for King's Lynn and a great supporter of the Glorious Revolution, having declared for the vacancy of the throne following the fall of James II. Afterwards, he was Gentleman of the Horse to William III, whom he attended at the Battle of the Boyne in Ireland. He seems to have been an honourable politician, until he lost his position as a Norfolk MP in 1698 – whereupon he voiced open resentment towards Oliver le Neve, Esquire, of Great Witchingham Hall.

Le Neve denied making any offensive comments and a formal challenge to settle the matter by combat was agreed. The first fight at Reepham was aborted, so the duel was reorganised, the terse, but polite, civilities between the two enemies illustrating the business-like fashion with which such matters were sometimes handled.

The spot where Sir Henry fell is marked by a monument.

Le Neve wrote to Hobart:

'Honoured Sir, I am very sorry I was not at Reifham yesterday, when you gave yourself the trouble of appearing there, that I might not only have further justified the truth of my not saying what is reported I did, but that I might have told you that I wrote not that letter to avoid fighting you; but that, if the credit of your author has confirmed you in the belief of it, I am ready and desirous to meet you when and where you please to assign. If otherwise, I expect your author's name in return to this, that I may take my satisfaction there; or else conclude the imputation sprung from Blickling, and send you a time and place; for the matter shall not rest as it is, though it cost the life of...

Your servant, Oliver Neve
20 August 1698'

'When' was Saturday, 21 August, the next day, and 'where' was Cawston Heath, east of Cawston village. The two men battled with swords, Sir Henry wounding le Neve in the arm, before the latter got the upper hand and rammed his weapon into Sir Henry's gut, mortally wounding him. The politician died the following day, leaving a widow and three daughters. He was interred in the vault at Blickling.

Le Neve took the decision to flee to Holland in the wake of the killing, remaining there until a friend of his, Mr Lombe, became Sheriff of Norfolk in late 1699. Lombe made efforts in December to persuade him that, if he returned and put himself on trial, he would only be convicted of manslaughter. These entreaties proved successful, and le Neve was tried at the following assizes – where he was acquitted. The slaying of the Whig politician is considered to have been Norfolk's last duel.

Chapter 5

Town and Countryside Murders

Assessing crime and murder away from London can be problematic, particularly during the first half of the seventeenth century. In some instances, where we have the full story, the only source may be a London-printed chapbook or pamphlet, the details of which are sometimes so Shakespearian that one wonders if they are reliable. One such case was reported in 1624 in a booklet called *The Crying Murther*, by Edward Allde. This explained that Mr John Trat, the curate of Old Cleeve in Somerset, had been deliberately ambushed on a local road around Midsummer Day that year. His attackers stabbed him twice and carried his body back to his own house, where they set about disposing of it in a 'strange and fearefull manner'. First it was dismembered with sharp implements and completely disembowelled, before the victim's decapitated head was burnt along with his 'privy members' (genitals). His flesh was partly boiled and salted up to look like cuts of meat. After two weeks, Trat's house was searched and the mutilated remains discovered, the killers not having had enough time to complete their work.

There were four conspirators. These were young Peter Smethwicke, of a prominent local family; Andrew Baker and Alice Walker, servants to the Smethwicke family; and a hired labourer called Cyril Austen. Smethwicke nursed an inveterate hatred of Trat over a number of issues, including the loss of certain parish revenues. He also believed that the curate had thrown his own wife to her death while limpet-picking with her in the Bristol Channel. To this end the young man invented a convoluted scheme to murder his enemy and dispose of the cadaver completely. One of the conspirators – probably Smethwicke – also rode off in the direction of Dorset, stopping at various locations and impersonating Trat, in an attempt to suggest the curate had left the country. The conspiracy was Machiavellian, with the plotters believing they could imply Trat had left Old Cleeve because he had murdered an Irish beggar; but in the end all four drew attention to themselves in one way or another. Smethwicke was the most obvious, since he seemed to know which route 'Trat' had taken when he vacated Old Cleeve, and single-

90

The murderers about their grisly work: a reproduction of the illustration on the cover of The Crying Murther.

handedly produced useful witnesses who believed they had met the curate during his supposed flight. Of course, these witnesses had actually met an imposter and this became apparent to the two investigating justices.

The four plotters were tried at the summer assizes in 1624 and sentenced to death by Lord Chief Baron Tanfield. At eleven o'clock on the morning of 24 July they were brought from Taunton Gaol 'unto Stoane Gallows' where they were all hanged – dying 'obstinate and unrepenting sinners.' Stone Gallows Hill is southwest of Bishop's Hull.

That this story isn't wholly an invention seems clear, because a 'Petr. Smithweeke', at least, is listed in the parish records. He was the patron of a previous Old Cleeve incumbent, Edward Brickenden, in the early seventeenth century and may have been the murderer's father. Mr Brickenden is mentioned incidentally in *The Crying Murther* and called 'Brigandine'. Chief Baron Tanfield was a famous political figure of the time. The true question mark is over the melodramatic details of Trat's violent end.

Murders reported in this indelicate manner were often of questionable authority, although one particularly intriguing case is that of Francis Cartwright, for whose crime there does seem a clear foundation despite a lack of corroborative data. We are told that in August 1602, Cartwright, the heir to one of the lords of the town, happened to be present during a sermon in Market Rasen, Lincolnshire, presided over by the Reverend William Storre. He quickly became infuriated by Storre's views on a local land dispute and shouted out, 'The priest deserveth a good fee, he speaketh so like a lawyer!' Francis was a young man with an ungovernable temper and his anger festered until 30 August, when he attacked Reverend Storre with a large sword on the road leading south from Market Rasen, hacking at him so violently that the injured man died after languishing in agony for six days.

The crime had been very public. Cartwright took refuge in his father's house, where constables seized him. But although he secured his freedom after payment of 'a very slender bail' and later earned a pardon from King James I, the ramifications of his actions haunted Cartwright for the rest of his life.

This event was first reported in 1603 in a sensationalist chap-book. But William Storre was certainly a real person; his name appears on a list of vicars and curates for the parish of St Thomas, Market Rasen, between the years 1597-1599 and it seems he continued to preach at the church in the town. Francis Cartwright's name also appears in historical records, in conjunction with the sale of his lands at Rasen and Linwood to Sir Julius Caesar in 1613. It is perhaps no coincidence that a new version of Mr Storre's murder was published in this year, Cartwright's straightened circumstances probably having renewed interest in his crime; not to mention the fact that around this time he killed another person, a man called Rigge in Grantham, although this was judged to have been in self-defence. That Cartwright was demonstrably a real person adds authenticity to a 1621 pamphlet reporting: *The Life, Confession and Hearty Repentance of Francis Cartwright, for his Bloodie Sinne in Killing of One Master Storr, Minister of Market Rason.*

As these two examples suggest, one often has to dig deep to even partially substantiate the violent episodes alleged by the era's sensationalist booklets to have occurred in the English countryside. In some cases, the problem can be of a different nature, however. Certain murders can be considered as genuine historical events, because of their appearance in trial depositions and the like, but the data may be of such a fragmentary nature that it is often difficult to ascertain the entire picture. An incident that occurred in Lancashire during the reign of King James I is typical.

Located by the River Ribble can be found Osbaldeston Hall, the ancient seat of a great family going by the same name. A 1911 survey of Lancashire notes that the west front of the house bears a carving dated 1593, although the hall is certainly older than even this date.

Around 1606 a crime occurred in a room here arising out of a family quarrel, when Thomas Osbaldeston of Cuerdale stabbed his youngest sister Elizabeth's husband, Edward Walsh, to death during a communal gathering. Some accounts suggest that Walsh was the curate of Blackburn.

The murderer was seized and imprisoned almost immediately, for the crime had been very public. Osbaldeston was found guilty of the killing at Lancaster Assizes on 7 April 1606. However, since he had somehow escaped into exile in the meantime, there was little the court could do other than brand him an outlaw.

We know he was still missing by January 1612; his name crops up in the *Calendar of State Papers* for that year, in relation to the forfeiture of his estate. The reason for relating this anecdote is that it illustrates how much data remains undiscoverable in certain cases. It is not clear what led to the killing, or how Osbaldeston managed to escape justice. It also eludes us where he died, and when; the point being that it would not have taken a great deal more for this incident to have vanished from the pages of history entirely.

Perhaps this is not surprising; after all, literacy was a precious gift in the seventeenth century. But it does also suggest that a great many more documents from the era might have become obliterated forever by war, fire, accident, carelessness or age, thereby denying us corroborative information.

In particular, one wonders what to make of stories like that of the infamous Doone clan. The earliest references to this notorious band of seventeenth century Exmoor plunderers only appear to date to 1853, when they were mentioned in T.H. Cooper's *A Guide Containing a Short Historical Sketch of Lynton and Places Adjacent*. He recorded that the Doones were supposed to have been 'men of distinction and not common peasants' who, having been disturbed by 'the Revolution' (the civil wars), suddenly entered Devon and made the deserted medieval village on Badgworthy Hill their home. They became the terror of the countryside for miles around, conducting raids and escaping with their plundered goods across the wild hills of Exmoor. In the course of their marauding, they attacked a house in the woods called the Warren and murdered a man known as 'the Squire' who lived there. Then:

'A farm house called Yenworthy, lying just above Glenthorne, on the left of the Lynton and Porlock road, was beset by them one night; but a woman firing on them from one of the windows with a long duck

93

The Doones were not the county's only bandit clan. Fuller's Worthies of England *(1662) refers to a lawless tribe called the Gubbins, who inhabited Dartmoor during the time of Charles I; a number of them are said to have been hanged on Gibbet Hill, seen here, north of Mary Tavy.*

gun, they retreated, and blood was tracked the next morning for several miles in the direction of Bagworthy; they entered and robbed a house at Exford in the evening before dark, and found there only a child, whom they murdered; a woman servant, who was concealed in the oven, is said to have heard them say to the unfortunate infant, the following barbarous couplet: "If any one asks who kill'd thee, tell 'em 'twas the Doones of Bagworthy". It was for this murder, that the whole country rose in arms against them, and going to their abode in great haste and force, succeeded in taking into custody the whole gang, who soon after met with the punishment due to their crimes.'

Stories about the Doones were later woven into R.D. Blackmore's classic tale *Lorna Doone* (1869) and ever after separating fact from fiction has been difficult. That the Doones may have been Scottish in origin was suggested in 1901 by Ida M. Browne, who produced a small pamphlet (via the Western Somerset Free Press) entitled *A Short History of the Original Doones of Exmoor*. Ms Browne argued that the Doones originated with Sir Ensor Doune, who was supposed – along with various members of his family – to have settled in the Oare valley upon being exiled from Scotland in 1620. It was his descendants who later became so hated and feared throughout Exmoor until their return to Perthshire *c*.1699. Rather more intriguingly, according to the historian Cooper, the weapon used to shoot one of the clan still existed: 'The gun was found at Yenworthy, and purchased by the Rev. W. S. Halliday.' This antiquity is still kept at the farmhouse to this day.

One is tempted to believe that Cooper was recording a genuine tradition in 1853, albeit one that may have become corrupted over the generations. Be that as it may, nothing in the literature of the period appears to substantiate it and to date his version is the starting point.

Many of the following cases do bear elements of uncertainty in their own right – alleging supernatural intervention, missing details, or having uncertain conclusions, for example. However, they also paint a vivid picture of the type of crimes that occurred in the English countryside and the resultant trials that took place in the provincial assize towns.

THE TRAGEDY OF BOHELLAND FARM

According to a news pamphlet, *Newes from Perin in Cornwall,* published in 1618, a privileged young man from Cornwall left his place of birth for an adventurous life on the seas around 1603. Taking up with a brotherhood of roving pirates, their vessel was accidentally destroyed and the young Cornishman forced to swim for his life towards the shores of the Greek island of Rhodes. Upon reaching land, he was condemned to death as a pirate, before escaping his captors in a pitched battle and managing to get on board a London-bound vessel. In the English capital, he was pressed into travelling to 'the Indyes' (the East Indies); there, his talent as a surgeon allowed him to amass enough money to buy his freedom and return to his family in Cornwall. By this time, it was 1618. Even then, the adventures weren't over; his vessel, sailing westward from London, was cast ashore and once again the young man was forced to save himself by swimming for his life.

Eventually, this lucky fellow reached his sister's house in the West Country. Although she initially mistook her brother for a poor stranger, she was amazed when he revealed himself; even more so when he disclosed that he had amassed a small haul of gold and jewels during his travels, which he carried with him in a 'bow case'. He also announced his intention of travelling further west to 'Perin' (Penryn) to see his father and step-mother. His intention there was to pass himself off as a stranger and then make a great reveal at a family get-together a day or so later when his sister and brother-in-law had had time to arrive.

Bohelland Farm stood in the vicinity of Bohelland Road.

In Penryn that September, the young man found his father's house more dilapidated than he recalled and the old couple appeared in very reduced circumstances. Still, they were hospitable enough to put him up for the night, despite the fact that they did not recognise him yet for who he was. Their good will was on account of the fact that he produced a piece of gold to pay them with. The young man enthralled his unwitting father and step-mother with tales of piracy, drama and escape that evening, before retiring to his bed chamber – no doubt in a state of high anticipation of the reunion that would shortly be unveiled.

That night, after all his adventures, the young man met a cruel and brutal end. He was bloodily murdered with a knife by his own father, at the instigation of the step-mother, for the purposes of robbery; afterwards, the pair heaped clothes onto the corpse to hide it until they could dispose of it.

The denouement to this tragedy occurred the following day, when the murdered man's sister arrived at her father's house in Penryn in a state of great excitement. She casually enquired about the 'sailor' under their roof; of whom the old couple denied any knowledge. In her persistence, the sister was forced to reveal that the 'sailor' was in fact their son, and asked to know what had become of him. She knew the traveller to be her brother, she said, because of a familiar sword wound he had shown her. Realisation began to dawn upon the father as to what he might have done and he rushed upstairs to the bed chamber where the body lay. After ascertaining that the dead 'sailor' was indeed his son, he cut his own throat in grief and died in the same room.

When the 'Mercilesse Step-mother' went upstairs, she found the two bodies next to each other. Realising there was no disguising the crime, she picked up the murder weapon and committed suicide with it herself. Finally, the daughter went up and saw how the bed chamber contained the bodies of her family – the shock of which caused her to collapse and die herself.

These facts reportedly reached the ears of King James I, who was enthralled by the horror. When the story was printed, the family concerned were not named out of respect for a Cornish neighbour of repute, who happened to be a relative of theirs. The incident supposedly occurred at Bohelland Farm, St Gluvias, which has long since disappeared.

THE SIEGE OF BRADLEY MANOR

In 1630, a small parish in Hampshire was the scene of a violent siege. The origin of the dispute was the acquisition of Bradley Manor, nine miles south of Basingstoke. In 1629, Bradley Manor's owner was forced to deliver the property into the hands of the king for a debt of £1,001 and one shilling. This followed a legal suit in the Star Chamber in London. Thereafter, Sir Kenelm Digby, a courtier and diplomat, became one of Bradley's two new lessees, the other being Sir John Savage. Digby was apparently persuaded to invest in the estate as 'his Majesty's farmer thereof' through the agitation of his friend Sir Henry Wallop, a local dignitary, who in all likelihood had his own designs on Bradley Manor by proxy.

However, Bradley Manor was at that time already let to Thomas Taylor, who had previously been granted a lifetime tenancy. Therefore, Taylor steadily refused to deliver over the manor-house and he, his wife Elizabeth and their sixteen children prepared to defend the property. To this end – Taylor being quite wealthy and influential in his own right – the manor-house of Bradley was garrisoned with a small army of soldiers and sailors sent immediately from the capital.

In the autumn of 1629 two attempts were made by the Sheriff of Hampshire, Sir Francis Dowse, to take possession of the manor, but these were ineffectual. In January 1630, two more attempts were made to obtain the house, directed by Dowse's successor, the afore-mentioned Sir Henry Wallop. On the fourth occasion, four shots were fired at the house, although this did not intimidate those inside, who became so menacing that the besiegers were forced to retreat in fear of their lives. Thomas Taylor was by now threatening openly to shoot anyone who came near his property.

It was not an idle threat. On 23 January 1630, Sir Henry Wallop led 200 men, with cannons procured from London, into the parish of Bradley. When Wallop ordered a shot to be fired at the manor-house's chimney stack, those inside opened fire on their attackers. In fact, they fired relentlessly for several hours throughout the day and into the night, wounding two of the sheriff's men badly. A report at the time stated that Taylor was assisted by 'a tumultuous body of sailors, under the command of a captain, who defended the house in a warlike manner.' One of the wounded men died after being hit by a poisoned bullet.

It was not until the house was rendered completely uninhabitable that it was surrendered. The following month Taylor also petitioned the king, complaining that he was being stripped of his estate by the oppression of Sir Kenelm Digby; Digby, meanwhile, attempted to procure warrants for Taylor and the other defenders on a charge of murder. For his part, Taylor pleaded his distressed state eloquently, arguing that his case was not properly understood, and everything he owned was now at stake. He also prayed that he might not be condemned unheard.

Whether anyone was made to pay for the shooting of the sheriff's men is uncertain, because about two years later Thomas Taylor was apparently re-granted the manor-house by the Court of Exchequer.

THE CRIME OF TWO SISTERS
According *to The Faithful Annalist,* the 1666 chronology of British history:

> *'William Calverley of Calverley in Yorkshire, Esquire, murdered two of his own children, at home at his own house, then stabbed his wife into the body, with full intent to have killed her; and then instantly with like fury went from his house, would have killed his childe at nurse, but was prevented. He was pressed to death at York the fifth of March (1605).'*

This report, though brief and perhaps slightly inaccurate, illustrates that some crimes caused much more of a stir than others. Calverley's case had been made famous at the time thanks to a subsequent stage play, *The Yorkshire Tragedy* (*c*.1608), and was still infamous enough sixty years on for its inclusion in the chronological history. Local folklore, in fact, has never really forgotten Calverley, of what is now Calverley Old Hall. Tradition says that his body was stolen by his servants and secretly interred in St Wilfrid's Church, Calverley. And in 1885, the antiquarian James Burnley found that 'at the restoration of the church a few years ago' a man's skeleton was discovered embedded in plaster. It had not been in a coffin. On the other hand, certain crimes – deeper and more intriguing than Calverley's act of violent, drunken desperation – have been all but forgotten.

Murderesses Elizabeth and Helen Drysdale, aged 26 and 24 respectively, came from a large family in Tadcaster, North Yorkshire, consisting of themselves, their parents, four brothers and two sisters. What the exact motive for their crime was remains unclear but they were, it seems, being courted by two men; their remarkable behaviour may have been a sibling act aimed at preventing their sisterly bond from being broken.

These two suitors were a joiner called Robert Boss, of Heslington, and Robert Blanchard, a wool-comber from Walmgate in York. Perhaps the women thought these trades insufficient security for their future, but at any rate, after a lengthy courtship, the sisters purchased some oxalic acid from Mr William Brooks, a chemist in Stonegate, York. This was on the morning of 16 February 1647. Later that day, the Drysdale sisters met their beaus at the house of Dame Robinson, beneath the sign of the Maypole, in Clifton, then a rural village outside York.

Here, the two unsuspecting men were administered the deadly poison by the siblings, both dying writhing in agony an hour-and-a-half later, despite the best efforts of surgeons to try and help them. It seems the two men realised what had happened to them, since before expiring they freely forgave the young women for what they had done, and left their fates in the hands of God.

The Drysdale sisters were very quickly taken into custody, tried and sentenced to death, meeting their fate with resignation and composure. On 10 April 1647, they were both executed at the gallows of St Leonard's, Green Dykes, outside Walmgate Bar. Afterwards their bodies were presented to the surgeons of York for dissection and anatomization.

The motive for their bizarre and desperate double murder – which they appear to have understood they had little hope of getting away with – is now a mystery open to interpretation. Interestingly, the scene of their crime, the Maypole Inn, burned to the ground the following year; it stood on what is now the site of the Old Grey Mare. Grace Bland, an employee at the place aged 29, was executed on 30 April 1649 for arson, weeping bitterly as she was 'turned off'.

EXECUTION FARCES

On 14 December 1650, a woman named Anne Green was taken forth to the gallows to be hanged. This dismal spectacle, however, which was enacted at Oxford's castle, was fated to become memorable for an entirely different reason.

Anne, a serving-maid, had been convicted of infanticide, having given birth to 'a bastard-child' begotten by her master, Jeffrey Reade, grandson to Sir Thomas Reade of Duns Tew in Oxfordshire. Immediately after the child was born, Anne had allegedly murdered it, although she denied this all the way to the gallows. The child was found 'on top of the ordure' (dung, or manure), and appears to have been born prematurely, as it was reported to be 'scarce above a span long, of what sex not to be distinguish'd'.

Some accounts suggest Anne was hanged from a cross-beam in Oxford Castle's yard; wherever it was that her body dangled after she had been launched into oblivion, she is said to have hung there for perhaps half-an-hour. Not only this, but during her execution she was subjected to all sorts of rough and violent treatment by her friends, who acted with a view to putting her out of her misery as quickly as possible. Her friends, in fact, hung with all their weight upon her legs, sometimes lifting her up and then pulling her down with a sudden jerk so as to try and break her neck.

After Anne was cut down and placed in a coffin, Mason, a tailor, observed her breathing and stamped with all his force upon her breast and stomach to end her suffering. A soldier named Orum also struck her forcefully with the butt-end of his musket. After this she was declared completely dead and was carried away to be anatomised by some young physicians within Christ Church Anatomy School. However, when she was laid out, all present were utterly astonished to observe the barest signs of warmth in the woman's body. Several professors overseeing the dissection – Drs Bathurst, Clarke, Willis and Petty – then began the process of attempting to re-animate the woman's motionless form.

After much perseverance, they and their scholars managed to restore Anne to life; Sir William Petty thereafter not only prevented her from being hanged a second time but actually procured a pardon for her. Afterwards, the miraculous matter became the sensation of Oxford, and later the whole country.

Young poets from the University very quickly produced pamphlets outlining the event, under the title, *Newes from the Dead: or, a true and exact Narration of the Miraculous Deliverance of Ann Green, etc*. Another very rare tract reporting the incident speaks volumes, for it went by the title: *A declaration from Oxford of Anne Green, a young woman who was lately and unjustly hanged in the Castle-yard, but since recovered, her neck set straight, and her eyes fixed orderly and firmly in her head again.*

When she had recovered a little, Anne was questioned about her escape. She claimed to have no memory whatsoever of her chains being knocked off, nor of being led from the gaol to the ladder she was to climb. Similarly, she could not remember whether she had sung psalms, and recalled no pain during the whole episode. However, when she became conscious, it was 'as if she had awakened out of a sleep.' Her speech appears to have returned not by degrees but in one moment.

Anne Green gradually recovered and relocated to Steeple Barton, where she married. In the years following her ordeal she produced numerous offspring and when she died in 1659, it was apparently in good repute. Her deliverance a decade earlier had, in fact, prompted many to consider her innocent of the murder charge laid against her.

Another person who cheated the executioner was John Bartendale, who was hanged on the York gallows outside Micklegate Bar on 27 March 1634. Bartendale was interred alive afterwards, having been improperly executed. He was saved when a horseman happened to ride past his grave only to see the earth shifting as Bartendale struggled to free himself. Later, when he was asked to explain what it was like being hanged, Bartendale replied that 'when he was turned off, flashes of fire seemed to dart into his eyes, from which he fell into a state of darkness and insensibility'.

Incredibly, Anne Green's case was not unique in Oxfordshire. Elizabeth – the servant of Mrs Cope of Magdalen parish – was hanged in 1658 at a place known as Green-ditch after being convicted of killing her bastard child and hiding it in the privy. Elizabeth's body was left hanging from a very high gallows for some considerable time and when she was cut down she plummeted to the ground with great violence. While she lay in a coffin at the George Inn, however, life was perceived in her and, a vein being bled, Elizabeth gradually began to recover. Her escape made no difference to her fate, however, according to Robert Plot's 1677 *Natural History of Oxford-shire*:

> *'Having no friends to appear for her, she was barbarously dragg'd the night following by the order of one Mallory, then one of the bayliffs of the city, to Glocester-green, and there drawn up over one of the arms of the trees, and hang'd a second time till she was dead.'*

Of unjust executions, perhaps the most famous case concerns the 'Campden

Wonder' of 1660. An elderly man, William Harrison, living at Chipping Campden in Gloucestershire, having gone to the neighbouring village of Charingworth, completely disappeared. His servant, John Perry, was sent to go and look for him. The following morning, 17 August, Mr Harrison's son went out to look himself and met Perry returning from Charingworth. William Harrison's hat, comb and collar were soon afterwards found at a local roadside, bloodied and slashed; Perry was taken into custody to be examined about what he might know of the man's disappearance. At first, Perry denied any wrongdoing, but after a few days he expressed a desire to unburden his conscience in the presence of a magistrate. He then presented a most minute and detailed account of how Mr Harrison had been strangled during a robbery attempt committed by himself, his mother Joan Perry and brother Richard Perry. He identified a cord with a noose that was found in Richard's pocket as the murder weapon and stated the body had been thrown into a field. Although Mr Harrison's corpse was not found in the place specified – and remained unfound – and the circumstantial evidence was less than convincing, John Perry's confession saw to it that he, his mother and brother were all tried for murder at Gloucester Assizes in September 1660.

All three were cleared, but soon after they were encouraged to confess to a robbery at Mr Harrison's house a year earlier on the assurance they would go unpunished because of Charles II's Act of Free Pardon, Indemnity and Oblivion following the Restoration. This was an act of general pardon for all crimes committed during the civil wars and Interregnum, with the exception of certain offences like witchcraft, piracy, rape and 'unauthorised' murder. The Perrys confessed to the burglary on this basis, but their confession constituted new evidence in the case of the missing man and forced a second trial for Mr Harrison's murder in March 1661. By now John Perry was claiming his original confession had been a fabrication, but it was too late; all three Perrys were hanged on Broadway Hill, within sight of Chipping Campden, at the spot where Broadway Tower now stands. John Perry's body was hung in chains from a gibbet post at the same spot.

The fact that old Joan Perry was also accused of witchcraft doubtless did not help their case. It only remains to be said that some years after his disappearance, Mr Harrison returned alive to Chipping Campden, giving a romantic and rather unlikely account of his absence, for which he may have had his own reasons.

THE MURDER OF A TRANSYLVANIAN PRINCE
Cossuma Albertus was a Prince of Transylvania, in the dominions of the King

of Poland, who – being beaten by German forces – was compelled to exile himself to England. Here, Charles II gave him a kind reception and provided him with a sufficient maintenance.

On the evening of Tuesday, 15 October 1661, the prince was approaching Rochester, Kent, in his carriage, accompanied only by his own footman and the coachman. These two had previously entered into a conspiracy to rob their master, so when the vehicle became stuck fast in the mire at Gadshill, about a mile from Strood, it presented them with an ideal opportunity.

The prince resolved to sleep in his coach and after a while he drifted off with his coat wrapped around him to keep out the cold. By midnight, he was deep in slumber. The coachman was a Jew, Isaac Jacobs, who very stealthily moved the sleeping man's body so as to obtain the prince's sword, which was being used as a head-rest. Jacobs then cold-bloodedly stabbed Prince Cossuma in the heart with that very same weapon.

With the aid of the footman, whose name was Casimirus Karsagi, he dragged the prince's body out of the coach and decapitated it, next cutting off at least one of the limbs and throwing all the mutilated remains into a nearby ditch. The pair then took all of the money their victim had on him before taking the coach and horses to Greenhithe, where they left them to be called for. The two murderers thereafter made their way further west into London.

The following Saturday, the arm of the dead man was found by a dog belonging to a Rochester doctor, who happened to be passing that way on horseback. The dog brought the limb to the doctor in its mouth and when a further examination of the area was made, the other mangled remains were discovered. It was observed at the time that the victim had been dressed in scarlet breeches and gold-laced stockings with pearl-colour silk hose under them; although some clothing had been taken from the cadaver by his attackers, what remained was enough to identify the prince. On 22 October, the prince was interred at Rochester Cathedral during a lavish ceremony attended by thousands of common people. A memorial tablet in the cathedral records his death and burial.

The two murderers were very quickly apprehended in London, largely due to the diligence of a Leadenhall Street grocer called Nathaniel Mannock, who was among those who went to see, identify and handle the prince's remains post-mortem. Mannock was naturally familiar with the prince, since the latter lived conspicuously at the George Inn in nearby Lombard Street, back in London. Therefore, when Mannock bumped into Jacobs trying to sell the murder weapon, as well as a picture owned by the prince, in Birchin Lane,

Thousands attended the prince's funeral service at Rochester Cathedral.

he was automatically curious. Mannock questioned Jacobs as to why he should sell those items and received an unconvincing excuse by way of reply; taken with the fact that he knew the prince to be dead, Mannock's suspicions were so great that he caused the coachman to be apprehended. Karsagi, the footman, was arrested shortly afterwards.

Having seized the suspects, Mannock saw to it they were brought before the Lord Mayor of London, Richard Brown, in whose presence the footman -younger and weaker than his accomplice- reportedly confessed. Here it became apparent that both men knew the prince to be returning to the Continent and therefore his complete disappearance from London society would not be remarkable. However, they had not counted on the body being found so quickly, or done a good enough job in rendering it unidentifiable. During one particular arraignment, which occurred at the Sessions House in the Old Bailey on 13 December 1661, both suspects repeatedly impeached each other. The court then present directed them to be conveyed to Maidstone in Kent. Both men were tried at Maidstone Assizes before Sir Orlando Bridgman and sentenced to be executed: following this, Isaac Jacobs's cadaver was duly hung in chains at Gadshill. The case was afterwards reported in a London-published news pamphlet, *A More Exact and Full Relation of the Horrid and Cruel Murther Lately Committed upon Cossuma Albertus.*

THE MURDER OF A YORKSHIRE 'WITCH'

The seventeenth century is synonymous with allegations of witchcraft. In 1612, for example, a feud between two Lancashire clans headed by ancient women called Old Chattox and Mother Demdike led to accusations that they were witches responsible for a vast array of improbable crimes. These included causing a number of deaths through incantations and curses in the district of Pendle Hill. Demdike cheated the executioner by expiring in Lancaster Gaol, but a zealous local magistrate, Roger Nowell, nonetheless managed to collect enough evidence to see to it that other 'witches' (comprising three generations) were all hanged in a grim mass execution on Gallows Hill outside Lancaster.

Similarly, Joan Vaughan and her mother, Agnes Browne, were both hanged on 22 July 1612 at Northampton. Having been slapped during a disagreement with a gentlewoman called Mistress Belcher, Joan, of Guilsborough, had vocally vowed revenge; shortly afterwards, both Mistress Belcher and her brother became afflicted with fits and convulsions. During their trial at Northampton Castle, Joan and Agnes were accused of witchcraft and an additional charge of using a spell to cause a child's death. Executed at the same time were Arthur Bill of Raunds, accused of using witchcraft to murder Martha Aspine; Hellen Jenkinson of Thrapston, accused of using witchcraft to cause a child's death; and Mary Barber of Stanwick, accused of bewitching a man to death over a petty disagreement.

*Guilsborough's village sign depicts the witches riding a flying pig –
something they were actually accused of at the time.*

Another purge was enacted in the East Midlands in 1618 when Joan
Flower, her two daughters and three others were accused of using curses and
enchantments to remotely murder the two young sons of the Earl and
Countess of Rutland. The two daughters had formerly been employed by the
earl at Belvoir Castle, but dismissed; both were hanged at Lincoln on 11
March 1618, while Mother Flower died choking on her own indignation as
she was being transferred from Rutland to Lincoln Castle.

When the cloud of witchcraft settled on a rural community or district, any
maliciously-minded neighbour might level ridiculous accusations of sorcery
at someone they bore a petty, superstitious grudge against, in the full
knowledge it was likely to be taken seriously. Provided the accuser could act
the part in court, they were often able to manoeuvre their enemy's death
through the judicial system, making cases like those already mentioned truly
perverse. In effect, the accused – who were frequently of pathetically low
circumstances – were often murdered legally by their accusers with the
abetting of the justice system, who usually managed to levy a charge of

106

murder by witchcraft against those they accused. This was to back up evidence against the prisoners that was of such a fantastic and supernatural nature that it was sometimes barely credible even during those confused times. Neighbours blaming someone for such things as livestock deaths or crop blight were brought before the courts as reliable witnesses; in some cases, the coerced testimony of small children against older relatives became admissible in court.

In eastern England, no announcement terrified a village more than word that Matthew Hopkins – the 'Witch Finder Generall' – was paying them a visit. Throughout the years 1644, 1645 and 1646 Hopkins, of Manningtree, Essex, went from town to town through many parts of Suffolk, Norfolk, Essex and Cambridgeshire discovering alleged witches. With his accomplice John Sterne, Hopkins is believed to have been responsible for some 400 executions – although the blame was not his alone, since without the original accusations made by parishioners he could not have performed his singularly horrible work.

It is important to remember that, when all is said and done, a genuine fear of witchcraft was so ingrained in the English psyche at the time that such vigilance was, without doubt, viewed as absolutely necessary by most rural

Effigies of Rutland's two young sons at Bottesford, Leicestershire: both were supposedly killed by witchcraft.

communities. And one detail of an otherwise unremarkable killing in 1662 illustrates the hold that witchcraft continued to have over a great many peasants in the counties of England.

The crime happened at an alms-house in Rotherham, Yorkshire, where the poor, infirm or aged of the parish were lodged. A simple falling-out among those dwelling there precipitated the matter; word reached a labourer named Henry Thompson that an aged widow, Margaret Hill, had been complaining that his sister had stolen some apples. At eleven o'clock on the night of 30 December Thompson attacked the old woman, striking her in the face and repeatedly hitting her on the head with 'a rod or staffe' for an astonishing hour and a half. At one point, Thompson said he would kill her, forcing Widow Hill onto her knees in front of him so as to beg his forgiveness. What is noteworthy is that Thompson bore a pre-existing grudge against his victim; he charged her with being a witch, who had cast spells upon his mother.

Widow Hill died of her beating on 18 January 1663 and another inmate at the alms-house – a spinster, Anne Ashmore – presented the authorities with testimony of what had occurred. This woman had been laid in bed near Widow Hill while the assault took place, but she had feigned sleep lest Thompson start attacking her too.

Rotherham's alms-house was sited in the Chapel of Our Lady on the Bridge. A Coroner's Inquest was held on 19 January, at which Thompson was indicted, although that he was hanged for murder appears unlikely. There seems to be no record of his execution and it is just possible that, in view of his claims that Widow Hill was a witch, there was a tacit reluctance to proceed with the matter any further.

RUTHLESS JUSTICE AS ENFORCED IN CORNWALL
The parish records of St Columb Major, a town in rural mid-Cornwall, shed a little light on a monstrous double murder that occurred there in 1671.

An entry for 23 June reads:

'Anne, daughter of John Pollard of this parish, and Loveday, the daughter of Thomas Rosevere of St Enoder, were both most barbarously murthered the day before in the house of Captain Peter Pollard at the bridge, by one John, the son of Humphrey and Cissily Trehemban of this parish, about eleven o'clock in the forenoon upon a market day.'

There is little more observed of this matter; although it is certain the crime occurred, because the murders are also referenced briefly in the *Calendar of State Papers* for the year 1671. Since both the killer and his victims appear to have been young – Trehemban was around 21 years old – we may cautiously assume the murders perhaps stemmed from some frustrated advance. Quite where the crime occurred is also a little vague, although the parish registers as published in 1881 observe that the bridge referred to 'is at the lower end of the town'.

John Trehemban's death does not seem to have been recorded in the registers and the 1881 edition observes, 'Traditions relative to the murder still exist in the parish.' These included the belief that Trehemban initially attempted to deflect suspicion from himself by joining a party on horseback who set out to hunt down the murderer. The group were accompanied by a pack of bloodhounds and when Trehemban's hat blew off and landed on the ground the dogs gathered around it and refused to leave it alone.

Accounts of a trial also appear lacking. But following a confession, Trehemban was supposedly gibbeted at Castle-an-Dinas, an ancient hill-fort high on the rugged land to the east of St Columb Major. The fact he was not

The wind-blasted height of Castle-an-Dinas.

109

buried in consecrated ground perhaps explains his absence from the parish burial records.

Furthermore, according to an article in the *Western Antiquary* (June 1881) by Richard Cornish, Trehemban allegedly suffered the punishment of being gibbeted while still alive. This awful fate allowed him to starve to death after his body was strapped immobile in irons (or perhaps put in a cage) and placed upon a large, flat rock out on the wind-blasted heights of the old hill-fort. If this is true, then the punishment was of a rare and cruel nature even by the standards of the time, also suggesting that if there was a trial then it was something akin to summary lynch-mob justice. A large stone at Castle-an-Dinas is said to have been the one that the murderer was placed onto before being simply left to die.

A SERMON AGAINST MURDER IN BERWICK-UPON-TWEED

It is recorded that the Reverend John Smithson, vicar of Berwick-upon-Tweed, Northumberland, was executed on 24 August 1672 for murdering his wife Sarah. This is a tradition that few histories of the town ignore. Some fanciful accounts suggest that Smithson, having killed his wife shortly beforehand, preached against the sin of murder during a sermon one Sunday in April 1672. At the end, he fainted inside St Mary's Church and when the townsfolk carried him home they found Sarah dead inside the rectory, which was awash with blood. This led them to realise Smithson had been publicly confessing his own crime that morning.

Whether this is correct or not, Berwick was at the time riven by religious schisms that impacted upon the municipality. Smithson had been Berwick's vicar for about eight years when he committed the murder, and there is a record on 2 May 1672 of a burgess refusing to watch over him while he languished in gaol. The burgess, Leslie Forside, gave the Town Guild 'saucy words' when asked to guard the prisoner, seeming to imply that his imprisonment may have been contentious.

Following his conviction, Smithson was drawn upon a hurdle to the place of execution where he was hanged. Public executions were at the time carried out near the castle, above Tommy the Miller's Field. His wife was reportedly the daughter of Mr Rosden, the lessee of the rectory; two months after his execution all Smithson's worldly goods were appropriated by the Town Guild.

THE WINDERMERE 'FEVER'

Thomas Lancaster, who lived at High Wray, a hamlet located on the picturesque western side of Lake Windermere in Cumbria, was married to Margaret Braithwaite on 30 January 1671. It seems that the union was somewhat speedily arranged, since the new Mrs Lancaster had apparently agreed to be married that very day (or soon after) to another.

Lancaster's greed had become excited by his new father-in-law's wealth and after the wedding the old man conveyed his estate to Thomas 'upon him giving security to pay several sums of money to himself and his daughters'. It was to avoid paying this that Thomas Lancaster committed what was described at the time as 'the most horrid act that hath been heard of in this country'.

Lancaster's covetousness over these matters and other payments drove him to poison – with white arsenic – not only his father-in-law but also his new wife Margaret. However, it didn't stop there, for Margaret's three sisters (Agnes, Elizabeth and Ruth), her aunt, a male cousin (who was the man originally intended as her husband) and a servant boy called William Beck also joined the list of victims one by one.

The hamlet of High Wray, where the murders occurred.

The principal victim of the scheme was Lancaster's new father-in-law, John Braithwaite. Towards the end of March 1671, the old man grew violently ill, his condition worsening until he died on 10 April. Immediately prior to his sickness he had partaken of some figs procured for him by his son-in-law during a trip to Kendal. When one of John's daughters, Elizabeth, ate part of a fig she also fell sick, as did Elizabeth's young daughter after being given a piece to try.

Elizabeth was among the first to observe that the figs looked somewhat rotten and tasted funny. But eventually she died also, thanks to Thomas Lancaster's machinations, for his poisoning spree continued beyond John Braithwaite's death in April and lasted weeks. The other six people stricken with sickness during this period also died writhing in agony and vomiting copiously. Most of the victims lived at High Wray Bank, not far from Lancaster's farm.

A continuance of the murders was all part of Lancaster's scheme. He may also have contrived to poison several of his neighbours, who grew sick but do not appear to have died – all to give the impression that a violent fever had overtaken the neighbourhood and so tragically claimed his nearest relatives.

Such a sequence of events could not occur without the suggestion of a plot and Lancaster's providential avoidance of illness throughout all this must have attached suspicion to him. In November, he was brought before a justice of the peace, Sir Daniel Fleming of Rydal.

Fleming committed the prisoner to Lancaster Castle, afterwards writing to Sir Joseph Williamson on 24 November:

'[I] shall take what more evidence I can meet with or discover against the next assizes that he may there have a fair trial, and – if he be found guilty – [suffer] such a punishment as the law shall inflict on such like offenders.'

In this correspondence, Fleming also makes reference to the aforementioned eight victims all having died.

At the following county assizes Thomas Lancaster, originally of Threlkeld, was found guilty of murdering eight people by poison and sentenced to be executed, then hung in chains 'untill such tymes as hee rotted everye bone from other…'

On 8 April 1672, he was carried to High Wray and hanged in front of the door to his very own house, High Wray Farm. Afterwards, his corpse was brought in a cart to the Coulthouse meadows near Hawkshead where it was strapped in iron and hung from a gibbet post erected for that very purpose. It stood, we are told in 1899 by Hawkshead historian Henry Cowper, near Pool Bridge, with an adjacent piece of land becoming known as Gibbet Moss as a consequence.

On 23 April 1672, Sir Daniel wrote to Sir William Wilde, Judge of the Common Pleas, stating that Lancaster had ultimately confessed to murdering 'the old woman' (presumably meaning his wife's aunt) using arsenic. He claimed to have been bribed with £24 by a mysterious legitimate heir to her estate, which was worth £16 per annum. However, his confession does not seem to have extended to an admission of guilt in the deaths of the other seven. Perhaps this was a late attempt by the cold-blooded murderer to confuse the entire matter anew, and sow doubt upon his culpability.

This was not the only time such a ploy was attempted. Two contemporary tracts (one called *The Poysoners Rewarded*) explain how a nurse and apprentice maid poisoned the household of a Plymouth dyer named William Weeks by putting mercury in the broth one Sunday. Two ladies of the house died in agony and others fell dangerously sick; however, the two domestics appeared to be faking their symptoms and it later transpired they both bore petty grudges against their deceased mistresses. A jury in Exeter heard their performance had been designed to deflect suspicion away from themselves and on 30 March 1676, both were executed at Plymouth. The nurse, Philippa Cary, was hanged, but the maid, Anne Evans, was hanged and then publicly set on fire.

'KILL ALL, AS ANDREW MILLS DID'

On 25 January 1683, a horrendous and inexplicable crime took place under the roof of John Brass's farmhouse, a place located on a hillside near Ferryhill in County Durham. The exact location of the Brass home was a few fields to the north of the lane from Merrington to Ferryhill, on the northern brow of the hill. This would place it where the building known as High Hill House currently stands. The details of the crime are a little confused, but the reality of the event is beyond question, recorded as it was by a Durham diarist called Jacob Bee, among others.

It so happened that John and his wife Margaret were away from the house on the day in question, paying someone a late Christmas visit. They had left their three children at home, Jane (aged about 20), John (aged about 18) and Elizabeth, aged just 11. The Brass family appear to have been relatively well-to-do and the children were well-educated. All three were kept company by the family servant, a youth of 18 or 19 named Andrew Mills (or, variously, Miles or Millns).

Mills is said to have been a generally quiet and inoffensive lad, although possessed of a deranged or deficient intellect. It had previously been observed how he had a particular attachment to Elizabeth, the youngest child; however, there had hitherto been no suggestion of impropriety and Mr and Mrs Brass apparently felt comfortable leaving all four youngsters together unsupervised.

Sometime around nine o'clock in the evening Mills went utterly berserk with two axes and a knife. What actually prompted this is unknown, although the situation apparently started with an argument between him and the eldest daughter, Jane, which led to a physical struggle. Mills's behaviour frightened Jane enough to make her seek refuge in an inner chamber, where the two younger children were at the time sleeping. She then attempted to barricade the bedchamber door from the inside.

Andrew Mills followed her. The enraged servant actually broke Jane's arm forcing an entrance and in a frenzied attack he struck both her and her brother, John, with the axe before slicing their throats. Eleven-year-old Elizabeth, however, begged for her life after seeing her siblings butchered, offering Mills bread, butter, sugar and all her toys if he would leave her alone.

Mills then left the room; but almost immediately changed his mind, returning to the bed chamber and grabbing young Elizabeth from underneath the bed, where she had hidden. He bloodily murdered her as he had done the others, then simply sat waiting among the bodies of the dead for the return of his master and mistress.

Another account, however, states that Mills ran to the inn at Ferryhill, where those gathered were playing cards and announced that the Brass household had been murdered by burglars. The landlady, seeing his bloodied attire, replied in shock, 'Oh, Andrew, thou's the man!'

Great numbers of people hastened to the Brass property, with Mills being taken there also under a firm suspicion of committing the murders. Along with the murdered youngsters, the two axes were found, both awash with blood; and when Mills was searched, a bloodied knife was found on his person, with which he had cut the throats of all three.

Quite naturally, the carnage shocked the entire county. It seems Mills was induced to confess by the coroner, who promised to save his life if he admitted what he had done. Once it was clear there was no escape, he admitted his guilt, stating that neither robbery nor revenge against his employers had been the motive. Furthermore, his confession suggested the entire episode had merely been due to a sudden impulse on his part.

In fact, the nearest thing to an explanation that Mills ever provided was that 'the enemy' – the Devil – had appeared to him bodily and coerced him into doing what he did by repeatedly saying, 'Kill all! Kill all!' When Mills had left the bed-chamber half-way through the massacre, a demonic impulse had overtaken him, compelling him to return so that no-one in the room might be spared. This impulse, Mills quantified, took the form of a hideous creature he encountered in a passage that looked 'like a fierce wolf with red fiery eyes, its two legs were like those of a stag, its body resembled an eagle, and was supplied with two enormous wings.' This apparition addressed Mills 'with a most unchristian croak', telling him to return and murder the remaining child.

However, it is also written that the eldest daughter was to be married at Candlemas and in all probability, Mills's latent, jealous passion was aroused, with some form of sexual assault or spurned advance perhaps leading to the crime.

Andrew Mills was tried and afterwards executed on 15 August 1683 at Durham. Later that same day, his cadaver was hung in chains from a 30-foot-

The tomb of the three murdered children in County Durham.

high gibbet post on common ground by the roadside, about half-a-mile to the north of Ferryhill and in full view of the house where he had enacted the tragedy.

In the decades following this horrific crime, an oft-repeated tradition developed that Andrew Mills was in fact gibbeted while still alive. That is to say, he was bound in irons and simply left hanging there, exposed to the elements while suffering an agonizingly slow death by starvation. Cruelly, it is said: 'A loaf of bread was suspended before him, guarded by an iron spike, which pierced his neck whenever he attempted to allay the cravings of hunger.' In some versions of the tale, a peasant girl attempted to feed Mills every day using sustenance attached to a pole. Although this is unlikely to have been the case, Sir John Edward Burke (whose 1850 article *The Ferryhill Tragedy* thoroughly assessed the case) thought it at least possible Mills was gibbeted alive.

The gibbet was a landmark for some considerable time, although after a while pieces of it were chipped away by locals who believed such splinters were a cure for toothache. It became known as Andrew Mills's Stob and a portion of it seems to have remained well into the nineteenth century, until the field in which it stood was ploughed and enclosed. What happened to Mills's body is unknown, but the crime spawned a grim local saying: 'Kill all, as Andrew Mills did.'

Chapter 6

Robbers, Bandits and Highwaymen

Confederacies of bandits were commonplace throughout the seventeenth century. In 1605, it was reported in a chapbook penned by 'B L' how 'a famous thiefe of England' called Gamaliell Ratsey had lately met his fate; Ratsey's story contains many basic elements that may be considered representative of this particular lifestyle. He came from Market Deeping, Lincolnshire, but despite a good education he had something of a restless nature. This led him to turn to highway robbery, in the process forming an organised gang; going about armed and masked, he committed audacious robberies in places as diverse as Lincolnshire, Northamptonshire, Suffolk and Bedfordshire. Ranging from county to county allowed Ratsey and his gang to sidestep the law until he was dangerously wounded by one victim during a hold-up a few miles outside Bedford. After that, the group fragmented, and Ratsey was ultimately betrayed by one of his comrades, called Snell, when the latter was apprehended in Duck Lane, London, for an unrelated horse-theft. In the end, Ratsey, Snell and a third man named Shorthose were all hanged at Bedford on 26 or 27 March 1605.

Ratsey had enlisted as a soldier around 1599 and is believed to have fought in Ireland under the Earl of Essex before returning to England and becoming a land pirate. This detail is interesting from the point of view that large sections of England's regular army behaved like common marauders, even when stationed at home during peace-time. Barely controlled by their senior commanders, undisciplined young soldiers would frequently inflict the most horrendous abuses upon the helpless communities where they were billeted. In fact, a 1628 Petition presented by the House of Commons to Charles I suggested English troops were little better than the plunderers of the Viking era:

Modern view of Bedford, where Ratsey and two others were condemned to death.

> *'The people in many places durst not repair to church, lest in the mean time the soldiers should rifle their houses... that tradesmen and artificers had been forced to leave their trades, and employ their time in preserving themselves and their families from cruelty; and that robberies, assaults, batteries, burglaries, rapes, rapines, murders, barbarous cruelties, and other abominable vices and outrages were complained of from all parts where soldiers had been quartered.'*

Following the civil wars, we are told that some English gentlemen on the losing side became Royalist highwaymen, attacking their latent enemies' messengers and baggage-trains. Such men entered Royalist folklore, preceding a strange phenomenon – the advent of brigands around whom a cult of celebrity developed.

Some highway robbers earned themselves popular nicknames, such as John Bennett, also known as the Golden Farmer. This gang leader was hanged on 22 December 1690 at the junction of Fleet Street and Salisbury Court, having murdered two people while being run to ground the previous September. He had eventually been subdued by a mob in Southwark, who

118

beat him with bricks. Bennett's notoriety, however, failed to stand the long-term test of time, unlike John Nevison and Claude Duval – both of whose names became public property.

Far from diminishing, however, the problem of banditry in England began to grow worse as the century drew out. What is immediately apparent from the observations of the diarist Narcissus Luttrell, writing in the aftermath of 1688's Glorious Revolution, is how organised and warlike some companies of freebooters became. Spectacular robberies were regularly committed on the highway by small armies of brigands, and – from their behaviour and language – there emerged a disturbing suggestion that many confederacies consisted of former soldiers who supported England's exiled king, James II. Therefore, the plague constituted a direct threat to the current monarchs, William and Mary, who had ousted James. The activities of highway robbers have acquired a certain air of romanticism, disguising the terror they inspired and the violence they were capable of. In truth, all were ruthless, most were dangerous, and some appear to have even been sociopathic monsters.

PILLAGING LIKE VIKINGS ON THE ANGLO-SCOTTISH BORDER

In 1602, Andrew Tate was tried and convicted of the murder and robbery of several people at Burn Hall, an old mansion near Sunderland Bridge in the county of Durham. Tate was hanged on the high road a little to the south of the scene of his crimes, at the point where the route to Bishop Auckland and Ferryhill divided.

Little more is readily available on this, although a statute of the English Parliament enacted in 1601 illustrates how lawless the north-east of England was considered at the time. This declared that all within the county of Northumberland and the bishopric of Durham who kidnapped for ransom, committed fire-raising while marauding, or extorted by means of blackmail would be declared guilty of a felony and condemned to death. For good measure, those who were forced into paying the blackmail would be similarly dealt with too, for encouraging banditry.

The Anglo-Scottish border suffered greatly from the ravages of so-called 'Border Reivers', marauding bandit armies consisting of adherents to English or Scottish families that pillaged all but openly with little regard for nationality or law. Huge gangs on either side pillaged livestock and plundered homesteads, usually on the supposition they would be safer from justice and retaliation once they had crossed back into their own country. However, with the accession of James I to both thrones, it was no longer desirable to have one side of the border stirred up against the other. In 1605, a new Anglo-Scots Border Commission was created to try and control the semi-lawless regions between the two countries. Great numbers were executed by the new commission, and the law in those parts was at times almost as ruthless as the criminals themselves. According to Sir Walter Scott:

> *'Numbers of border riders were executed, without even the formality of a trial: and it is even said, that, in mockery of justice, assizes were held upon them after they had suffered.'*

Such examples had become necessary, particularly in view of the awesome level of raiding, plundering and murder that immediately followed Queen Elizabeth's death. So open became the lawlessness that the period of her death earned the name 'Ill Week' along the border. In one instance, for example, more than 200 men from the Western Marches of Scotland pillaged as far south as Penrith, Cumbria.

The executions without trial soon became known as 'Jeddart justice', after the Scottish border town of Jedburgh, and Sir Walter Scott observed of the purges:

> *'By this rigour… the border marauders were, in the course of years, either reclaimed or exterminated; though nearly a century elapsed ere their manners were altogether assimilated to those of their countrymen.'*

As this infers, the clampdown did not altogether suppress the banditry. What seems to have been a late exercise in the practice occurred six years after the establishment of the Anglo-Scots Border Commission. On 25 May 1611, a party of seventy heavily-armed Scots – comprising Armstrongs, Elliotts and others – attacked the home of Lionel Robson at Leaplish, near Kielder Water in Northumberland. Breaking into his home with axes, they proceeded to utterly wreck the place and plunder whatever they could. Robson was shot in the chest and fatally wounded during the incident, and a woman called Elizabeth Yearowe also died after being shot in both thighs and one arm. Thirteen others, including a pregnant woman, were wounded during the rampage, some critically. There is some suggestion that the incident was the culmination of an ongoing feud between Robson and the two Scottish families.

Whether anyone was punished for this particular rampage is unclear, although state papers imply that the culprits were certainly identified. A list of two dozen names was drawn up, and Rowland Yarrow, an informer, was later violently assaulted in Jedburgh for going to the authorities regarding the authors of the raid. Yarrow may have been a relative of the murdered woman.

Robert Elliot, of the 'Redheugh' in Liddesdale, was named as the leader of the criminals; however, the only punishment he appears to have suffered was an exile to Fife. His actions, it is thought, were something of a final gesture of defiance aimed at the king's commissioners, who he believed were unjustly attempting to enforce change upon a legitimate and centuries-old past-time in the border country. The Victorian North Tyndale historian Edward Charlton concluded: 'We find no more documents regarding this outrage, nor do we know that any tradition of the event has come to our time.'

This state of affairs was at its worst in the early years of the seventeenth century, when thieves and robbers flew from one country into the other and back again almost with impunity, although by the middle of the century they were still bold enough to launch assaults upon straggling Parliamentary forces in the region, following the abatement of the civil wars. In 1650, Cromwell was forced to issue a Proclamation against the Reivers – or moss-troopers, as they sometimes went by – because, 'Many of the army were not only spoiled and robbed, but also others barbarously butchered and slain, by a sort of outlaw, not under the discipline of any army…' Thomas Fuller, the English churchman and historian who died in 1661, observed of these brigands:

'They are called moss-troopers because [of] dwelling in the mosses and riding in troops together. They dwell in the bounds or meeting of the two kingdoms, but obey the laws of neither. They are a nest of hornets; strike one, and you stir all of them about your ears.'

Earlier in Fuller's lifetime these bandits had numbered in the thousands, making a living by robbing their neighbours, but by mid-century, 'the ringleaders being destroyed, the rest are reduced to legal obedience'. One particular victory against these freebooters was scored by the Parliamentarian General John Lambert and his ally General George Monck in 1650, who assaulted a moss-trooper stronghold at Dirleton House, between Gullane and North Berwick, crushing them and summarily executing their captain, called Waite. In fact, maintaining law and order in the region became one of the principal objectives of Oliver Cromwell, whose government passed an Act on 17 September 1656 'for the better suppressing of theft upon the borders of England and Scotland, and the discovery of High-way men and other felons'. Among other things, this relied on the encouragement of ten pounds to make people become informants.

GILDEROY

Around this time there operated in Scotland a noted robber and cattle-stealer going by the name of Gilderoy, whose activities earned him something of a mythological status. According to tradition, having inherited – and subsequently squandered – a Perthshire estate, he murdered his mother, sister and a maid before wandering the Continent as an adventurer and bandit. After returning to Scotland, he formed a gang that, among other violent crimes, lynched a judge from a four-point gibbet post on the outskirts of Edinburgh where the bodies of some of his comrades were suspended. Before he was finally brought under control, Gilderoy killed eleven of his captors and for her obvious treachery also stabbed his mistress.

Over the following 100 years, Gilderoy's name entered into legend. Popular ballads embellished his activities and appearance, so much so that by the late 1700s some commentators were inclined to doubt whether the man himself had ever existed. Typically, in 1791 the following lines were written:

> 'Gilderoy was a famous robber, who lived about the middle of the last century; if we may credit the histories and story-books of highwaymen, which relate many improbable feats of him, [such] as his robbing Cardinal Richelieu, Oliver Cromwell, etc. But these stories have probably no other authority than the records of Grubstreet.'

The truth behind Gilderoy's legend was helped a little by the findings of the nineteenth century MacGregor Clan historian Kenneth MacLeay, who understood the story to have its origins in the behaviour of a sect of MacGregors that lived as banditti entirely outside the law 200 years before his time. This group was headed by two brothers, James and Patrick MacGregor, and they existed by blackmailing protection upon communities and helping themselves to livestock etc. The descriptive term 'Gilleroy' ('red-haired boy') was applied to the brothers. If this is correct, then historical documents begin to shed light on the reality of 'Gilderoy'.

It appears that it was Patrick who was to become the more notorious. The Commissary Clerk of Aberdeen, John Spalding, recorded that in February 1636, eight of Gilleroy's followers were apprehended on suspicion of plundering the countryside around Craigievar. Their rampage was, apparently, 'under pretext of seeking James Grant for killing Patrick Ger.' They were seized by the Stewarts of Atholl; seven of them were later executed in Edinburgh before their heads were cut off and displayed around the city. The eighth prisoner managed to convince the authorities he had been an unwilling gang member and secured his life.

In reaction to this, Patrick MacGregor attacked some Stewart properties at 'Athole'. Some accounts suggest that John Roy Stewart of Kincardine in Strathspey, who had been instrumental in the earlier arrests, was murdered and his house set on fire by Gilleroy during this episode; this was in spite of Stewart's intimate connection to the MacGregor family through marriage.

In June 1636, a party under Archibald, Lord Lorne, ambushed and captured 'the arch rebell, Patrik McGregor, alias Gilroy'. He was presented to the authorities in Edinburgh along with nine captured comrades, including John Forbes, who may have been his lieutenant. James MacGregor, Patrick's brother, is not listed among the prisoners. They were charged with, among other things, housebreaking, kidnapping for ransom, livestock theft, and a number of murders. Among their crimes was a deadly shooting melee on 9 April at the house of James Anderson ('hangman of Strathbogie') in which two or three people died. These murders appear to have been committed while some of the gang were being run to ground.

On 27 July, the gang were tried before Lord Lorne himself and reportedly confessed in Gaelic, which had to be translated for the jury by James Stewart of Ardvorlich. All were sentenced to be hanged two days later, although Spalding observed that only Gilleroy and five other 'lymmars' (bandits) were executed. MacGregor and Forbes had the honour of being hanged from a gallows that stood considerably taller than the one their comrades died on, and afterwards the heads and right hands of the pair were fixed up at two different points in Edinburgh. What happened to the brother, James MacGregor, is unclear, although he may have been executed also at some point. James Grant, whose name is mentioned intermittently in the court records of Gilleroy's trial, subsequently earned a pardon despite his involvement in a number of crimes. This may have been because his victim, Ger, was himself a notorious 'lymmar'.

This would seem to be a plausible origin for the legend of 'Gilderoy' – although it does beg the question of why later writers transported him into Oliver Cromwell's time. It also suggests that many details concerning his exploits, such as his execution of the judge, were later elaborations.

THE ROYALIST HIGHWAYMAN

Following the civil wars, perhaps somewhat naturally, there is reputed to have been a surge in banditry among former Royalists reduced to penury.

One of the most notorious criminals of the era was Captain James Hind, the pro-Royalist son of a Chipping Norton saddler, who allegedly attacked Cromwell's entourage around the time of the king's execution in 1649. The ambush and robbery attempt was a failure, however. It occurred as Cromwell journeyed from Huntingdon to London, but he was at the time guarded by seven troops, who managed to apprehend one of Hind's accomplices, Thomas Allen. Allen – a noted highwayman in his own right – was afterwards executed. Hind barely escaped with his life.

Hind roamed from county to county ambushing republicans, and many stories are told of his adventures on the highway, including his hold-ups of coaches carrying noted regicides. One such victim was Colonel Harrison, who Hind robbed of £70 in Maidenhead Thicket, a wooded wilderness west of Maidenhead in Berkshire.

The outraged victim raised an immediate uproar over his treatment and information of this hue and cry was passed to Hind while he rested at a safe-house where the proprietor was an ally of his. As a result of his hunted state, Hind very soon afterwards shot dead a horseman called George Simpson at Knowl Hill, evidently in the mistaken belief the man was pursuing him with an arrest warrant; in fact, Simpson was an entirely innocent servant racing behind the highwayman upon an urgent errand of his own.

Hind also fought alongside the future Charles II at Worcester in 1651 and managed to escape the battlefield when the Parliamentarians secured victory. In the end, he was betrayed by an intimate acquaintance while lodging at a barber's opposite St Dunstan's Church in Fleet Street, London. As soon as he was apprehended, Hind was presented before the Speaker of the House of Commons, who then lived in Chancery-lane, before being lodged in Newgate Gaol.

He must have thought his luck was in when his trial at the Old Bailey's Sessions House on various charges collapsed on 12 December 1651. However, he was then transferred to Berkshire and on 1 March 1652, convicted at Reading of Simpson's murder, that particular crime plainly appearing to have been his work. Even then he escaped the noose, because an Act of Oblivion had by that time annulled all former offences except those committed against the state. However, the establishment was determined to see him executed, and so next conveyed him to Worcester – where Hind was condemned for treason, due to his having fought against the Parliamentarians there.

Captain Hind is a curious figure. He was formerly apprenticed to a butcher in Oxfordshire before persuading his mother to loan him the money to come to London, where after a while he became drawn into the political agitation and criminality that parts of the city seethed with. A 1674 account of his life by G Angus refers to his 'merry life and mad exploits', and it appears something akin to a cult of celebrity began to develop around him. However, despite being first and foremost a highway bandit, he was nonetheless a principled political one and many of the stories concerning him have an odd ring of truth about them. On 24 September 1652, he was hanged, declaring before he died that most of the robberies he had committed targeted the republicans, whose principles he abhorred. He also shouted that he was being executed by 'a rebellious and disloyal crew' who deserved hanging more than he.

After his execution, his body was quartered as a traitor to the new establishment. His decapitated head was set upon the bridge gate, over the River Severn, while his other body parts were put up at several locations around Worcester.

'SWIFT NICK', THE YORKSHIRE BRIGAND

Like Middlesex, the roads to the north also suffered from a proliferation of banditry. For example, four fellows were hanged together at York on 2 April 1660 for a highway robbery committed near Whitby the previous year; while two highwaymen were executed in 1661 for robbing a traveller called Melrose in the Forest of Galtres north of York and cutting off his nose.

Among the numerous road bandits who terrorised the north of England and met their fate on York's gallows, however, the name of John Nevison stands out somewhat. He is variously said to have been born at Upsall, Wortley, Pontefract or other places in Yorkshire. He was principally active in the counties between York and the capital, where his face became well-known in the market towns. Some later accounts of his life would have us believe that, in the manner of Robin Hood, he stole from the rich and gave to the poor; when circumstance forced him to hold up the poor he repaid them when better supplied by robberies from the rich! Be that as it may, Nevison became a terror to the drovers and carriers that travelled the roads. More often than not, he extracted protection money from them, ostensibly meaning that he not only left them alone but also protected them from other robbers where possible.

On one occasion Nevison allegedly committed a robbery somewhere near London about sunrise and, finding he was known, took the decision to escape north to York. This city he reached by sunset of the same day, arriving upon the same mare. When he was tracked and arrested for the south-east robbery he proved himself to have been at York's Bowling-green that very evening and a judge and jury found it difficult to believe he had ridden such an immense distance in so short a time. Therefore, they acquitted him – despite a number of witnesses having sworn positively he was the man who committed the robbery near London.

Charles II himself is said to have referred to Nevison as 'Swift Nick' upon hearing of this and the name stuck. This story is probably the most famous one associated with Nevison. It was originally noted in the 1720s by the traveller Daniel Defoe, who heard the robbery had been committed 'in the year 1676 or thereabouts' along Gads Hill west of Rochester, Kent.

Some versions of his story insist that Nevison's real first name was William, not John. And although many accounts of his life infer the opposite, Nevison does not appear to have been a lone highwayman. At one hearing in York, for example, he was found guilty on 3 March 1676 of committing highway robbery, alongside others. The court heard he used the alias of John Bracey, or Brace and although he was condemned for a crime possibly committed at Wentbridge, south-east of Pontefract, the trial depositions are a little unclear on whether he was convicted *in absentia*. A witness, George Skipwith, told the court, 'that this Nevison is now married and *lives* beyond Pontefract.'

Nevison certainly suffered imprisonment around this time, perhaps as a direct result of this hearing. However, he subsequently earned a remarkable reprieve alongside a woman called Jane Nelson, in the expectation he would reveal details of his accomplices. Whether Nevison gave up any of his comrades is unknown, but he suffered a lengthy spell of imprisonment instead of execution. Eventually, he was drafted into a regiment under Captain Graham destined for Tangiers *c.*1681. The freebooter soon deserted, however, and thereafter subsisted wholly by highway robbery.

By this time, Andrew Tucker, another notorious Yorkshire highwayman, had been hanged on the gallows outside Micklegate Bar on 28 July 1680 for holding up the London mail as it was passing through Knaresborough. Examples like this – not to mention his own brush with the gallows – taught Nevison little and, if anything, he became bolder and more desperate. He terrorised not only Yorkshire but Derbyshire, Huntingdonshire, Lincolnshire and Nottinghamshire. On Sunday, 31 July 1681, after encountering a small crowd of people bent upon his capture, Nevison committed murder when he fired his pistol at a butcher named Darcy Fletcher in Howley Park, near Morley.

The exact site of the killing is said to have been 'near the footpath on the road between Morley and Howley Hall'. On this spot – at least as late as 1881 – a square stone sunk into the ground announced 'Here Nevison slew Fletcher'. Fletcher may have been acting in the capacity of parish constable. Seeing the shot man drop, the rest of the posse – including the victim's brother – backed off.

According to an 1865 history of Howley Hall, it was local knowledge at the time that Nevison was having an affair with a married woman at nearby Dunningley. The Fletcher brothers managed to trap him (and his horse) in a barn there, although the bandit escaped out of a window and into a pile of manure, leading to a pursuit. The compiler of this history, Norrisson Scatcherd, actually knew an elderly man in his own time ('old Robertshaw'), whose grandfather had claimed to know Nevison in person. Through family traditions there was a firm conviction that Nevison had in fact stabbed his victim to death, rather than shooting him. The bloodied weapon was supposedly thrown onto the thatch of a cottage at the top of the park as the murderer escaped, where it was later discovered.

Be that as it may, Nevison's appearance was becoming well-known and an interesting description of him appeared in a news-sheet the following month. This read in part:

'He is a man of a middle stature, and brown hair'd, inclining to be fat, aged above thirty years, and is thought (if he have left his old roads in the West-riding of York-shire) to be gone towards the sea-ports westwards.'

After committing this murder Nevison became England's Public Enemy No.1, and an appeal to catch him was printed in the *Gazette* on 31 October 1681. A reward – at the time substantial – of £20 was offered for information, at the instigation of Sir John Reresby, the scourge of Yorkshire highwaymen. However, it says much about England's state of policing that, even though known to be a bandit, Nevison was able to continue marauding for another two-and-a-half years.

Nevison's downfall appears to have been set in motion by the arrest of a woman named Elizabeth Burton, who had allowed his gang to lodge with her at the Talbot in Newark, Nottinghamshire, in return for stolen clothing. After she was charged with stealing clothes at Mansfield, she expected her old comrades to rescue her; but they did not, so in January 1684, she named Nevison as the man behind several brazen robberies. She also gave up his

Lincoln's Castlegate, location of one of Nevison's numerous safe-houses.

confederates, men named Wilbore, Tankard, Brommett, Everson, and Bracey – this last fellow seemingly from whom Nevison took his alias sometimes. Elizabeth delivered over much useful information about the gang, including that they also hid out at a house in Lincoln's Castlegate. She further disclosed that she had given birth to a child by Bracey – 'which is deade'.

On Thursday, 6 March 1684 Nevison was finally caught at an alehouse near Sandal Magna, south-east of Wakefield, when he was ambushed by Captain William Hardcastle. It is likely that the fugitive was taken while asleep.

The location of the arrest was an old roadside inn called the Magpie. This inn, which afterwards became the Three Houses, stood beside the Barnsley road near Castle Terrace. It was later pulled down, to be replaced by a new Three Houses on the opposite side of the road. The captain had earlier perceived Nevison at a village called South Milford, while riding to Wakefield and after that had followed him. It is possible that Hardcastle, a local constable who lived at Milnthorpe, was aided in his initial discovery of Nevison by an informer who sent him a letter saying, 'Sir, the bird is in the cage.'

After his apprehension, Nevison was lodged in York Castle; following his trial for robbery he was sentenced to death. He was executed at the Tyburn gallows outside Micklegate Bar on 4 May 1684 (although dates conflict), aged about 43. He is said to have confessed to Fletcher's killing, claiming it was an act of self-defence, while resolutely refusing to incriminate any of his criminal accomplices. The parish registers of St Mary's Church, Castlegate, imply he may have been interred at that place in an unmarked grave.

FEMALE HIGHWAY ROBBERS

John Cussans, in his 1879 *History of Hertfordshire*, provides a curious footnote concerning an old manor house at Markyate called Markyate Cell. A 'religiously believed in' tradition suggested that there was a staircase near the chimney that led via a sturdy door to a secret chamber above the kitchen. This chamber was where the 'Wicked Lady Ferrers' changed into male attire before thundering out into the countryside to commit highway robberies on a coal-black horse with white fore-feet.

Being wounded on Nomansland Common (where there is a Ferrers Lane) during one of these exploits, she managed to make her way back to Markyate Cell, where she died attempting to gain access to the secret chamber.

The story of Hertfordshire's lady highway robber is a very famous one, although it is of such a circumstantial nature that it must at best be classed as unproven and at worst considered an absolute fabrication – particularly when taken into account with the fact that the story's development coincided with a number of Victorian ghostly legends about Markyate Cell.

The suggestion of a secret chamber appears somewhat plausible, however; and a tentative identity has been ascribed to the 'Wicked Lady'. Most believe her to have been Mrs Catherine Fanshawe, wife of Thomas Fanshawe, Esquire, who – according to the parish register of Ware, Hertfordshire – died in June 1660 in her mid-twenties. Catherine was the daughter of Knighton Ferrers of Bayford, Hertfordshire; but if she really was the 'Wicked Lady', then it is unclear what her connection to Markyate Cell was – since at the time of her death the place was in fact owned by the Coppin family; although Catherine had inherited the manor house as a child, she and Thomas had sold it years before 1660.

At any rate, the elements of this legend seem to have grown in the telling. Catherine, it is said, was not happy in her marriage, so took to disguising herself as a man, committing numerous daring robberies along Watling Street and taking a lover in the process. The killing of Caddington's parish officer was laid at her door; but the excitement couldn't last forever and one night she suffered a fatal wound while out riding, which some said was dealt accidentally by her lover.

Thomas Fanshawe had his errant wife buried at Ware. The secret chamber at Markyate Cell was bricked up and sealed off, its location having been discovered thanks to Catherine's proximity to it in death. Stolen valuables and jewels were found stored within the hidden room.

The following is recorded of her possessions after her death:

'1660. Oct. 19. Admin of goods of Catherine Fanshaw, late of Ware Park, granted to Thomas Fanshaw, husband of deceased.'

Might these goods have been the proceeds of Catherine's alleged robbery spree? It seems unlikely. Her mother-in-law's assessment of her was, apparently, 'She was a very great fortune and a most excellent woman.' However, the unknown circumstances of Catherine's early death will ensure that the legend continues to thrive.

It has to be said that this story has been endlessly recycled, assessed and dissected to such an extent that there is little left to impart, other than to reiterate that the yarn appears to have survived in oral tradition only for some 200 years until Cussans jotted it down.

One wonders if it is mere coincidence that another female highway robber, Mary Frith, otherwise Moll Cut Purse, infamously operated around this time nearer the capital. She committed mounted hold-ups dressed in a man's apparel and is said to have 'entered herself into the society of divers, otherwise called cut-purses, or pick-pockets; which people are a kind of land pirate.' A career criminal, on one occasion she allegedly shot General Fairfax through the arm during a robbery on Hounslow Heath before shooting and killing the horses of his two attendants. Following this crime, she was pursued to Turnham Green, apprehended, and thrown into Newgate – although she managed to procure her pardon by paying her victim the sum of £2,000. After this she took a house within two doors of the Globe in Fleet Street, where she lived as a 'fence'. She later declined into insanity, alcoholism and illness aggravated by her heavy smoking, and was buried in St Bridget's (Bride's) church-yard following her death in 1659. Although a marble stone with an inscription befitting of her notoriety was placed over her, this was destroyed in the great fire of 1666, according to the crime compiler 'Captain Johnson' in 1742.

Although female highway robbers were rare, they were not unknown.

Around 1680, for example, a farmer's daughter called Joan Phillips fell in with a career highwayman named Edward Bracey. Claiming to be man and wife, they lived by crime in the area around Bristol, later migrating to Nottinghamshire. Here, while robbing the carriage of a person of quality, Joan was caught and later hanged on Wilford Lane, Nottingham, in April 1685, aged in her twenties. She allegedly wore men's apparel habitually when out on the highway. Her 'husband', Edward Bracey, was afterwards fatally wounded during a skirmish when one of his former victims recognised a distinctive stolen white mare outside an inn he was frequenting. The location where this occurred is uncertain and some accounts also suggest he died on the gallows like Joan.

Of Joan, the Nottinghamshire antiquarian James Orange noted:

'Her body was given to her friends, and handsomely interred in one of the church-yards in this town [Nottingham], but which of them we have not been able to learn.'

HORROR PILED UPON HORROR

Around 1697, the noted traveller and diarist Celia Fiennes passed through the parish of Calverton, nine miles to the east of Buckingham. Here she paused at 'the rich Mrs Bennet's house, remarkable for covetousness, which was ye cause of her death – her treasures tempted a butcher to cut her throate, who hangs in chains against her house.' The victim was Mrs Grace Bennett, mother to the Countess of Salisbury and widow of Simon Bennett, Esquire and she lived alone in the rural sixteenth century Manor-house next to All Saints Church. All accounts suggest she was a miserly, unpopular lady, whose reputed hoard lured her murderer – a Stony Stratford butcher called Adam Barnes – to break into her house and kill her in the Servant's Hall when she disturbed him. The murder had been committed on 19 September 1694, and (according to both Luttrell and the Duke of Portland) Barnes was suspected almost immediately. He was subsequently found guilty of murder during a hearing held in a room at the Cross Keys Inn, Stony Stratford, and later sentenced to be hanged in Gib Lane near the house. After this had taken place, his corpse was strapped in irons and suspended at the same spot until – ultimately - it rotted and fell apart. Perhaps Barnes's cadaver was approaching such a tattered state of ghoulish disintegration when Celia Fiennes's eyes fell upon it three years later in 1697.

The societal position and reputation of the victim perhaps made her a natural target, but the case was by no means unique. England's evident

Barnes's cadaver was hung in chains near the perimeter wall of Calverton's Manor-house.

decline into criminality can be appreciated by a look at some of the appalling atrocities supposed to have been committed by common marauders during the course of robberies in the final decades of the seventeenth century.

In a work called *Bloody News from Yorkshire* (London, 1674) mention is made of a great robbery committed by twenty highwaymen upon fifteen butchers travelling to Northallerton Fair. Seven of the latter were killed during the hold-up, while three among the highwaymen also died in a fierce battle that ensued. The murdered butchers were named Thomas Simpson, Ralph Green, George Waterhouse, Gregory Smith, William Brand, Edward Hewit and Francis Miles. The gang stole £936 during this ambush, but were pursued and caught that night in a fight with parish officers during which four more of the robbers died. The other thirteen were imprisoned in York Castle, where two confessed to having previously ridden with the famed robber Duval.

Claude Duval, the French page of the Duke of Richmond, took to the road and became captain of a formidable gang, having the honour to be named first in a royal proclamation against notorious offenders. Duval, aged 27, was another early example of a celebrity criminal, reputedly the terror of men, while stealing away the hearts of women with his charming manners. That is, until he was arrested while intoxicated at the Hole in the Wall in Chandos Street, convicted of several robberies and executed at London's Tyburn in 1670. That very year, his life story was told in a London-published work called *The Memoires of Monsieur Du Vall*; the work was full of anecdotes concerning his exploits, and no shortage of exaggeration. For example, the *Memoires* firmly attested that, had he not been drunk when arrested, Duval could easily have shot and stabbed to death ten of his pursuers. However, Duval seems to have been something of a rarity – perhaps it was his avoidance of shedding blood that charmed and fascinated the public so much.

The Northallerton Fair robbery was just one horror among many perpetrated by highwaymen, footpads, thieves and burglars of every description in every part of the country. For some, murder clearly became habitual. For example, on 28 February 1673, William Blisse, of South Mimms, was tried at the Sessions-house of 'the Old Bayly, London' and sentenced to be hanged at Kitt's End for three murders. One of these concerned a drover's boy who was killed, robbed and stripped as he made his way to market. The case was published in a chapbook at the time, *A True and Perfect Relation of Three Inhumane Murders*.

At eleven o'clock on the night of 22 January 1680, a number of banditti broke into Upper Park House in Pontefract Park, West Yorkshire, and during a robbery they murdered Mr Leonard Scurr, his mother Alice and a maidservant. According to some accounts, Scurr managed to mortally wound two of the intruders before being killed; whether this detail is correct or not, the house was set on fire to disguise the crime afterwards. On 24 January, Ralph Thoresby, an antiquarian and diarist, went from Leeds to visit the crime scene. There, he observed that old Alice Scurr's body had been virtually burnt to ashes, although within the remains of the torso 'her heart [was] hanging as a coal out of the midst of it'. The skulls of all three were broken in the same place, proving that a horrendous crime had occurred. Furthermore, the maid had apparently been decapitated.

Scurr was a former reverend and lately a wealthy colliery owner, and one of his employees – named Holroyd – drew attention to himself the morning after the crime by turning up at the 'coale pitt' and wondering conspicuously loudly where Mr Scurr had got to that day. He further implicated himself by fleeing to Ireland shortly afterwards. There, he proved incapable of keeping his mouth shut and very soon his acquaintances were reporting to the Dublin authorities that his mistress appeared to be wearing the murdered Alice Scurr's gown and scarlet petticoat. Holroyd and his female companion were returned to England by Dublin magistrates and he was eventually hanged on Holbeck Moor on 14 August 1682 before 30,000 spectators. Although others were implicated, he seems to have been the only one to have been executed.

In 1691 news was published of a violent engagement between a new gang of highwaymen and several local people near Barnet, in which three of the latter were fatally wounded and several horses killed. Apparently, 'one that is supposed to be the chief' was arrested not long after, according to a London-published account, *Great Newes from Hertfordshire*. Similarly, the diarist Luttrell recorded on 7 December 1693 how five highwaymen had, a week earlier, murdered nine people on the road between Gravesend and Rochester, Kent, during a series of robberies.

Then there was the case of a common thief called Charles Pyne, who pulled his shoes off immediately prior to being hanged at Tyburn on 18 July 1694, so that he could prove those who said he would die with his boots on incorrect. Pyne was convicted of two murders during robbery attempts, but credibly suspected of committing four others.

In 1687, a psychotic highwayman named William Cady was allegedly hanged at Tyburn, having had his horse shot underneath him while holding up a gentlewoman on Finchley Common. Cady was suspected of six murders at various locations around the country, including the barbaric mutilation of a woman on Blackheath, who he shot in the head after she swallowed her wedding ring.

In 1692, another criminal monster was hanged at Old Heath, just north of Shrewsbury. This was Jocelin Harwood, the ungovernable son of an honest Kentish family, who supposedly stabbed to death Sir Nehemiah Burroughs, his wife and two daughters at their remote home in Shropshire. He was caught shortly afterwards because his two accomplices, allegedly horrified by his actions, shot his horse and left him tied up by the roadside with a tell-tale piece of stolen plate beside him.

Perhaps worst of all was Thomas Austin, a Devon farmer whose extravagances forced him to turn highway robber. Having held up and fatally shot Sir Zachary Wilmot between Wellington and Taunton Deane, which earned him a mere 46 guineas and a silver-hilted sword, Austin appears to have utterly lost his mind. He made his way to his aunt's house where he murdered her and five of her children with a hatchet and razor, before returning to his own home at Cullompton and butchering his wife and two small children. He is said to have been wrestled under control by his uncle, who had called round incidentally and was not yet aware his entire family were also dead. After being imprisoned in Exeter Gaol Austin was executed in August 1694, to the end uncomprehending of the magnitude of what he had done, since his last words were:

'I see yonder a woman with some curds and whey, and I wish I could have a pennyworth of them before I am hanged, as I don't know when I shall see any again.'

In the interests of accuracy, it is worth pointing out that these last three examples bear the stamp of unreliability, for to date no contemporary evidence appears to corroborate them. The accounts were first laid out in works published early during the following century, compiled by the likes of 'Alexander Smith' and 'Captain Charles Johnson' (pseud). At worst they are complete fabrications, but it is just about feasible that the accounts were misremembered or exaggerated examples of real events from two generations earlier where the chroniclers had no access to a primary source.

Support for this, at least in the case of Thomas Austin's rampage, comes from the fact that at the same time as his alleged spree a strangely similar massacre occurred elsewhere in Devon, which was reported at the time. According to a London publication, based on a letter from 'an eminent dealer in Combe to a worthy citizen' in the capital, a father had lately killed his son and three daughters. The attack happened on 30 March 1694 at a village near Combe, the father beating all the children's brains out with a mattock while they knelt in front of him imploring him to spare their lives. The man then attempted to commit suicide by hanging himself, but was prevented by the timely appearance of some neighbours, who apprehended him. His wife was also reported to be in a deplorable condition, having barely escaped a murderous attack herself. Following his confession before a justice of the peace, the murderer was committed to Exeter Gaol to await his fate.

Perhaps Thomas Austin's rampage was a misremembered version of this report? At any rate, one incident chronicled in the works of Captain Alexander Smith is worth including for its sheer outrageousness. That it contains even a glimmer of truth would be remarkable. But at the very least it suggests the phenomenon of seventeenth century banditry was real enough for such stories to be taken credulously two generations later by those who perhaps felt their own era's lawlessness had been inherited from those times.

AN ATROCITY COMMITTED BY A 'DEAD MAN'
Patrick O'Brien hailed from Loughrea, County Galway, and in his youth, he came to Britain to enlist in the Coldstream Regiment. Here, he proved himself

to be a shameless borrower of money, his multiple debts leading him first to become a footpad and then a mounted highwayman. One of his early victims was allegedly Nell Gwynne, an actress and mistress of Charles II, whose carriage he held up on the road to Winchester. Another dubious story about him is that he attempted to rob a man named Clark on Primrose Hill but when the victim appeared to transform before his eyes, O'Brien feared he had encountered the Devil and ran like fury. Clark, it is said, was in fact a famous performing contortionist who had the ability to morph his body and features into all manner of weird and frightening positions.

O'Brien gathered around him a band of land pirates as desperate as he and lived fully by crime. One of the gang, Claudius Wilt, was caught and hanged at Worcester and O'Brien was himself arrested for a robbery committed two miles from Gloucester. Although he was sentenced to hang in that town, the process was carried out inefficiently – and the stories would have us believe that a tiny flicker of life was espied in O'Brien after his body had been delivered over to friends. With the aid of a surgeon, who bled his neck, the bandit was revived, and the matter kept secret.

This narrow escape from justice did not affect O'Brien's behaviour, only in so far as it made it worse. About a year later, on horseback, he ambushed the victim of the Gloucester robbery a second time, telling him he was O'Brien's ghost; as the man looked on in disbelief, O'Brien shot him in the head, then dismounted and stabbed him several times with a rapier.

Around 1687, the Irishman, together with four other rogues, broke into the isolated home of Lancelot Wilmot, Esq, which was to be found about a mile or so from Trowbridge, Wiltshire. They bound and gagged five of the servants, as well as Mr Wilmot and his wife, who were at the time of the burglary asleep in their bedchamber. Next, O'Brien went into Mr Wilmot's daughter's room, where he raped the young woman before stabbing her to death when she resisted. Having gone this far, he and his companions next murdered the incapacitated Wilmot and his wife in cold blood. They then plundered the house of some £2,500 worth of gold, silver and plate before setting the building ablaze. The five servants, also incapacitated by their bonds, burnt to death in the conflagration.

This atrocity remained unsolved for two years, until one of those involved was hanged at Bedford for another crime and chose to make a confession before he died. His evidence named O'Brien as the man behind the killings and he told the authorities where O'Brien now had lodgings. The Irishman was taken by surprise during a raid on his house in Little Suffolk Street, London, approximately where the Haymarket Theatre now stands.

O'Brien was conducted to Salisbury, Wiltshire, where he was tried and convicted of murder. He was hanged on Tuesday, 30 April 1689, aged about 31, and afterwards his corpse was suspended from a gibbet post near where the massacre had occurred.

'THE CAPTAIN' OF THE CAPITAL'S BANDITTI

The celebrated criminal James Whitney came from Stevenage, Hertfordshire. In his youth, he was apprenticed to a butcher, and he appears to have seen his apprenticeship through to its conclusion. However, no sooner had Whitney become his own master than he fell irreversibly into a criminal lifestyle, before taking to the roads as a mounted robber. In his lifetime, he received such notoriety that he gained the nickname 'the Captain'.

It is said that Whitney somewhat relished his image, taking care to affect a generous and noble appearance. On one occasion, he robbed a man named Long of £100 in silver on Newmarket Heath, along the Cambridgeshire/Suffolk border. When the victim complained that he had a long journey ahead, and needed travel expenses, Whitney told him to take as much as he needed. Long in fact greedily grabbed back all the silverware he could carry, but rather than antagonising Whitney, the latter apparently found it comical, declaring, 'I thought you would have had more conscience, sir!'

Remarkably, Whitney was able to sidestep the law for some thirteen years, perhaps on account of his moving from place to place. During this time, he gathered a band of likeminded marauders and formed a dangerous gang. All the while, however, he was becoming more familiar to the authorities, a wound on his face and a missing thumb having made his appearance quite distinctive. By late 1692 he had become England's most wanted highwayman.

Whitney was finally arrested in December that year. It appears his position was betrayed by a prostitute called Mother Cozens, who ran a brothel in Milford Lane, near St Clement Danes in the capital. According to the diarist Luttrell, he was ambushed in Barnet (then a distinct village) on 6 December by a party of horse sent out that very morning to pursue and arrest him. There followed a sharp battle in which Whitney (or someone with him) fatally wounded one of the troops and injured a number of others before being overpowered. He was taken to London and thrown into Newgate on the orders of a magistrate, and such was his notoriety that the king himself was kept informed of events.

In the run-up to Christmas there was a curious development. Whitney ransomed himself – in other words, he was granted bail – after promising two examining lords that he would raise an army of thirty brother highwaymen, and as many horses, to serve the king faithfully if he were but granted a pardon and given a sum of money. It is possible that his interrogators thought it worth the risk to free him on this ridiculous understanding, perhaps briefly, to see if Whitney led them to further members of his gang, who do not appear to have been taken with him at Barnet. So, before long, England's Public Enemy Number One was once more walking the streets of the capital.

Whitney – predictably – immediately attempted to go into hiding, but was spotted in Bishopsgate in the City of London by a spy called Hill, who discreetly followed him to his dwelling. Hill summoned assistance, and for an hour or so there was a siege, which was ended by the arrival of a party of officers from Newgate. Whitney eventually surrendered, but managed to stab Hill with a bayonet during a violent melee before being cuffed, shackled in irons and recommitted to Newgate. But the authorities' ploy had worked to a certain extent: the following day two members of Whitney's gang, one of whom kept a livery stable in Moorfields, were similarly apprehended and committed.

Whitney's notoriety by this point exceeded that of any robber in the capital since Colonel Blood and rumours circulated that he had somehow engineered a second escape from Newgate, although Luttrell makes it clear on 7 January 1693 that the highwayman was immobile, loaded with forty pounds of irons on his legs. Nonetheless, Whitney's attempts to confuse and avoid his fate beyond this became nothing short of remarkable. Whitney was tried and convicted of robbery at the Old Bailey on 16 January.

By now awaiting a death sentence, his first scheme was to employ a tailor to make him a rich embroidered suit, as well as a striking wig and hat at the cost of £100. However, his gaoler disallowed him from wearing these items because he believed Whitney was trying to disguise his appearance and confuse witnesses. Next – since the remainder of Whitney's gang were still defiantly active upon the highway – the prisoner offered information on his former accomplices and throughout January 1693 Newgate began to fill with the criminals arrested on Whitney's testimony. On 27 January, seven highwaymen were carried to Tyburn and hanged alongside a 'clipper'. James Whitney was taken to Tyburn at the same time, ostensibly to suffer the same fate as the others, yet he mysteriously received a reprieve while at the foot of the gallows and afterwards was taken back to Newgate with a rope ceremonially draped around his neck. Luttrell recorded that a vast concourse of curious, suspicious Londoners followed him back to the notorious gaol.

The reason Whitney had earned a reprieve was his last-minute promise

A loose engraving of Whitney from around 1700. (Mary Evans Picture Library)

to deliver more information on the highwaymen continuing to rob the mails so often. That very night he was carried in a sedan to Whitehall, where he was interrogated about this and what he knew concerning an emerging plot to assassinate William III himself. Whether such a plot existed or not is unclear. But it is possible that as Whitney saw his liberty slip through his

139

fingers he sought to portray his former confederates as traitorous assassins, in an effort to secure his freedom by becoming a prosecution evidence in a political plot. His disclosures were taken seriously, as the proliferation of robberies had long been suspected to be the work of Jacobite malcontents. However, he was returned to Newgate after his examination, the validity of his claims being questionable.

Whitney's execution was scheduled to be re-set. In the run-up to this, he dashed off five letters promising explosive details of the alleged plot – the last to Algernon Capell, 2nd Earl of Essex, who considered its contents serious enough to seek the urgent advice of the Lord Chief Justice, Sir John Holt, then on the bench at Westminster. Whitney's letters hinted that he had been one of twelve men who had gathered in Windsor Forest in order to ambush and assassinate the king while he was out hunting, immediately upon the monarch's recent return to Windsor Castle from Flanders. However, when he was examined a second time, he demanded a full pardon before presenting any more data on this 'plot' and the authorities (seeing Whitney's claims as a contrivance) finally lost patience with him. They signed a warrant ordering his execution to take place the following day – 1 February 1693.

Although Whitney was sentenced to be publicly hanged at the Maypole in the Strand, this location was switched at the last moment to 'Porter's block, near Cow-cross in Smithfield'. Luttrell noted that the prisoner was in the cart for half-an-hour before it drew away and he was 'turned off'. He seemed to die very penitently. Whitney was about 34 years of age and reputedly very handsome, although at the time of his death he had a cap pulled over his face.

A PLAGUE OF BRIGANDS

What is remarkable is that Luttrell, in recording the story of Whitney, makes it clear that 'the Captain's' detention made next to no difference to the violence of the banditti who by this time terrorised many parts of the country. The plague was truly breath-taking in scale, for companies of armed men committed spectacular robberies almost daily, and – as often as not – dealt out violence or themselves died in clashes with those attempting to defend the stagecoaches and mail. On 7 December 1693, for example, the diarist recorded how a group of highwaymen had held up several people near Beaconsfield, south Buckinghamshire, the previous week; following the robbery, the people of that parish chased the bandits and shot their chief, called Reynolds, who was carried away by his comrades fatally wounded.

Tellingly, Luttrell also suggested that ten men who held up the Earl of Dorset's coach in July 1699 between Fulham and Chelsea were 'disbanded

The inscription on this neglected grave in Melbury Bubb, Dorset, states that Thomas Baker was 'barbarously murdered'. Baker, a yeoman farmer, was killed by two footpads on Bubb Downe Hill on 10 November 1694; his attackers were caught and hanged in 1701, after being overheard accusing each other of the murder in an Evershot tavern.

soldiers'. By this, he perhaps did not mean men from the king's army, but 'Jacobites' – those who had supported the exiled former monarch, James II. Indeed, the size of some of the gangs, not to mention the astonishing bravado and military-style ambushes they practised, led to a general suspicion that many were comprised of pro-James revolutionaries and former troopers. Overall, Luttrell's diaries make for staggering reading, his entries suggesting as they do a breath-taking level of robbery upon the public highway that seemed frighteningly organised.

As an example, on one occasion around this time, fifteen butchers going to Thame, Oxfordshire, were held up, robbed and forced to drink to the health of King James II in brandy. The audacious theft of £4,000 of the king's money from the Worcester waggon at Gerrard's Cross (four miles west of Uxbridge) also no doubt helped fuel such conspiratorial rumours. This ambush occurred in December 1691, with some sixteen highwaymen taking part.

Luttrell recorded in July 1692 how the Oxford stagecoach was plundered in broad daylight after a bloody fight in which one of the bandits was killed. The criminals were so deliberate in their actions that they even took time to bury their comrade in a wood before escaping. The *London Gazette* of 12 January 1693 reported how a waggon laden with £15,000 – an astronomical sum in those days – was held up and ransacked. The robbery took so long that any fellow travellers who happened upon the incident were seized and held captive while the operation proceeded. When the booty had been secured, the criminals released their hostages, but either shot or hamstrung their horses – to the number of sixteen or eighteen – to prevent anyone following them. Also, according to the *London Gazette* of 19 December 1692, the Portsmouth mail was robbed twice in one week by men heavily armed and well mounted – this crime was linked to Colonel Blood's son. In Essex, a group of squires jovially chasing a hare were themselves hunted down by a band of marauders and systematically robbed.

It became necessary for the Lords Justices to order that horse and foot guards patrolled all the roads leading to the capital, both day and night, although this had the effect of simply scaring the criminals somewhere else. Despite numberless arrests throughout the 1690s, the surge in robberies continued unabated. Without question, England was entering its great era of lawlessness, an age of highway robbery with which the late seventeenth century was to become thoroughly synonymous. To travel throughout certain districts was to gamble with one's own life; and it was a situation that would not end for decades.

Chapter 7

Britain's Earliest Serial Killers

In the seventeenth century, most serial killers were driven by one motive – avarice. In fact, it would be realistic to say that the majority were not serial killers as we might understand the term, rather robbers who simply kept committing murder until they were uncovered.

As an example of this, there was the case of Thomas Shearwood and Elizabeth Evans, otherwise 'Country Tom' and 'Canberry Bess'. This couple had met in London's notorious Turnbull (now Turnmill) Street after migrating to the capital from Staffordshire and Shropshire respectively. Elizabeth had at one time enjoyed a promising future as a maid in a gentleman's service, but drifted into prostitution after a disastrous fling with some young rake. Thomas's profession was husbandry but he became corrupted by drunkenness, as did she. By 1634, they were operating in those urban areas on the fringes of the city that seethed with prostitution and criminality, their ploy being to haunt the alehouses and dingy clustered streets looking for gentlemen of quality to assault and rob. The method they employed was chillingly simple. Elizabeth would lure their target like a 'decoy ducke' to some secluded semi-rural location, using 'deceitfull smiles, and salutes' whereupon Thomas would materialise out of the darkness and assault the tricked gentleman.

During the course of these muggings they brutally murdered at least three men. In the autumn of 1634, they killed Michael Lowe, a lord mayor's son and employee of the Corporation of London, on the slope of a hill going down to Hockley-in-the-Hole, Clerkenwell. Then, on 22 January 1635, Rowland Holt was murdered in 'Clerkenwell field'. On 2 April 1635, Lieutenant Thomas Claxton encountered the pair in Bloomsbury, and after a drink accompanied Elizabeth Evans alone to a place 'neare unto Lambs Conduit' where Shearwood reappeared and violently assaulted him. At least two of the victims were beaten to death with a ferocious wooden club spiked with iron.

After murdering Claxton, the couple stole all his money and even his clothes, including his scarlet coat, boots, shirt and hat, before taking the decision to get out of London. First, however, they attempted to sell Claxton's distinctive coat in Houndsditch, precipitating their arrests. According to some accounts, Shearwood – in view of witnesses – suffered a huge nosebleed when he was brought to view Claxton's corpse on display. Such an occurrence was viewed suspiciously by those present, it being believed that this was a divine sign of guilt. It appears that Shearwood also believed providence had pointed a finger at him; he and Elizabeth were imprisoned in Newgate, where he in particular apparently accepted his life was over from that moment on.

Both admitted many crimes, and following a swift trial Shearwood was hanged on 14 April 1635. At the gallows, he confessed once more and asked for a song, *Lamentation of a Sinner*, to be sung for him. Shortly before his execution near Lambs Conduit he 'joy-fully embraced' his own death; afterwards, his corpse was hung in chains at Battle Bridge, Saint Pancras. Here, such was the volume of people who came to see his body that surrounding fields and crops were trodden into mire, forcing the removal of the gibbet post bearing his remains to the Ring-Cross beyond Islington. It probably didn't help that a butcher had been ambushed, stripped, robbed and bound to the gibbet post by hooligans while it had stood at its original location.

Elizabeth Evans followed him to the gallows on 17 April. Afterwards, her cadaver was dissected at the Barber Surgeon's Hall and 'her bones [p]reserved in a perfect forme of her body which is to be seene, and now remaines in the aforesaid Hall'. Her partner's skeleton later ended up at the hall in Monkwell Street as well, ensuring both their names became notorious for several generations.

What seems reasonably clear from the earliest account – Henry Goodcole's *Heavens Speedie Hue and Cry Sent After Lust and Murther* - is that the murders they committed were incidental. A contemporary ballad suggests that Shearwood and Evans attacked a number of others in the same manner although these had the good fortune to survive the violent strikes from his vicious spiked truncheon. Homicidal impulse was not behind the attacks, it could be argued, merely a brutal, selfish desire to scratch a living at the callous expense of the lives of others.

Perhaps the most interesting feature of the case is Elizabeth Evans's role as an inviting, persuasive, calculating decoy, which contrasts sharply with Shearwood's unsophisticated savagery. Indeed, in some ways it is the instances of female serial killers that are rather more interesting, for their victims were more often than not helpless children, while their attempts to avoid detection were at least as deliberate as those of their male counterparts, if not more so. Nonetheless, in most cases, it was still the desire to obtain income that drove the female serial murderer.

There were, of course, exceptions to the rule. One was a series of murders that occurred in the East End of London in 1691, in which the barbarity of the crimes suggests that the perpetrator was a psychopath, the accompanying robberies perhaps merely a secondary motive. Another was the case of Elizabeth Ridgway, of Leicestershire – who appears to have fallen into the habit of murdering people simply because she considered them an annoyance.

'THE BLOUDY MOTHER'
In 1610, a pamphlet, *The Bloudy Mother, Or, The Most Inhumane Murthers, Committed by Jane Hattersley* by Thomas Brewer, told how a horrific murder case had lately reached its conclusion in West Sussex. The pamphlet explained that Jane Hattersley, serving maid to Adam Adamson, of East Grinstead, had been seduced into an affair with her master. This liaison over time resulted in several pregnancies, and (as per the pamphlet) Jane committed 'the most inhumane murthers… upon divers infants, the issue of her owne bodie'. These poor creatures were secretly interred in an orchard around a specific tree.

Jane had begun her adulterous relationship with Adamson around 1599, following his seduction of her. However, when he found she was pregnant for the first time, Adamson's panic forced him to order her out of the house and into the dwelling of a neighbouring family called King. They quickly recognised their new guest was pregnant, despite her attempts to conceal it – but scandal turned to horror when they chanced to find young Jane simply holding the lifeless body of her new baby a few days after she had given birth.

The King family believed that, since the infant had been born healthy, Jane had smothered it to regain the affections of Adamson – and Adamson did indeed invite her to return to his house so as to resume their affair behind his wife's back. An attempt to prosecute Jane Hattersley for murder failed, the authorities deciding that the baby's death was a sad accident. Adamson, who was a man of some standing, levelled counter-accusations against the King family, accusing them of thieving from Jane while she had lodged with them.

Over the next decade, it was regularly gossiped among the local community that Jane had more than once become pregnant by Adamson and they had contrived each time to murder their unwanted newborn babies. Neighbours claimed to have heard the screams of a newly born infant silenced on at least one occasion and Jane herself was overheard to rage at Adamson during an argument that she knew she had the power to send him to the gallows, if she made the 'discoveries in the orchard' public.

When the orchard *was* searched, the remains of three infants were found and Jane was arrested. Adamson was arrested on suspicion too but thanks to his position he secured his release and next used a plausible argument to persuade Jane that she should admit full responsibility for the infant deaths. He suggested to Jane that she should wilfully lie in court, exonerating him and subsequently leaving him free to arrange her acquittal. Of course, nothing of the sort happened – Jane was convicted of murder and hanged in June 1609, while Adamson was simply acquitted.

Despite having gained his freedom, however, Adamson subsequently fell sick. The pamphlet explains how 'the unlawfull begetter of those unfortunate babes [was] being eaten and consumed alive with wormes and lice.' He died within a year of Jane's execution, probably through some wasting disease, although naturally God's hand was seen in his fatal decline.

Interestingly, East Grinstead had seen another multiple child killing not long before these events. On 15 July 1606, the *Faithfull Annalist* tells us, the wife of Richard Homewood 'murdered her own three children, and threw them into a pit, and then cut her own throat likewise'. There was no known cause for her actions.

THE BODY PIT

Another news pamphlet, *The Cry and Revenge of Blood Expressing the Nature and Haynousnesse of Wilful Murther*, written by Thomas Cooper and printed in 1620, told of another grim story which had lately drawn to a conclusion in Suffolk.

The case centred around a man named Norton, who lived in the town of Halesworth, eighteen miles south-west and inland from coastal Lowestoft. Although a man of 'faire possessions', Norton was nonetheless 'of a very foule and evill favour', and greedily sought the land of a neighbour, the Widow Leeson, who had four grown-up children.

Norton, it was reported, sought to ingratiate himself with the Widow Leeson, worming his way into her affairs, simultaneously lending her money while corrupting her family with his crude and drunken pastimes. After a while she found herself mortgaging some of her land in order to secure certain necessary funds from Norton. Norton's influence was such that when the eldest Leeson boy reached his majority and looked to his inheritance as a way of earning a livelihood, the former had him imprisoned on a spurious legal charge. The youth died while languishing in gaol and it is suggested that Norton somehow engineered this through a plot with the jailer.

When the second son, John Leeson, inherited the land in his brother's stead, Norton apparently began to bribe him in an effort to get him to renounce the claim. This ploy did not work for long and so, in around 1612, Norton plotted with two other men – a servant of his called Worlich and a weaver called Land – to have the youth murdered.

The nature of Norton's relationship with the Widow Leeson is uncertain, but what is clear is that by the time he decided upon this course he firmly believed her estate was due to him, if not legally then by murder. To this end, the hired men – Land and Worlich – took John Leeson to a tavern 'up at the Mill-hill', where they plied him with drink before taking him outside into the night and bashing his head in with a heavy stick. The body was dragged to a local pit full of water, where it was weighted and sunk. An illustration on the tract's cover suggests the body was further secured in the depths by use of a stake.

Around 1614, the Widow Leeson's third son reached the age of majority and he attempted to untangle Norton's influence in his family's financial affairs by obtaining a writ ordering the latter to attend court. In attempting to nail this writ to Norton's front door, both this young man and his sister were seized by Worlich and Land, who murdered them both before dragging their corpses to the same pond where their elder brother, John Leeson, had earlier been deposited.

Three of the Widow Leeson's children had disappeared by now, not to mention her first-born who had died in gaol, and the explanations Norton and his cronies provided were of such a laughable nature as to insult the intelligence. Worlich, for example, claimed John Leeson had died after suddenly travelling to the Continent, while the last two victims – it was alleged – had unexpectedly taken themselves off to Ireland for no reason and without telling anyone. It appears Norton was of considerable standing and influence within his local community; despite the general suspicion, most parishioners were either cowed or bribed by him.

Six years later, however, the pond was unexpectedly cleaned, dragged and drained by the farmer who owned the land and the skeletons of the three murdered siblings were found. When the remains were laid out, 'the helpe of a chyrugeon' was employed to establish the level of violence sustained and to look for evidence that might suggest who the victims had been. One set of remains was forensically identified as belonging to John Leeson – he had been unusually tall – while one of the skulls was missing certain teeth that suggested it belonged to his younger brother.

Word spread like wildfire that the Widow Leeson's children had all been found dead in the pond. Land, one of the hit-men, panicked. He procured the youngest son's skull and took it first to a barber-surgeon, and then a smith – on each occasion trying to persuade these people to remove more of the teeth in an effort to cast doubt upon the head's identity. Both the barber and the smith refused to help him, however; and furthermore, Land had infallibly pointed the finger of suspicion at himself.

The other hired killer, Worlich, next betrayed himself by absconding to the coast, but he was easily traced and apprehended after falling sick while there. As the conspiracy began to unravel, members of the intimidated community came forward to provide evidence against Worlich and Land. In the end – following their trial at Bury in 1620 – both were sentenced to be executed for the three murders.

How this matter concluded itself is a little unclear. On the day of judgement, Land was hanged, but Worlich earned a temporary reprieve – in the hope that he might make a greater confession implicating Mr Norton, the instigator behind the whole affair. The tract makes it plain that Norton's involvement was well known; but the evidence cannot have been such as would ensure his conviction, if there was a need to elicit a further confession from Worlich.

Frustratingly, this is the point at which the tract was printed at the behest of 'John Wright, dwelling in Pie-corner', and any data beyond this appears lacking.

A GLOUCESTERSHIRE INNKEEPER'S PRIVATE GRAVEYARD

In 1675, a chapbook entitled *The Bloody Inkeeper: Or, Sad and Barbarous News from Glocester-shire* reported how an innkeeper and his wife from 'Putley' (probably meaning Putloe, Gloucestershire) had lately taken the decision to relocate to Gloucester and open a larger establishment there. This surprised their former neighbours, because the couple's original inn had been a small one; obviously, they had exceeded their expectations and made more money over the years than anyone thought possible.

The truth of the matter was revealed when a smith moved into the recently-vacated house at Putloe. While digging in the yard to set up his anvil, he and some neighbours discovered seven corpses – of both men and women – buried in the garden. All were in various stages of decomposition and

148

appeared to have been put there over several years while fully clothed.

One of the bodies had a knife rammed in its chest, easily suggesting what had occurred. Given that many of their visitors would have been Bristol-bound merchants, the innkeepers had obviously murdered their customers occasionally when they felt it was safe to do so.

Initials carved on the knife's handle matched those of the (un-named) absent innkeeper, who is said to have been a former Parliamentary solder who had served in Scotland. His wife was reportedly Scottish and many victims may have been Scottish cloth merchants who deliberately sought out the Putloe inn on their travels, thinking it friendly.

As we have seen elsewhere, cases of this nature were frequently reported as a 'true relation' of some provincial horror. However, many are today unverifiable because corroborative evidence is lacking. What is particularly annoying in the case of the Putloe murders is that the chapbook came out before any trial - meaning the outcome of the case is unknown. We learn that the author of the chapbook opted not to name the suspect in order 'that I may not seem to prejudice him'.

'WHY TALK TO ME OF HEAVEN?'

Trials where felons were sentenced to death for what might be termed a lesser crime, while remaining un-convicted of more serious ones they were strongly suspected of, were another curious feature of the age. In December 1679, for instance, two men named John Dell and Richard Dean were sentenced to death at the Old Bailey for stealing a mare worth 26 shillings.

Dell hailed from 'Edger' (Edgware) in Middlesex and Dean was his servant. Both were thought guilty of murdering Dell's brother-in-law, a tanner whose body had been found near 'Redlion-fields' the previous year. They were also suspected of quietly smothering Dell's 80-year-old father-in-law, Daniel Ball, as well as murdering Dell's own wife.

Dell claimed he and his wife had been attacked by three thieves while riding near woods in Barnet. He had managed to scramble away, despite his hands being bound together; and after he found some country people to untie him, his wife was discovered to be dead. She had suffered a fearful wound to her head, although it appeared she had in fact been forcibly drowned – her upper body was soaking wet, and there was a pond nearby.

Investigators believed the whole incident had been staged. Slashes and rips in Dell's clothes and hat seemed to have been made on purpose; he himself had no serious injuries despite claiming to have been viciously assaulted. One witness stated Dell's hands were so poorly tied that he should easily have been able to free himself, had he so wished. And his loyal servant, Dean, could give no convincing account of his whereabouts at the time, implying he may have abetted in the wife's murder in some way.

It was suggested all three murders stemmed from a dispute over land. However, contradictions and mere circumstantial evidence led to both men being acquitted; so they were next put on trial for the theft of a mare in Hertfordshire. Their guilt appeared plainer in this matter, thanks to some credible witnesses, and livestock theft at that time was a capital offence.

Both Dell and his servant continued to deny any guilt in the three killings they were suspected of and their behaviour prior to execution was sullen and un-cooperative. The servant even tried to set his prison cell on fire twice the night before his execution. And when Dell was pressed by ministers to confess his wicked acts, he said back, 'Heaven! There is not one of a thousand goes to Heaven, why talk you to me of Heaven?'

Dell was hanged at Tyburn on 19 December 1679, angrily denying any guilt, and after this his servant, Dean, followed him to the gallows. The latter was pressed one last time to make a confession and he grudgingly suggested that his master *may* have murdered his wife. However, he continued to deny any guilt himself, and so – further data not being forthcoming – he was likewise launched to his death.

A WOLF IN A LAMB'S SKIN
Elizabeth Ridgway was born in the neighbourhood of Ibstock, west of Leicester, sometime around 1655. She was the daughter of a farming couple called Husbands and in adulthood she developed a very good reputation locally, being 'a religious maid, and a follower of the Presbyterians.'

However, Elizabeth was – as per a contemporary pamphlet published by George Croom, *A True Relation of Four Most Barbarous and Cruel Murders Committed in Leicestershire by Elizabeth Ridgway* – a 'wolf in a lamb's-skin, or rather, a devil in the shape of a saint'. Around 1681 (it would later transpire) she murdered her own mother, Mary Husbands, using poison, following some petty argument they had had over the household affairs.

About a year later Elizabeth went into service and shortly afterwards had a disagreement with a fellow servant, a young man. She apparently tolerated his spite, but privately plotted his removal by putting white arsenic into his broth. Unlike the case of her mother, there was great surprise when the young man died, because he had been in rude health and showed no signs of illness until a few hours before he died. In both cases, Elizabeth appears to have escaped suspicion on account of her pious reputation and also the fact that she had not entered into wholesale public feuding, but rather allowed her rage to simmer privately while she plotted revenge.

By the summer of 1683, Elizabeth entertained two suitors in Ibstock, both of whom wished her hand in marriage. Accepting the proposal of William Ridgway, a local tailor, she coldly decided to get rid of her other suitor, a servant named John King, for no other reason than that she considered him a nuisance. Under the pretence of wishing to enjoy his company, Elizabeth poisoned Mr King's beverage around the middle of August 1683, killing him and so claiming a third victim.

Elizabeth was married to William Ridgway around Christmas-tide that year. Within a week, the newlyweds were arguing. Elizabeth immediately began to conceive a plot to get rid of her husband. She used her usual method, pretending the matter was forgotten while dutifully accompanying her spouse to the market at Ashby de la Zouch; but, three weeks into the marriage, she stirred some white arsenic into William's broth. Ridgway ate heartily and later complained in the presence of his servants that the broth tasted funny, and 'grated in his teeth'. He died in excruciating agony two days later, in early 1684.

This time there was great suspicion in the neighbourhood that Elizabeth had had something to do with the death. So widespread did the suspicion against her become that when she presented her youngest apprentice-boy, Richard Tully, with some broth, he refused it. This enraged Elizabeth and she threw the broth away with a great display of hysterics. This, it seems, was what she was like when her true character overtook her for a few moments.

There is some suggestion that she had been trying to kill her apprentice-boy for some time, as well as another apprentice she kept. Young Richard apparently believed his master, William Ridgway, had been murdered, so had taken to watching his mistress with a great deal of attention; this may have been the reason she decided to poison the boy also. In the end, he took his suspicions to his father, who in turn went to a neighbouring justice of the peace, Sir Beaumont Dixey.

Elizabeth was arrested. Eight days after his burial, William Ridgway's body was exhumed. She was forced by her father-in-law to touch the corpse, there being an old belief that a corpse would bleed in the presence of its murderer. To everyone's astonishment, her husband's corpse gushed blood from its nose and mouth, 'as fresh as if new stabbed', and Elizabeth was committed to Leicester Gaol on suspicion of murder.

From the outset, she persistently denied any wrongdoing, but the circumstantial evidence was not in her favour when she was tried at the next county assizes. It did not help her case that she was proved infallibly to have

Elizabeth Ridgway, the Ibstock serial murderer, following her arrest – a later imagining.

purchased white arsenic during her trip to the market in Ashby de la Zouch with her late husband.

Elizabeth was convicted of murder and sentenced to be burnt to death 'at the common place of execution for that county'. On the morning of her execution, she finally admitted killing all her four victims and it is a sign of the times that her confession was interwoven with suggestions she had been led by a supernatural agent of evil. This took the form of a 'familiar spirit' who appeared to her around 1676 and tried to persuade her to poison herself. The demon-spirit had next encouraged her to consider murdering anyone who annoyed her; to this end she had begun concealing a bottle of poison in the bunches of her hair. Elizabeth subsequently confessed she had also intended to poison both of her apprentices and afterwards commit suicide. However, she appeared very reluctant in her confession, admitting only the four deaths she was questioned about. This recalcitrant attitude led the authorities to firmly suspect she may have murdered a great many others by poison over the last eight years, but – because the details were not known – she preferred not to bring them to light.

On the morning of her execution, 24 March 1684, 'two eminent divines' offered to accompany her and assist her, but she scorned this by saying she could read and pray as well as they. Persistent attempts were made to bring Elizabeth to confess to other murders, but still she stubbornly refused, even when she was tied to the stake in preparation for being set alight. The day was particularly eventful; she was forced to watch the execution by hanging of two brothers, who had been convicted of other crimes at the same assizes. One had actually been offered a reprieve if he would participate in the execution of his sibling and set Elizabeth afire, but he turned down this opportunity for what might loosely be termed 'mercy'.

Being forced to watch these executions had no other effect on Elizabeth other than to prompt her to request hanging. The authorities were aware she might make a further confession if this was permitted, but the law prescribed she *must* die by burning for petty treason – the deliberate killing of her husband. Therefore, the pile of woodchips at her feet was set on fire and when the first flames touched her she gave a loud shriek; whereupon the town executioner began to slowly garrotte her with a rope from behind. Afterwards, Elizabeth's body was left tied to the stake to become consumed by the flames.

THE EAST END MURDERS

On 17 January 1691, a crime was committed at East Smithfield that both appalled and terrified the East End of London. The gruesome discovery was made by a woman who turned up at the Loyal Coffee House near what is now Wellclose Square. Finding the door already open, the woman entered and found a scene of utter carnage within. Mrs Sarah Hodges, the wife of Thomas Hodges, had been attacked while naked in bed, her murderer dashing her skull in and cutting her throat. Both of her ears had also been slit so as to take out her gold earrings.

Not only that, a lodger called Elizabeth Smith was also found murdered; she was naked too, and her hands had been bound before someone had stabbed her repeatedly in the head and ear. Finally, the body of a maid called Hannah Williams was discovered. She had been repeatedly stabbed before her throat was cut. All three bodies were discovered in two rooms on the first floor, which was awash with blood.

This part of London was already highly agitated following the recent unrelated massacre of an aged gentlewoman, a maidservant and a little girl on 13 January, during a robbery at Captain Gidding's house in Wapping. A servant, Robert Congden, arrested trying to sell stolen plate, was tried and hanged on 27 February.

In April that year, James Selbee of Whitechapel was tried at the Old Bailey for the murder of Mary Bartlett (alias Bartley). Mary was the keeper of 'a common bawdy house' in Goodman's Fields, near present-day Leman Street, and Selbee had attacked her on 22 March with a knife he had purchased for one penny. With this basic weapon, he had cut her throat to a depth of four inches and stabbed her several times in the forehead. Following his trial, Selbee was hanged on 2 May near where he had committed the crime.

The proximity between the two murder locations – they were only several streets away from each other – as well as the timing and the method employed in the crime, suggests that there may have been a link between them. A contemporary ballad on the Selbee case also hints that this is so, since it suggested Selbee murdered Mrs Bartlett while drunk and disgusted with himself for cheating on his wife. Tellingly, it also observed that Selbee attempted to kill another woman on the premises, Mrs Bartlett's 'nurse', although she got away. This woman had her throat cut and was dashed on the head, but not effectually enough to kill her, and after Selbee had run off into the night, her cries of 'Murder!' brought the watch running to her assistance. Since he had left his hat and gloves next to Mary Bartlett's corpse, the watchmen quickly scoured the area looking for a hatless suspect, and found the drunken Selbee trying to climb over some railings near the house, covered in blood.

Although it is not clear, there is some suggestion that the scene of the first murders – the Loyal Coffee House – doubled as a brothel, with Sarah Hodges acting as a procuress while the two other victims were prostitutes in her employ. If Selbee had been at that locale suffering from a similar attack of drunken shame and rage, it might explain the brutality meted out on the three original victims.

However, the matter is a little complicated by the fact that Sarah Hodges's former lover – a butler to Catherine of Braganza, Charles II's wife – had been brutally murdered in the Tower Hamlets area in 1689. According to a 1694 report by the Society for Reformation, Sarah had been suspected of involvement: 'Several great evidences were produced in order to [secure] her conviction, but all ineffectual.' This led some to suppose that Sarah Hodges's own murder was somehow connected to that affair.

'THE BLOODY MIDWIFE'

Even by the standards of the time, the discovery made in Poplar was a horrifying one. At this time, Poplar was a Middlesex hamlet in the parish of Stepney. By August 1693, Madame Mary Compton (alias Norman) had lived there for around two years, alongside Mary Compton the younger, described as the former's 'maid' although in actual fact her daughter. The older Mary, according to a subsequent ballad, had practised midwifery for thirty-three years, making her perhaps around 55.

It was Madame Compton's custom to take bastards, orphans and other unwanted children into her household to raise them as her own, a not-unusual practice in many large parishes during those times. However, Madame Compton, despite being a midwife, and thus holding a somewhat elevated position in Poplar compared to many of her contemporaries, nonetheless appears to have made little effort to fit in, avoiding church while drinking and entertaining gentlemen callers in the evening.

Her crimes came to light when it became necessary to remove three of her young wards from the house because of accusations they were suffering severe malnutrition. This order was given by a Poplar minister, based on the emerging concerns of neighbours and local church-wardens and he presented the task of removing the three children considered at risk to a local nurse. She in turn collected the three children from Madame Compton, finding them shockingly malnourished. Moreover, the nurse reported that there were numerous other children under the Compton's roof, all looking as though they were in various stages of poor health.

Despite this precaution, one child died after three days and the concerned nurse who had taken the child away originally later returned to Madame Compton's house to inform her of this development. It was while there, as the nurse and Madame Compton exchanged words, that a little boy inside the house blurted out that another child (his brother, in fact) was also dead within and would the nurse be so good as to see he got a decent burial?

Other versions aver that the authorities were alerted when children called out to passers-by from the windows of the house, upon Madame Compton and her 'maid' venturing to leave. Very possibly, the two incidents that supposedly brought the matter to light occurred more or less simultaneously. The Poplar authorities naturally took an immediate and closer interest in the situation and Madame Compton's house was searched by parish constables. What they found shocked them beyond belief, for the midwife had been abusing her responsible position in an almost unheard-of manner.

The remains of two dead children were found in a hand-basket which had been placed on a shelf in the cellar. Both corpses were in a dreadful condition, the eyes, skin and parts of the flesh having been consumed by vermin and maggots. The cellar and the garden were subsequently excavated, with one contemporary pamphlet reporting that the skeletal remains of six more children were discovered buried at the former location. There is a suggestion that at least one more body might have been buried in the garden at some point, although the true number of victims is unclear, since the remains appear to have been somewhat jumbled. However, the fact that numerous other living children existed under the roof of this house of horror merely added another grim dimension to the case.

Madame Compton was arrested alongside Mary Compton the younger. Both were charged with 'destroying, starving to death and famishing several poor infants', while a servant named Ann Davis was also arrested on suspicion of being an accomplice. A number of neighbours were rounded up to appear against the women. These included some who had long entertained grave suspicions that abuses were occurring under Madame Compton's roof; other witnesses consisted of those who had been present when the house was searched.

The younger Mary was eventually persuaded to become a prosecution witness against her mother. When Madame Compton learned of this in mid-September 1693, she attempted to poison herself while awaiting trial in Newgate. The attempt was unsuccessful, and the following month the midwife was found guilty at the Old Bailey of starving four infants to death. To what level the servant Ann Davis was involved is unclear, but she was burnt upon her hand after being judged complicit to a lesser degree. The court decided that the 'bloody midwife' had deliberately and callously starved the neglected children to death in order that she might have room to take more in – since, of course, she was paid £5 on each occasion by the parish.

Madame Compton is reported to have been lame and in a state of general ill-health when she appeared at the bar of the court to hear her sentence pronounced. The convicted woman appeared to have little comprehension of her crimes, apparently believing that she had done nothing she could be hanged for. When it became apparent that she was to suffer death, she continued in her stubbornness; on the morning of her execution she even had the audacity to claim that she had been visited by an angel in her cell the night before, who had absolved her. The Ordinary of Newgate, to whom she told this, reminded her that her soul was by no means safe, for Satan frequently deceived sinners in the guise of an angel.

On 23 October 1693, Madame Compton was placed in a cart and taken from Newgate to Chancery Lane-end, Holborn, stopping beneath a specially erected gibbet. A noose from the beam was secured around her neck, and – because she continued to deny the gravity of her crimes – little time was wasted in drawing the cart away, leaving her kicking at nothing until she died. The execution occurred near 'Old Southampton Buildings', according to the diarist Luttrell.

Sadly, this was not the first time something like this had occurred. Thirty-five years earlier, Abigail Hill, a parish nurse residing in Southwark St Olave, on the southern banks of the Thames, had murdered in a 'barbarous' manner four children who she had undertaken to look after. This heartless woman even covered up the disappearance of her infant charges by deceitfully 'borrowing of other children of her poore acquaintance, whom on every quarter day she would bring to the over-seers of the parish, and receive her quarters pay for them, as if they had been the same children which had been committed to her charge to nurse.'

Hill was tried for the four child killings at the Old Bailey sessions of 15 December 1657, and hanged on 22 December somewhere near Wood Street, Cheapside. According to an account of her case, *A True Relation of the Most Horrid and Barbarous Murders Committed by Abigall Hill*, published in 1658, her execution was a disgraceful spectacle, for she jeered the executioner and in her final moments was 'strange and stubborn'. She condescended to admit she had throttled one of her charges, the infant being ill, but that was as much of a confession as was forthcoming.

This case was all the more shocking because Abigail Hill had been looked upon as a responsible person. She had been respected by many in the community for several years, and there must have been great shock when it was learnt the woman was, in fact, a deceitful, cold-blooded murderer. In the end, it was her suspicious neighbours who gave her away to a parish constable; it is perhaps the case that over the years she disposed of many more children than the four she was convicted of murdering.

Chapter 8

Coastal Crimes

Charles I's unpopularity grew with his extension of the 'Ship money' tax in June 1635. This was a dictatorial law levying the tax to pay for warships upon inland areas – not just ports and coastal towns, which had previously been the case when the nation was threatened by war. The cause of the move, moreover, was not war but the perceived national threat posed by pirates in the Channel. The policy was also carried out without the backing of the House of Commons, since Charles had dissolved Parliament in 1629 following a violent uproar against his authority in the chamber.

This is not to suggest there was no threat from piracy. In 1666, the *Faithful Annalist* recorded that the problem had been deeply entrenched for years:

> '*July the eighth 1605, Proclamation was made against pyrates, and other English mariners and souldiers, who under pretence of serving the states, robbed divers English men and others, who made complaint thereof to his Majesty. Now this is the third Proclamation against pirats.*'

Under Charles's predecessor, James I, the problem had been judged a quasi-political one, because not only were English pirates attacking the vessels of their own countrymen but those of other nations, 'especially upon the Florentines and Venetians, wherewith his Majesty was much grieved'. In 1608, these seafaring bandits were pronounced rebels, traitors and peace-breakers and English merchant vessels were authorised 'to proceed severely in justice against all such offenders' with the backing of 'the Judge of the Admiralty'. As a result of this offensive, it was reported, 'December the two and twentieth [1608], nineteen pirates were executed at Wapping.' Hangings such as these, at Execution Dock on the Wapping shoreline, were customarily carried out in such a way that the felons' bodies were left suspended in the water of the Thames until three tides had washed over their heads. The grim spectacle also had the benefit of being seen by every single vessel – domestic

A pirate's end at 'Execution Dock'. (Courtesy of Madame Tussauds, London)

and foreign – that sailed up the Thames in the direction of the Tower and City of London.

The problem was much more widespread and complicated than this suggests. Freebooters of all nations and types were involved, as were certain English merchant vessels – which were in some cases complicit with pirates in the organised trafficking of stolen goods under the pretence of commerce, 'to the great cherishing of those malefactors, and dishonour of this nation'. The public's grievance with the king's extension of the 'Ship money' tax was that it was so obviously a money-spinning scheme, having been instituted suddenly to tax the whole nation for a 'national emergency' that had always been a threat. At the time, to suggest that such a threat could be eradicated by merely extending the tax was unthinkable.

THE PIRATE THREAT
The British Isles suffered from a proliferation of piracy throughout the seventeenth century, both home-grown and non-domestic. Freebooting vessels circled and waited out at sea like sharks, launching ambushes on

159

smaller trading vessels and committing the oceanic form of highway robbery.

Although the problem of seaborne looters later became somewhat complicated and magnified through their evolution into the more patriotic 'privateers', in the early 1600s the motive of seafaring bandits was rather more straightforward; that of common plunder. Such plunder could take the form of goods, vessels or even people.

There were numerous guises that threats could assume for ordinary vessels, not even taking into account the obvious natural dangers of making a living out at sea. In fact, the seas around the British Isles were nothing short of a criminal free-for-all. Some freebooters were considered domestic, as in the case of the 'English pirates' who assaulted London merchant vessels off the Scillies around July 1611, or the bark 'taken by English pirates, and run ashore at Lydd (Kent)' *c*.1618. Some were of unclear origin, such as 'the pirates who molest the coast near Milford Haven' around August 1634 during a gathering of merchants at St James's Fair, Bristol. The Welsh coast suffered as greatly as any; it was communicated by the Lords of the Admiralty around this time that Pembrokeshire 'was much infested with pirates'.

There was also naturally great fear of pirates coming ashore, as per this 1607 declaration from the archives of the justices of Devon:

'The county justices complained to the Lords of the Council that the harbour of Salcomb was infested with pirates, who often landed and came into the town in great numbers armed, and that the inhabitants were in great danger.'

Even the British navy caused problems. Sir William Uvedale complained in July 1634 how 'men belonging to the King's ships' had raided Pewit Island in Portsmouth Harbour, where Sir William bred pewits and harvested their eggs. The seamen thoroughly vandalised the island, also threatening to stab Sir William's servant (who protected his royalties there) to death. Bizarrely, this seems to have been done for the sport of it, rather than plunder, but the incident illustrates the manner of those supposed to be keeping order off the coast.

Some pirates were clearly non-domestic. Word was communicated to the Admiralty in June 1634 of:

'a small Biscay man-of-war or two, with two or three shallops, which lie pilfering between Lundy, and Mount's Bay, which rob small vessels that trade between Ireland, Wales and that place.'

The Pembrokeshire coast was menaced by pirates.

The previous year Sir Bernard Grenville had reported to the Secretary of State that a Spanish man-of-war, out of Biscay, had landed eighty armed men on the Isle of Lundy, off the north Devon coast. These brigands killed a man named Mark Pollard during some skirmishes with the local people, before thoroughly plundering the island of everything of worth. Lundy appears to have been a continual magnet for pirates of various nationalities, either for use as a base or as a hiding place from which to launch ambushes. This was until Captain John Penington, of the *Vanguard*, was ordered to end these incursions. His imposition of martial law on the island met with some success, although it was not an indefinite one. Two decades later, Generals Penn and Blake mentioned that they had been forced to send a ship to patrol the waters around Lundy because Brest pirates were threatening shipping.

The greatest threat all round seems to have come from the so-called 'Barbary Pirates', or corsairs – plunderers, kidnappers and slaver-traders who sailed from the region of Algiers, Tunis and Tripoli. Some also came from Turkey. Much of Europe was terrorised by these more-organised, warlike freebooters, including Britain. Around 1618, the people of Dorset petitioned for the protection of 'Swanwhich [Swanage]Bay' from 'dangerous pirates, especially the Turks'. About this time there occurred a great raid by Turkish pirates 'on a seaport borough not named', leading to calls for a fort to be built there for future defence. The appearance of unfamiliar foreign vessels filled

161

A corsair vessel menaces the coast.

coastal communities with terror, because shore raids were not unknown during which villagers were kidnapped and taken out of the country, never to be heard from again.

England's south-west suffered particularly heavily. In July 1636, a veritable fleet of fifteen Turkish vessels had done 'much mischief' lately:

> *'These Turks daily show themselves at St Keverne, Mount's Bay, and other places, that the poor fishermen are fearful not only to go to the seas, but likewise lest these Turks should come on shore and take them out of their houses.'*

A ship out of Topsham, the *Lark*, had also lately been commandeered and the master murdered. One incident around this time speaks to a massacre having been committed:

> *'A ship was taken by the Turkish pirates within three leagues of Dartmouth; £5,000 loss was sustained by Exeter, besides the loss of the ship and the seamen.'*

The terror these men-of-war caused can be gleaned from the pleas of the Cornish justices in July 1636 to the king. They begged his majesty to listen to the:

'complaints lately received from the sea coast of Cornwall, and particularly from East Looe and West Looe. About two months since, three barks of the said towns, on a fishing voyage upon the coasts, were taken by the Turks, and 27 persons carried away into miserable slavery, which loss falls more heavy upon the said towns, by reason of their former losses in two preceding years, wherein they lost four barks and 42 persons…'

There is also an astonishing suggestion that some skippers drove their boats onto the rocks deliberately, preferring to lose their vessels – and perhaps their lives – rather than their liberty. At the time of the plea to the king:

'The Swan, of Topsham, was set upon by two great Turkish men-of-war near the Scillies, and the crews were obliged to run ashore to save themselves.'

SHIPWRECK LOOTERS

However, in some cases, it was the British coastal dwellers themselves who were dangerous. Often tough people who knew no other life than that of the seas, they believed that whatever washed up along 'their' stretch of coastline was brought to them by God. Abandoned ships cast ashore, or poorly piloted onto the rocks, were considered gifts sent to these communities by providence.

Riotous scavengers collectively called 'wreckers' would often descend onto the beaches like a pack of wolves, to plunder shipwrecked vessels with callous disregard for the plight of any human survivors. Certain communities even formed mutually-beneficial alliances with the pirates we have already observed. In June 1634, Sir John Pennington communicated to the Lords of the Admiralty that the pirate vessels and small men-of-war which menaced all parts of the south-western coastline were also trading with coastal communities in return for protection. Lately, for instance, disguised pirate vessels had been spotted 'in Mount's Bay, at anchor within Mouse-hole'.

But these people also committed their own violence. In February 1635, an armed and rioting crowd from Mousehole and Marazion, crying 'One and all!' prevented the Admiralty Court's commissioners from recovering booty from a cast-away Spanish galleon. The mob forced the officials into scrambling down a steep cliff to save their lives, before looting everything they could. The king himself ordered these 'sea-mutineers' and 'rebellious rascals' to be supressed and the offenders exemplarily punished.

Marazion, Cornwall: in 1635 an armed mob assaulted the Admiralty Court's commissioners.

'Wrecking' occurred elsewhere too, other than along the Cornish coast, with which it is primarily associated. On 10 February 1638, for example, it was corresponded how four men brazenly boarded and looted two vessels cast on shore at Dartmouth, Devon. The vessels were at the time under the possession of the officers of Sir Edward Seymour, a Vice-Admiral of Devon: but the thieves stated they 'did not care a pin' for the Vice-Admiral's warrant, and threatened to throw his officers overboard.

Sometimes even those authorised to recover goods from shipwrecks on behalf of the government could not be trusted. In December 1633, a Dutch ship driven ashore near Holland Haven, Essex, was plundered by (probably local) 'covetous persons' actually employed by the Court of Admiralty to assist in the recovery.

These sorts of practices bred many a tradition of 'wreckers' deliberately luring ships onto the rocks with false lights, and murdering shipwrecked mariners in cold blood. The Victorian Cornish historian Alphonse Esquiros observed:

> *'[Wrecking] consisted in killing and torturing passengers who had escaped the sea, in order to take advantage of their misfortune. If such a custom ever existed in Cornwall (and unfortunately certain stories which appear authentic leave little doubt on this point) I can confirm it ceased long ago.'*

The greater portion of these stories are anecdotal, however, and in truth it appears that the more-vicious crimes were committed away from land by piratical boatmen – rather than by coastal communities as a whole.

SHIPBOARD MASSACRES

Sometimes, a ship did not need to have been wrecked for it to be looted by those desperate or ruthless enough. It appears that on occasion, vessels lying at anchor off the coast were attacked. At around four in the morning on 6 January 1600, a group of men plundered the *Nancy*, at that time lying in the port of Hull, East Yorkshire. During this they murdered Captain Thomas Fletcher, Guy Foster (the ship's mate), and two seamen, Forest and Fowler. There was never really any chance the criminals would evade justice, as all were local men involved in smuggling, and the very next day they were rounded up and imprisoned in York Castle. On 2 April, seven men were hanged for the massacre at St Leonard's, Green Dykes, by Walmgate Bar, in front of a crowd numbering 6,000. Those executed included 59-year-old George Wolstenholme and 48-year-old Thomas Wilson, Esquires, who appear to have been of a certain standing and may have been the ringleaders. Afterwards, their bodies were delivered to surgeons in York and Hull to be dissected and anatomised.

Such outrageous crimes were not, apparently, confined exclusively to England. In around the year 1683, a Swedish vessel bound for the west coast of England happened to cast anchor 'near the mouth of Kylscow' on the extreme Scottish north-western coast. The vessel's exact location was at a place called Poleghaun, or Stirk's Pool; while it waited there, a force of banditti sailed out and stealthily clambered aboard under the cover of darkness. They massacred the crew and carried off all the money they could find, wrapped up in a Highland plaid. However, upon manhandling the plaid into their own boat, a corner of it 'slipt off' and most of the money poured into the sea.

Lord Reay and others went to great lengths to discover the perpetrators of this vicious seaborne robbery but although several men were suspected, no proof could be levelled against them. However, in line with the superstitions of the times, it was generally believed that those suspected fell afterwards into great poverty and misery.

The eighteenth century teacher Robert MacKay wrote in his *History of the House and Clan of MacKay* that in 1783 he worked at a school in 'Edderachillis' near Badcall Bay where he found the story to be common knowledge. The local people explained that the crime had occurred the same year a local figurehead, Duncan MacKenzie of Rhiroy, was born: and by 1783 he was in his 100th year. A local legend had it that the Swedish captain had been forewarned by a fortune-teller in his native land to steer clear of Whiten Head and Cape Wrath. However, strong winds forced him to anchor at Poleghaun, and when the local people told him where he was, the captain exclaimed, 'Then I am gone!'

THE RISE IN SMUGGLING

Though shipwreck looting was communal and opportunistic, another burgeoning crime among coastal dwellers became vastly more organised. Throughout the 1600s, royal proclamations prohibiting the exportation of wool, among other things, meant an extensive smuggling network evolved to sidestep this law. 'Wool-running' was sometimes aided and abetted by those in higher society, so consequently, few convictions took place. The coast-men would habitually defy the law, openly carrying immense quantities of wool at shearing time on horses' backs to the sea shore where French vessels waited to pay for it. They also attacked fiercely anyone who ventured to interfere.

It was from Romney Marsh, Kent, that the greatest percentage of fleeces was smuggled out of the country. The contraband was put on board French shallops by night, and protected by armed Kentish men so threatening that the writer Andrew Marvell went so far as to call them a 'militia' in 1677. These men went by the name 'Owlers', either through their working at night, or because they imitated the hoot of an owl to warn their confederates.

Around this time, Canterbury and Dover were reputedly 'villainous dens infested with atrocious smugglers'. Their operations were often disguised by the fog and storms of the coast and although the work was dangerous, the seamen were bold and experienced. The French and Dutch bid high for English wool, while in reciprocation, the enormous duties imposed upon imported French and Dutch liquor and fine silks allowed for the illicit smuggling of vast quantities of this contraband into England.

Of course, the revenue suffered hugely and by 1662, the losses to the government were so great that the penalty for anyone caught smuggling wool had been made death. However, the law was ineffectually enforced, since many magistrates, attorneys, clerks and under-sheriffs were involved to a greater or lesser extent with the gangs, whose operations also extended into Sussex, Hampshire, Essex and other places.

The smugglers' fierce opposition to the law can be gleaned from an incident in 1688, when a Kentish gentleman named Mr W. Carter narrowly avoided assassination. For years Carter had declared the quantity of wool stolen out of England to be the nation's 'great misery', and in December – having procured the necessary warrants – he descended on Romney Marsh, where he seized eight or ten men engaged in smuggling. The Mayor of Romney, however, bailed those arrested and Carter and his men thought it wise to retreat to nearby Lydd.

There, they were attacked on the night of 12 December and forced to retreat further towards Rye the following day, pursued by fifty armed horsemen intent on assaulting them. Having missed the Guldeford ferry, Carter and his men only made it to Rye thanks to the providential assistance of some local boatmen in this waterlogged region. Had he been caught it is likely Carter would have been severely beaten, and probably murdered, for 'many of the exporters were desperate fellows, not caring what mischief they did'.

Quite naturally, this form of organised crime operated its network inland on an immense, industrial scale, although it was those on the coast who took the greatest risks and proved the most war-like. Luttrell recorded in 1699 that a Herculean attempt had been made to patrol the coastline:

> *'The owling trade is in a manner supprest by the diligence of the officers appointed for that purpose, who are posted all along the sea coasts of England and Wales.'*

But, as is well known, smuggling continued to develop almost Mafia-like throughout the following century and beyond.

'PRESSING' POOR SOULS
A major concern of the inhabitants of the great port cities – such as Bristol, Portsmouth and London – was the threat of being violently forced into the government's navy. Men were frequently 'pressed' by bodies of armed seamen known as 'press-gangs' into sea service, just as military agents 'pressed' other men into land service. This forced recruitment, with or without notice, naturally caused equally violent resistance among the common people.

As an example, Narcissus Luttrell wrote in his diary on 11 April 1695 that, two days before, an uprising against Mr Tooley, provost marshal to the army, had broken out among Londoners. This had caused them to march from the wrestling ring at Lincoln's Inn Fields to Holborn to 'sett at liberty 200 men that were pressed, to sell for recruits to Flanders'. Tooley's house was ransacked but soldiers soon arrived and opened fire, killing one among the mob and wounding others. On 10 April, the people assembled again, launching an attack on the house of another provost marshal in Drury Lane; however, they were prevented from rescuing their 'illegally detained' fellow subjects by the fact that the prisoners had been removed earlier. The mutiny began to spread and was only reined in by the threat of a general massacre by the guards. The fact that the revolt started when the Middlesex under-sheriff attempted to serve a writ of execution against Tooley on behalf of the people and was wounded by sentinels in a shooting melee, illustrates how confusingly volatile the matter was.

What is shocking is that two years earlier, in February 1693, the House of Lords had advised William and Mary 'to regulate for the future the disorderly pressing of men.' Though they replied that they would consider it, clearly nothing changed. In one incident, recorded by Luttrell on 27 October 1694, a Major MacKinsey stabbed to death a clerk during a town council meeting in Glasgow. MacKinsey, of the Lord Lindsey's regiment, was in the process of being interrogated about 'pressing of soldiers contrary to the usual method' and the clerk had rebuked him. After the stabbing the major attempted to escape on horseback, but was caught and taken into custody.

But by now citizens were also being criminally kidnapped for other reasons. The cruelty of ordinary English people is exemplified by the number of abductions of young people of both sexes who were violently carried onto ships. On board, they were held captive with intent to transport them to the plantations and sell them to the planters of the West Indies, or the American mainland. It is reckoned that only one in twenty managed to escape these transportation vessels, often thanks to the vigilance of their father or employer, or through having money enough to have 'brought their *habeas corpus*'. Society, however, was generally indifferent – as indicated by the relatively lenient punishments imposed upon the percentage of miscreants and kidnappers who appeared in the dock at the Old Bailey. Rather than death, 'man-stealers' suffered fines, imprisonment or the pillory, often escaping worse through their powerful and wealthy connections. Perhaps there was also tacit government agreement that the plantations required greater populations to thrive and survive.

THE MENACE OF 'PRIVATEERS'

By the second half of the 1600s, a new threat menaced Britain's coastline in the form of 'privateers'. The distinction between these and pirates was that a privateer was an armed ship of any nation owned by private individuals, who held a government commission allowing them to attack or harass 'enemy' vessels. In reality, they were a warlike hybrid of pirate and patriot.

COASTAL CRIMES

Quite naturally, privateers of numerous nations – including Britain – roamed the seas around all parts of Western Europe. Typically, it was recorded on 19 April 1667:

'Several privateers between Pembroke and the Land's End much hinder the coal trade, there being no [British] frigates on the coast.'

While foreign privateers were seen as a piratical menace to merchantmen, British privateers who acted likewise against European vessels were often promoted as seafaring heroes who brought home 'prizes'. The scale of the problem is nowadays difficult to appreciate, for the seas were full of foreign and domestic privateers and men-of-war, which contested each other in continual skirmishes, while British government vessels also chased the 'enemy' ships and engaged them. *State Papers* (13 June 1667) recorded:

'A report of three French privateers near Lundy island put a terror into all vessels that were there; much shooting has been heard for three or four days past.'

Naturally, some collisions were catastrophic. News out of Portsmouth on 10 May 1667 reported:

'The Dragon *has brought in a French privateer of 16 guns taken off the Isle of Wight, after a long engagement in which many of the French were killed and the vessel much shattered.'*

Nearly 30 years later nothing had changed. Luttrell recorded on 10 May 1694:

'This day the York *frigate brought in a French privateer of 26 guns (but can carry 40) and 150 men, which he took on Monday off the Land's End, after six hours fight, wherein 30 of the French were killed, and on our side the lieutenant and three men, with fourteen wounded.'*

Quite naturally, this perpetual cycle of seaborne warfare was one factor that drove government naval impressing.

Sometimes, non-domestic privateers came terrifyingly close to coastal communities. On 13 June 1667, correspondence out of Dartmouth reported how a French man-of-war had chased a collier into Dartmouth harbour and had to be repulsed by a bombardment from the castle – but not before it had captured two vessels and killed the master of a fishing boat. And sometimes

English and Dutch forces pound each other in battle off the Scillies in 1666.
(Courtesy Doddington Hall)

a privateer's crew might actually come ashore. One Dunkirk freebooter named Jean Bart – the terror of the Dutch and English merchants trading with the Baltic in the summer of 1691 – was so bold as to actually land in Northumberland. His men, under a lieutenant called Forbin, plundered and set Widdrington ablaze before the trained bands could be organised to repel them during a violent skirmish at Druridge.

Some incidents were merely confusing, however. As Luttrell noted on 24 June 1693, a French vessel mysteriously approaching the Isle of Wight was deemed to be a threat – until it was discovered that it was piloted by some asylum-seeking French Protestants who had murdered the commander of their vessel. The briefness of this report really does not do the phenomenon justice, it must be admitted. The above data forms just the tiniest tip of the mightiest iceberg; the true picture of coastal and seaborne lawlessness can perhaps only be appreciated when one learns that all this merely continued as normal, month in and month out, throughout most of the following century too, as well as the century we are exploring.

Chapter 9

Riots, Disorder and Insurrection

One interesting element of the famous Gunpowder Plot of 1605 that is often overlooked is that it was more than merely an attempt to blow up the House of Lords and assassinate King James I; it was primarily an attempt to fully overthrow the status quo, facilitated by a simultaneous armed uprising in the English Midlands and Wales. General support for the insurrection failed to materialise when news of the failure in London swept across the country, however, and the traitors' ranks were further depleted by desertions among their panicking retainers in the Midlands. What might have become a nationwide conflict was actually contained to several instances of plundering by Robert Catesby and his supporters and a short, deadly battle at Holbeche House.

Nonetheless, another conflict *was* generated as a by-product of the plot. Around May 1607, it was brought to the attention of the authorities that lawless assemblies of men, women and children were being observed in Northamptonshire, Warwickshire and Leicestershire. When news of this reached the court it greatly alarmed the king, who feared a Puritan or Catholic insurrection was gaining ground.

It turned out to be nothing of the sort, although much of the agitation was in fact a knock-on effect from the Catholic Gunpowder Plot. The forfeitures of the estates of some of the gentlemen who had been involved in that conspiracy threw their lands into the hands of new proprietors, who enclosed many tracts – including parts where the former owners had allowed the peasantry right of common.

The ordinary people, aided by the blundering statutes against enclosures, felt themselves justified by law in resisting these measures. At 'Hill Norton' (Hillmorton, Rugby) around 1,000 assembled; elsewhere, they were even more numerous. The mob cut and broke down hedges, filled up ditches and laid open all enclosed fields such as had formerly been free and common. They called themselves Levellers, declaring themselves bound to 'level and lay open the old commons without exercising any manner of theft or violence upon any man's person, goods or cattle'. Their headquarters is believed to have been at Cottesbrooke, Northamptonshire. Entire parishes were at their mercy, but there was a certain order in the disorder and violent acts were largely avoided. This was, of course, until the authorities got wind of this 'insurrection'.

Placed at the head of the rebels was 'a base fellow', John Reynolds, nicknamed 'Captain Pouch' on account of a large purse he wore at his side. Reynolds managed to convince large portions of the illiterate and superstitious peasantry that he was sent by God to lead them and that the king himself had granted him the authority to destroy the enclosures. He even persuaded the deluded rabble that he was invulnerable to bullets and swords, on account of a magic charm in his purse that would protect them all – provided they refrained from evil deeds, blasphemy and uttering profanities.

Proclamations to disperse were ignored on this basis, so the lords-lieutenant attempted to galvanise the yeomanry – groups of men who held and cultivated small landed estates, and commanded the local militia. These proved reluctant to engage the peasantry; furthermore, certain gentlemen – whose interests were not affected – began to indicate sympathies with 'Pouch' and his supporters, which naturally bolstered their belief that they were in the right. Further support appeared in Leicester, where a gibbet had been erected in the market-place to warn the townsfolk against participating in the disorder. This was torn down during the night, and the town mayor refused to allow it to be set up again.

The king sent the Earls of Huntingdon and Exeter, backed by a considerable force of regular troops, to the Midlands to force the yeomen into doing something positive about this 'peasant's revolt'. Thus pressured, Sir Anthony Mildmay and Sir Edward Montague on 8 June 1607 confronted the rebels at Newton, between Corby and Kettering, while they were busy digging and levelling. They found Reynolds and his supporters armed with half-piked staves, long bills, bows and arrows, and stones.

Mildmay and Montague read the king's proclamation aloud – twice – in an attempt to get the peasants to halt their vandalism and disperse. They were completely ignored, more so when it became apparent there was great reluctance among the local militias to engage their fellow countrymen. Therefore, it fell to the mounted troops and the yeomen's own servants to charge into the crowds.

At the first charge, Reynolds and his men fought defiantly, but they were utterly annihilated and when a second charge was launched the rebels scattered immediately. The violence inflicted was horrendous; some forty or

A memorial to the revolt, outside St Faith's Church.

fifty people were slaughtered as the Northamptonshire countryside became a killing ground, with great numbers critically injured. Among these was Sir Henry Fookes, who led the foot into battle and was so badly wounded in diverse parts of his body that he was 'more likely to die than live', according to a letter written by the Earl of Shrewsbury to Sir John Manners later that month.

The insurrection was utterly crushed and many prisoners were incarcerated in St Faith's Church, Newton. In the aftermath of the violence, a number of captured men were dragged before Sir Edward Coke and condemned to death as traitors for levying war against the king. Among these was 'Captain Pouch' himself, who was hanged, drawn and quartered. His body parts, along with those of a handful of others, were put up at Northampton, Oundle, Thrapston and other places.

Many more people were prosecuted for felony because they had not dispersed upon the reading of the proclamation. However, most survivors were granted a royal pardon, provided they presented themselves before Michaelmas to Sir Edward Montague and signed a submission document. Only around thirty were educated enough to actually *sign* their name, but the

173

pardon was extended to about eighty more who left some form of mark on the document.

Upon searching Captain Pouch's valuable purse, it was found to contain merely a piece of cheese.

As this episode illustrates, it seems quite clear that the common people of England were frequently prepared to go to war over any number of issues, large or small – merely adding another element of instability to life in a nation that, for much of the century, already had the threat of complete implosion hanging over it.

WARS WITHIN WARS

During the reign of Charles I there began a violent revolt in the Isle of Axholme, a large region sited approximately between Doncaster, Scunthorpe and Gainsborough in Lincolnshire. It had come to the monarch's attention that the great swathes of marshy fenland in this place might be put to better use agriculturally if they could be drained via an immense system of dykes and ditches cut across the wetlands. Prior to this, such land – much of it common land at that – had served largely to provide the inhabitants of this harsh environment with an easy means of netting, fishing, fowling, harvesting reeds and, where possible, pastoral farming. In 1627, a renowned Dutch drainage engineer, Cornelius Vermuyden, was commissioned to drain the Isle of Axholme and for his efforts was granted one third of the land to be drained; while the king himself – who was lord of the four principal manors there – enclosed another third for himself as his 'right of improvement' dictated. To finance the enterprise, Vermuyden invited European investors into the project, including fellow Dutchmen, while a small army of Dutch engineers, besides a number of Englishmen, were recruited for the manual labour the immense operations would require. Miles and miles of deep trenches were cut across the wet landscape, into which water was drawn from immense pools like those standing near Hatfield and Thorne.

These arrangements left the local inhabitants with just one third of what had formerly been common land; seeing a traditional way of life deliberately eroded before their very eyes, protests and riots erupted in many places. It also appears that during the draining of Hatfield Chase and other places, some inhabitants' homes were deluged with water that had been turned into channels unable to cope with the volume. Very quickly the people took the law into their own hands, breaking down the embankments, destroying sluices and assaulting the European workmen. Typically, on 21 August 1628 it was communicated to the Duke of Buckingham - who at the time had a vested interest in the project - that 'great riots have been committed by the people', resulting in a bloody skirmish somewhere near Tickhill Castle in which an Englishman was fatally wounded by a Dutchman. These disturbances involved not only the common people but also landowners. In 1629, for example, Robert Portington, a justice of the peace who came from an ancient Barnby Dun family, was indicted with others for beating, wounding and killing several workmen employed on the project. He was, however, merely bound over to keep the peace.

The first wave of disturbances subsided after a royal proclamation mingled with threats of violent repression was delivered to the mutinous local people by a sergeant-at-arms and fifty troops. Some accounts suggest Vermuyden also put up temporary gallows structures as a warning. In fact, the local rebels not only backed down, but were actively encouraged to participate in work on the dike which they had fifty times destroyed and thrown into the River Idle. This did not quell the trouble entirely, however. Following new outbreaks in 1636, a number of people were prosecuted by the Star Chamber. Epworth commoners William Torksey, Hezekiah Brown, John Moody, Henry Scot and other rioters were charged with having beaten the European workmen before throwing some into the River Torne where they were ducked with long poles. Heavy fines were imposed on the arrested rioters and they were ordered to pay 2,000 marks in damages to Cornelius Vermuyden. Some are said to have had their ears and right hands mutilated.

Nonetheless, during this period many Dutch families actually settled in the region, and worshipped in their own established churches. They were gradually joined by over 200 French and Belgian Protestant families escaping persecution at home. For several years, these new arrivals had cultivated their lands in peace, when suddenly their situation became extremely precarious through the troubles arising out of the English civil wars.

In 1642, a committee in Lincoln decided the best means of preserving Parliamentary interests in the Isle of Axholme was to break the dikes and pull up the flood-gates at 'Snow-sewer and Millerton-sluice' near Hatfield. This re-flooding of reclaimed land was intended to hinder the progress of Yorkshire Royalists under Sir Ralph Humby, who were intent on making military advances from that neighbouring county. The orders from Lincoln were enforced and assisted by local people the following Candlemas, who enthusiastically abused their position, using it as an excuse to take latent revenge upon the 'invaders' who, they still felt, had robbed them of their common land. Parts of the Isle of Axholme slowly began to sit under water again, as sluices were destroyed and dikes broken; worse, persecution against the European settlers began to become disproportionate. Their crops were destroyed, their houses ransacked and their churches vandalised. Around this time, the local people were encouraged in their backlash by the subsequent presence of the Parliamentarian Colonel Lilburne, who occupied Sandtoft and allowed his troops to stable their horses within the settlers' chapel. The local people came to an agreement with the colonel, granting him 2,000 acres of Epworth Common on condition that they kept the rest. Because of this arrangement, the colonel abstained from prosecuting them too harshly for their abuses against the European settlers – who by now were struggling to survive.

These appealed to the House of Commons, but during this period the Isle of Axholme entered a state that can realistically be described as near communal warfare. On one occasion, a sheriff acting on behalf of the European settlers, commanding 100 men, battled an army of 400 locals led by Daniel Noddle (or Noddel), a local solicitor to the common people of Epworth. Noddle was certainly of the firebrand revolutionary mould, telling the local people at one point he would draw up his demands (to settle the matter legally in their favour) and nail them to the door of Parliament; but if no-one should acknowledge them, he would see to it that those inside were dragged out by their ears.

For years, the Dutch attempted to pursue the matter legally through the courts, but in this they found themselves simultaneously fighting a governmental system that was in itself continually handicapped by the excesses of the civil wars. It took a new Parliament in 1653 to begin addressing the matter with any degree of efficiency. Noddle, the lawyer, is said to have died of a sudden illness around this time – his disappearance from the theatre of war curiously coinciding with the employment of a dynamic barrister called Nathaniel Reading, who acted on behalf of the dispossessed European settlers. Also, by this time the powerful Colonel Lilburne had been forced into exile thanks to various squabbles, both political and personal; after this the situation began to clarify itself.

Cromwell's Parliament, finally seeing the agricultural worth of the land, decided to end the conflict once and for all by adjudicating in the European settlers' favour. Nathaniel Reading was employed on behalf of the Court of Sewers and ordered to seize the local people's cattle in lieu of rates and tolls imposed upon them which they were refusing to pay. During one violent incident late in 1655, a Hatfield parish constable named Haddon, who accompanied Reading, was almost killed by an armed crowd of people. Following this an order was finalised in Whitehall on 21 August 1656

Almighty drains, like this one here near Sandtoft, helped the region develop its striking 'flatness'.

authorising Edward Whalley, Lincoln's administrative major-general – who answered directly to Cromwell – to disarm the rioters by force. It also allowed for the restoration of the European settler's rights and freedom to exercise their religion peaceably.

Nathaniel Reading was placed in charge of the repression. He obtained writs of assistance and deputations from the sheriffs of the three counties affected by the disturbances, Lincolnshire, Nottinghamshire and southern Yorkshire. He hired men, provided arms and horses; he even enlisted a surgeon. Then, after thirty-one set battles, during which several of his men were killed, Reading subdued the mutinous local people to obedience. He subsequently repaired the church at Sandtoft, settled another minister, restored the congregation, and made the Levels quite safe and flourishing.

Reading's quelling of the insurrection in the Isle of Axholme was not without consequence. He was tried in the Court of King's Bench, Westminster Hall, for killing one of the rioters, later enduring violence and persecution for vigorously attempting to prosecute others. Remarkably, Mr Reading continued to live in the region, despite more land disputes flaring into violent disturbances throughout the remainder of the century. During an outbreak of disorder in the early 1690s, after Mr Reading had accepted a lease of land in Epworth parish, rioters assaulted him and his sons and servants regularly, shot at him desperately, and killed and destroyed his cattle. His dwellings were repeatedly attacked, including an incident on 15 April 1697 when his house near Sandtoft, in Belton Plains was set ablaze. The disguised arsonists had stopped up the key-holes with clay, preventing an easy escape by the occupants and it was only by forcing an exit that Reading and his household escaped being burnt to death. Several of the attacks were actually led by a local landowner's wife, Mrs Popplewell, whose husband eventually interceded and agreed to part-pay £600 in damages to Reading – probably in an effort to save his wife from being gaoled, or worse.

Despite the perpetual threat against him, however, Nathaniel Reading died in 1716, aged nearly 100, and was buried at Belton in what is now North Lincolnshire.

Violent disturbances among local people over the issue of draining 'their' land for agriculture also occurred around the same time in Cambridgeshire, Norfolk, southern Lincolnshire and other parts. In one atrocious episode, farmers and labourers who had settled in the West and Wildmore Fen district between Tattershall and Boston were attacked by a great mob of fenland rebels collected together from the surrounding districts. Under the pretence of gathering for a game of football, they ran riot, levelling the enclosures, burning the cornfields, setting the houses on fire, slaughtering livestock and murdering many of the settlers. The crowds then proceeded to destroy the drainage works by cutting across the embankments and damming up the drains, inundating the countryside and restoring it to its original waterlogged state. The engineering historian Samuel Smiles suggests this occurred about the year 1640.

The Isle of Axholme was in a state of chaos for thirty years, the disorder aggravated and encouraged first by the excesses of war and then by a paralysed system of government after the fact. It may be argued that it was almost a war within a war. It is only thanks to the heroic level of perseverance attributable to Vermuyden, and engineers like him, that these drainage projects were ultimately seen through to completion, allowing the landscape in parts of Lincolnshire and Cambridgeshire to ever after present the unique flatness it does today.

THE BATTLE OF THE EMBASSIES

Towards the end of September 1661, a quarrel arose between the Spanish Ambassador to England, Baron de Batteville, and his French counterpart, Godefroi d'Estrades, Marshal of France. Both resided in the capital and both, it seems, were keen to fight for precedence upon the arrival of the Swedish Ambassador in London on 30 September. Impressing, chaperoning and, indeed, intimidating, newly-arrived European dignitaries was, it appears, a frequent cause of quarrel between the various foreign embassies located in

London; Charles II – considering this particular matter a private quarrel between the Spanish and the French – forbade any Englishman to get involved.

In allowing the situation to run its course, perhaps Charles did not foresee what might happen, although it was later speculated that it was in his own political interests for the two European powers to quarrel upon British soil.

Samuel Pepys, rising early on 30 September, understood that some form of violence was likely from the hundreds of armed English soldiers and Londoners who bustled about certain parts of the city in a state of great anticipation. However, wherever he travelled, Pepys remained unmolested and he quickly realised the simmering antagonism was between the attendants of the two European ambassadors. Of course, prior knowledge of what was coming had excited the London population greatly, as though it were a sporting event of some kind.

Following his morning's business in Chelsea, Pepys was returning home via Whitehall when he observed 'great preparations' among employees of both the Spanish and French embassies as they assembled their rival entourages. The Swedish contingent does not yet appear to have set foot in London.

What followed thereafter was nothing short of a battle, although Pepys did not see it personally. The posturing and antagonism that had been simmering all morning finally exploded in a bloody collision around mid-day, between hundreds of armed attendants from both the Spanish and the French sides. Although the French 'ranted most' and greatly outnumbered the Spanish, the latter were better prepared; they had lined their horses' harnesses with chains of iron so they could not be cut, while simultaneously employing soldiers to guard their entire entourage, coaches and all. The French were not so vigilant and the Spanish exploited it, launching a ferocious assault upon the poorly-defended French retinue. They cruelly slaughtered three of their rivals' coach-horses and massacred several Frenchmen, while they in turn managed to kill one or two among their attackers. An Englishman who had become caught up in the violence was fatally wounded by a bullet. The Spanish victory was all the more remarkable in that they were armed mainly with swords, while the French had dozens of pistols.

When word of this bloody victory swept London, the people rejoiced, for as Pepys put it, 'We do naturally all love the Spanish, and hate the French.' He was in Cheapside when he heard the news, so swiftly 'took oares' along the Thames to Westminster Palace. Here he found the streets full of people, and followed the Spanish victory procession first to 'the Mewes' (near Charing Cross) and then to York House in the Strand. There, it ceremonially collected the Spanish Ambassador and went on its way, to the cheers of the English soldiery, who had followed the contest eagerly throughout the day. What the Swedish Ambassador thought of this titanic riot brought about by his arrival does not seem to have been recorded.

The affronted French subsequently blamed the English for aiding the Spanish victory, and d'Estrades – whose own son had been wounded in the battle – sent a messenger to the King of France to air his grievances. The diplomatic fallout of the affair need not side-track us too much, since the English continued to deny it was any of their business; suffice to say that an outraged King Louis XIV eventually managed to redress the affront through the threat of war with Spain, which had the effect of subjugating them somewhat. Louis also attempted to get any Londoners who had 'insulted his ambassador' punished, as well as arguing for the dismissal of Baron de Batteville. But the British king simply refused to pay it any heed; it appears no-one was imprisoned for this strange episode in diplomatic posturing.

THE 'FIFTH MONARCHISTS'

In 1661, there occurred an insurrection of a remarkable nature in London. Five years after the event it was chronicled as follows in *The Faithful Annalist:*

> *'January 6. Certain chiliasts, or Fifth Monarchy men, having as their leader one Venner, a wine-cooper, rose in arms; and with a desperate intention fought to destroy all those that were not of their opinion, shooting a man in Paul's church-yard and killing a headborough [parish officer]in Beech Lane; and having done other mischief, marched into Cane Wood [Kenwood]. After three days' time they returned again, and with such a desperate boldness set upon the city, as is hardly to be credited: that a handful of wild-brained people should dare to undertake such an attempt against the metropolis of the kingdom, which a well-governed potent army would not without good advice be driven to! After a most desperate assault and resistance, having killed 22 of the king's men, and 22 of them being killed, the rest – with much ado – were taken and dispersed.'*
>
> *'On the nineteenth of the same month, four of them being arraigned and condemned, were hanged, viz. Thomas Venner, their leader, and Roger Hodgkins, a button-seller in St Clement's Lane, who were executed over against their meeting-house, in Swan Alley in Coleman Street. Next, one Giles Pritchard, a cow-keeper, and another of them*

in Cheapside; and on the Monday following, being 21 January, nine more of them were executed at five several places, viz. two of them at the west end of St Paul's, two at the Bull and Mouth in St Martin's, two at Beech-lane, two at the Royal Exchange, and one – a notable fellow named Leonard Gowler – at Bishopsgate.'

Venner's actions are believed to have been driven by a kind of religious fanaticism, which apparently developed some twenty years earlier while he had been in New England (then colonial America). Having returned to London, Coleman Street became Venner's base for a conventicle – that is, an unlawful religious gathering – where he and others would preach from the Prophecies of Daniel and the Revelations. From these texts, Venner drew mystical revelations which persuaded him – and subsequently his followers – that the way forward was to take up arms in the name of 'King Jesus' and set up a 'fifth monarchy' (or reign of Jesus Christ on earth) in London. This belief was sometimes called 'chiliasm'.

Thomas Venner, ready for war. (after engraving by an unnamed artist published by Caulfield, 1794)

Venner must have been exceptionally persuasive, since he not only argued that Charles II, the Duke of York and General Monck were all illegally in government, but also declared that any weapons used against his followers would not injure them. Following the growth of their society, the Fifth Monarchists printed and distributed a declaration entitled *The Door of Hope Opened*, which outlined their vow not to sheath their swords until the monarchy (or 'Babylon') in London had been obliterated. After this, they predicted their fury would in turn spread to France, Spain and Germany, as the Fifth Monarchist revolution swept across Europe.

The number of those involved in this now largely forgotten London insurrection does not appear to have exceeded 100; and perhaps fifty or so participated in the violence on 9 January. Nonetheless, for a short time, certain places became battlefields where deadly skirmishes were fought with the capital's trained bands: Threadneedle Street, Bishopsgate Street and Wood Street – where Venner was knocked down and badly wounded – all saw action. The last of the rebels holed up in the Blue Anchor alehouse ('near the Postern'), which was besieged by Lieutenant Colonel Cox before being stormed with a great deal of violence. While some Fifth Monarchists were taken prisoner, others appear to have been summarily executed for refusing to tell their names.

Pepys implies that only a year or so earlier, the Fifth Monarchists had tentatively supported the Parliamentarian General Lambert, before he was gaoled in the Tower by General Monck prior to the Restoration of the Monarchy. Rumours of Lambert's brief escape energised them greatly and after his recapture their philosophy became more militant. One contemporary observer, Archdeacon Echard, noted:

> *'Thus ended a rebellion of a very strange nature, which was begun and carried out with such infernal rage, that if their numbers had been equal to their spirits, they would have overturned the city and the nation.'*

AN UNSTABLE NATION?

It is readily apparent that where the situation dictated it, civil disorder might be quelled with a great deal of violence. As far back as August 1643, for instance, a remarkable anti-war demonstration had been held in Westminster, during which a great many women – allegedly several thousand – blockaded the House of Commons. Wearing white silk ribbons on their bonnets, they had shouted 'Peace, peace!' and harassed Puritan politicians. Locally-raised trained bands were unsure how to deal with this mob of women, even though it apparently included some men in women's apparel; they only opened fire when brickbats were lobbed at them. Their shooting killed a one-armed ballad-singer and a completely innocent man during this confrontation. In the end, ten of Sir William Waller's mounted soldiers charged into the crowds, later followed by a troop of horse, meting out such violence with swords and cudgels that a great many of the women demonstrators were seriously injured. One woman had her nose struck off and two or three were fatally wounded.

By the second half of the seventeenth century, violent disorder among the common people was a regular occurrence. Attacks on 'Bawdy-Houses', or brothels, were hardly unknown in the capital; at least one bore the appearance of an anti-monarchy protest. On 23 March 1668, a great mob assembled in Moorfields and proceeded to ransack red-light districts, pulling down a number of brothels, looting the buildings and breaking open Clerkenwell Gaol. The crowds also violently confronted a contingent of troopers, shouting that if the king would not allow them 'liberty of conscience, [then] May-day must be a bloody day.' These details – combined with the trial accounts of a number of arrested rioters – make it clear the violence was some form of protest aimed at the licentiousness of the court. The trouble was drawn out over several days.

In some cases, violent rioting was tacitly allowed to run its course and burn itself out, although the 'Bawdy-House riots' of Easter 1668 were clearly seen in a more threatening light – four men named Messenger, Beasley, Cotton and Limerick were convicted of armed insurrection against the king and executed for treason.

Some riots were simply the result of the drunken, rakish times, however, occurring for no other reason than the sport of it. One typical incident took place on Sunday, 24 July 1687, when a great mob of loutish young hooligans took on the trained bands in Red Lion Fields. Quite who they were is unclear, as is their grievance – it appears to have had something to do with the imprisonment in Newgate of a cow-keeper. They regularly stoned the militia, who lost patience with them and opened fire on the night in question; the offensive was a disaster, for they killed one person, a completely innocent woman walking near the fray. Six or seven of the troublemakers were, however, seized upon and thrown into Newgate.

At the other end of the kingdom, another pitched battle occurred when James Bruce of Kennet, together with his drunken friends, fought Edinburgh's Town-guard on 4 May 1690 and killed three of them. The murdered men's names were Henry Linkletter, Alexander Simpson and Colin

Campbell. A contemporary judge, Lord Fountainhall, recorded how Bruce somehow earned a remission for these murders on 2 May 1691.

Food riots were a continual feature of disorder throughout the century, which speaks more to desperation than anarchy; nonetheless, such uprisings met with little sympathy, and market squares could become something akin to battlegrounds. Luttrell, for example, recorded in May 1693 that an uprising occurred in Worcester over the price of corn, cheese and butter. This became so serious that the mayor was forced to call the militia in.

However, this was not unduly unusual, and the overall picture of instability can be gleaned from the endless examples of lethal flare-ups throughout the kingdom. These today paint a combined picture of a barely-controlled nation ever ready to fight itself over any issue.

In 1673, eight men were killed at the foot of the stairs of Chester's common-hall during a volatile local election, for example. Throughout 1675 and 1676, reactionary Middlesex weavers broke into houses and destroyed engine weaving looms. In July 1691, a pro-James II mob led by Captain Francis Winter battled the sheriffs of London in Whitefriars, leaving three dead – Winter was hanged for murder in Fleet Street on 17 May 1693, according to Luttrell, who is also the source for the following incidents. In March 1693, about eight people were killed in a fight for control of Edinburgh's 'citty guard house' over the matter of forcibly 'pressing' land dwellers into sea service. A 'great scuffle' between townsfolk and soldiers in Shaftesbury, Dorset, left six dead in April 1693. A pitched battle in Newport on the Isle of Wight on 5 June 1693 between townsmen and soldiers claimed three lives, including Captain Juxton, who was killed by a stray bullet while going on board the *Neptune*. A mutiny among Colonel Cunningham's regiment as it marched from Scotland to England left several dead in March 1694.

In November 1695, a violent rebellion was reported from the Isle of Skye, off the western coast of Scotland. Thirty soldiers from Colonel Hill's regiment were sent from Fort William to assist the king's collectors in gathering taxes. However, 'The inhabitants fell upon them, and kill'd several of them.'

And so it went on. The threat of tumult was almost a way of life, and it would be possible to list a great many more examples of violent disorder throughout the seventeenth century. On this basis, it could be speculated that the precariousness and vulnerability of everyday life was so severe it prompted many among the common people to risk fighting their fellow countrymen – if to do so meant even the barest improvement in their circumstances.

Chapter 10

Clan Warfare

When King James VI of Scotland also inherited the English throne in 1603, he not long afterwards made his way south to London, where he established his court. He relied on a Privy Council in Edinburgh to enforce his rule during his absence, allegedly declaring in 1607:

> *'This I must say for Scotland, here I sit and govern it with my pen; I write, and it is done, and by a clerk of the council I govern Scotland now, which others could not do by the sword.'*

This was a rather broad statement, because in truth much of Scotland at this time was ungovernable from Edinburgh, with many regions in fact controlled by clan chieftains, who themselves often governed complicated hierarchies of immediate kinsmen, subordinate families, tenants and other dependants. These clans were frequently involved in violent disputes with each other, at all levels and feuding that bordered on warfare was often the natural recourse.

Three examples illustrate the differing forms of murder that ensued from the seemingly endless clan conflicts across Scotland.

Sir John Carmichael was, in the late 1500s, granted the important position of Warden of the West Marches of Scotland. This position was given to him by the Scottish regent, Morton, who hoped to use Carmichael to strengthen his own authority along the Borders. However, this occurred at the expense of the Border chieftains, who had been established in that part of the country for generations.

On 16 June 1600, Sir John was ambushed at a place called Raes Knowes, between Lockerbie and Langholm, and assassinated by a party of Borderers. He was on his way to hold a court of justice when he was attacked by around seventeen men said to have been returning from a football match, who staged an ambush and shot him in the body. Sir John was reputedly wounded a number of times by the men, who were armed with pistols and hagbuts – the latter a type of firearm with a long barrel.

It was reasonably clear from the start that a party of the Armstrong Clan, of Rowanburn, had been behind the murder. These had suspected Sir John of making preparations to round them up, and had even gone so far as to send a member of the family, Alexander Armstrong (alias Sandy's Ringan), into his camp to try and negotiate, or otherwise see what could be found out. But the triggering factor seems to have been something trivial; some foolish young men in Sir John's retinue filled Alexander Armstrong's sword scabbard with egg-yolk, making it messy and embarrassing when he unsheathed it. This insult he carried back to the rest of the clan.

A list of those believed to have been present at the killing was drawn up. At the insistence of the victim's brother, two of the ringleaders in the murder, Thomas Armstrong (known as Ringan's Tam, and son of Alexander Armstrong) and Adam Scott (called 'the pecket'), were tracked down, apprehended and tried at Edinburgh. They were condemned to have their right hands chopped off before they were hanged on 14 November 1601; their bodies were afterwards gibbeted on Burrowmure near the castle of Merchiston – possibly the first time such a post-mortem punishment like this was practised in Scotland. 'Pecket' was said to have been one of the most notorious 'thieffes' in the region.

In February 1606, another Armstrong – 'Sandy of Rowanburn' – was executed along with several others of that clan for involvement in Sir John's murder and other violent excesses. Rowanburn confessed his guilt in the murder, but claimed he was brought to it against his will, and following his conviction he too was sentenced to be hung in chains after his execution. Those sentenced to death alongside him would seem to have been his sons; the group as a whole were also convicted of border-raiding crimes.

In this case, a clan's answer to a perceived enemy was simply to assassinate him, irrespective of the victim's status and the wrath it might bring down upon them. But on other occasions they went to war. In February 1603, a body of the clan under Allaster MacGregor of Glen Strae penetrated southwards to Glen Fruin, a broad valley descending towards Loch Lomond which separated it from the Gare Loch. This march precipitated a disastrous skirmish of near-legendary proportions with the Colquhouns, who were headed by the Laird of Luss, which is sometimes called 'the Raid of Glen Fruin'. It may have been that the meeting of the two clans was pre-arranged, under the guise of a peace conference at which hundreds were present; in fact, the MacGregors appear to have launched an ambush, massacring their way through the Colquhouns and pursuing the Laird of Luss to the very gates of Rossdhu, the ancient seat of the Colquhouns on the western edge of Loch

Lomond. The MacGregors next set about plundering the entire area, helping themselves to livestock and burning the houses and barn-yards of Luss's tenants to ground level.

During this episode, the followers of MacGregor massacred around 140 people, including a party of students, whose curiosity led them from their studies at Dumbarton's Collegiate School to the scene of the confrontation at Glen Fruin. The students were brutally murdered after taking refuge in a barn, but by whom is an open question; the Clan Gregor apparently blamed the atrocity on a renegade member of their tribe called Dugald Ciar Mhor, otherwise known as 'the Dun Coloured'.

An Act of the Privy Council dated 3 April 1603 made it a punishable offence to bear the name MacGregor. Those providing said clansmen with food or shelter were also liable to receive severe punishment. To this end, those culpable were hunted like wild beasts, their houses were destroyed and every conceivable place of refuge they might possibly have escaped to was raided and ransacked. Since it was the Earl of Argyll who was hierarchically responsible to the Council for the MacGregors' conduct, the execution of these severe measures was entrusted to him and his men to carry out. On 28 April 1603, three MacGregor followers were hanged in the Burrowmure area of Edinburgh, while on 20 May three more participants were sentenced to be hanged on the Castle Hill – the first in a series of trials, convictions and executions.

Allaster MacGregor himself was arrested by the Earl of Argyll at Berwick-upon-Tweed, Northumberland, the clan chief having been tricked into believing the earl would help him pass safely out of Scotland. On 20 January 1604, Allaster MacGregor, along with several of his party, was brought to trial in Edinburgh. In particular, they were accused of being part of an army numbering hundreds, and murdering eleven people specifically as well as others not named while armed with swords, axes, pistols and other weapons. After their conviction, MacGregor and four others were taken to the 'mercat-croce of Edinburgh' (market cross) and ceremonially hanged; apparently, the post from which Allaster MacGregor himself was launched to his death was higher than the others by a length of some six feet. The sentence also dictated that all their worldly goods be appropriated by the state; rather more grimly, it further decreed that after death the felons' heads, legs, arms and torsos be separated from their corpses and 'put upon public places.'

A third case illustrates that these feuds sometimes passed between generations. The crime for which John Maxwell, the 30-year-old 9th Lord

Maxwell, suffered had its origins in a protracted feud with the Johnstones of Annandale, Dumfries and Galloway. As a consequence of engaging in continued disturbances, Maxwell, of Caerlaverock Castle, was imprisoned in Edinburgh Castle, from where he managed to escape after wounding the porter in 1607. He immediately sought an interview with Sir James Johnstone, at a location 'beyond the house of Beal', pretending he desired only to accommodate their differences. This was facilitated by Sir James's brother-in-law, a Maxwell; thus, Lord Maxwell and Johnstone met on 6 April 1608 'at a place called Achmanhill.' Each was accompanied by a single attendant.

Their negotiations quickly went downhill. The attendants began fighting and Sir James Johnstone turned his horse in an attempt to intercede and end the distraction, at which instant Lord Maxwell took the opportunity to shoot his enemy through the back with a brace of bullets, which may have been dipped in poison.

Lord Maxwell made an immediate escape to France. After cautiously returning to Scotland some years later, he attempted to alleviate his crimes by proposing a marriage between the houses of Maxwell and Johnstone. This ploy of alliance was unsuccessful and the murderous nobleman was eventually apprehended while lurking in the wilds of Caithness.

He was brought to Edinburgh to stand trial. Apart from being convicted of Johnstone's murder, Maxwell was also found guilty of fire-raising and killing several Johnstones during a raid at 'Dalfeble in Nithsdale' in 1602. According to ancient Scottish law, such a crime, if perpetrated by a landed gentleman, constituted a form of treason and warranted forfeiture of the felon's estate. King James I was by this time losing patience with Scottish lords like Maxwell, who had given him nothing but trouble since his childhood; he therefore determined to make an example of him. Lord Maxwell was executed in Edinburgh by being beheaded on 21 May 1613.

The clan vendetta had, in fact, claimed the life of Maxwell's father, while Johnstone's father had succumbed to the effects of the conflict too; it was also considerably aggravated by each clan swinging in and out of favour with the royal court.

As a point of interest, living in a city was no guarantee this sort of thing wouldn't erupt. On 17 June 1605, groups of men under the young Lairds of Ogle and Pittarrow fought for two hours between nine and eleven at night. The clash happened near Edinburgh's salt tron (weighing-beam), along what is now the Royal Mile. Many were wounded and one of Pittarrow's men called Guthrie was killed. An attempt was made to prosecute the lairds the following day, and although they were committed to prison it is unclear what long term punishment – if any - they suffered.

There is, in fact, anything but a favourable impression of law and order among the various Scottish clans during the first half of the century, particularly in certain Highland and Border districts. Loyalties chopped and changed, allegiances were formed and broken, clans were outlawed only to be reintegrated and feuds frequently resurrected themselves. The northernmost parts of Scotland appear to have been all but continually trapped in a perpetual cycle of broken allegiances, vendettas, treachery, massacre, pitched battles, assassination and tit-for-tat plundering.

THE ELIMINATION OF A WITNESS

In Ayrshire, John Muir, the Laird of Auchendrane, entertained a historic bitterness against a tutor called Sir Thomas Kennedy of Culzean, despite their differences having been publicly reconciled. Broadly speaking, the feud had developed in the late 1590s over Auchendrane's desire to raise the influence and extend the power of his own family at the expense of the House of Cassilis, whom Culzean had supported and encouraged. This local power struggle had led Auchendrane to attempt the assassination of Culzean in Maybole, although the threat of punishment apparently saw to it that Auchendrane and Culzean afterwards became friends.

In fact, it was all a deception on Auchendrane's part. In 1602, the laird received a letter from Culzean, alerting him to the fact that he would be travelling to Edinburgh on business. Knowing Culzean would be commencing his journey in Ayr ('at the Duppills'), Auchendrane ordered Walter Muir, Thomas Kennedy of Drummurchy, Kennedy of Bargeny and others to that place to ambush his latent enemy.

There, the group assassinated Culzean with pistols and swords on 11 May, before robbing him to the tune of £2,000. The laird's followers were subsequently outlawed, and although he himself was suspected of being the instigator of the killing it could not be proven.

Thomas Kennedy of Drummurchy, one of the murderers, was eventually punished for another violent episode. As part of the wider feud, on 18 May 1603 he led fifty armed men in an attack on the retinue of Jean, Countess of Cassilis. The countess and her attendants found refuge in the house of Duncan Crawford, of Auchingaul, in Carrick; however, her attackers set the place ablaze and when the besieged party escaped from the flames, one of them was murdered. Seven among their number were kidnapped, only being released when they agreed to pay large sums of money and forsake their chief, the Earl of Cassilis. For this violence, Kennedy of Drummurchy was summoned to appear before Parliament in April 1604. According to the Scottish historian George Chalmers, writing in 1824:

> *'This criminal person fled from Scotland; but, the process being continued, his estate, and life, were forfeited, on the 11th July, 1604.'*

For the Laird of Auchendrane, a dangerous witness remained in the form of the boy who had delivered Culzean's letter to him, William Dalrymple. Shortly before the murder, Dalrymple had been ordered by the laird to take the letter back to Culzean, with the false intelligence that the laird could not be found. The assassins probably followed the boy surreptitiously. Therefore, the fact that Culzean had been killed almost immediately afterwards and he had unwittingly become a party to the conspiracy, must have left a very strong impression on young Dalrymple.

Fearful that the youth would betray him, Auchendrane first took him under his wing at his home south of Ayr, before sending him on some pretext to Arran; next – as the boy grew older – he packed him off to the wars in Flanders, hoping he would never see him again. By 1607, however, Dalrymple was back in Scotland after several years' absence and living at Chapeldonan, nineteen miles south of Ayr.

Auchendrane immediately lost patience upon the lad's return, and so he deceitfully managed to convey him to the beach at Girvan around ten o'clock one evening in September. There, he murdered him with the assistance of his eldest son James and one of his tenants, James Bannatyne of Chapeldonan. It appears the son strangled the lad, before the group waded as far into the sea as they dared with the corpse and set it adrift.

When the body was found on the sands shortly afterwards, it was buried in Girvan churchyard under the assumption that it was that of a mariner who had met with tragedy at sea. However, a former employer of the murdered young man, John Kennedy, the Laird of Culzean, suffered a disturbing dream in which he imagined it might be the missing Dalrymple, who was identifiable by a particular mark on his body. In the end the corpse was disinterred and proved to have such an identifying mark. Following this discovery, the Laird of Culzean instructed all who lived nearby to come and touch the corpse 'as is usual in such cases'.

All came with the exception of Auchendrane and his son, although 'a young child of his' named Mary Muir came to see what all the fuss was about. When she came near the body, 'it sprang out bleeding' – and upon this perceived miracle Auchendrane and his son became strongly suspected of the murder.

In truth, it is probably the case that Auchendrane was already suspected. Around this time, he had been advised to escape by sympathetic kinsmen who knew what he had done, out of concern that such a common murder, if traced to him, would see him executed. Therefore, they suggested he commit a 'minor' crime – something not connected to Dalrymple's death – that would give him a reason to leave. To this end, Auchendrane settled upon the assassination of Hugh Kennedy – a participant in the earlier feud, and apparently a more 'legitimate' victim than Dalrymple. However, Auchendrane's assault upon Kennedy was a failure; his son was so badly wounded he almost lost his hand during this deception.

This disastrous ploy encouraged the warrant that was issued for Auchendrane's arrest. Following their apprehension, the son, and possibly the father too, were tortured to encourage them to confess. By now, Auchendrane had also further implicated himself by sending into hiding certain people who knew he had murdered Dalrymple, such as a servant called Cunningham; Lady Auchendrane herself; and Bannatyne, the man who had helped him kill the lad on the beach.

Bannatyne had been persuaded to go to Ireland, where he became convinced the Laird of Auchendrane was to have him murdered. To this end Bannatyne wrote to the authorities concerning what he knew of the matter and was eventually extradited from Ireland to Scotland for interrogation. The mysterious favours shown by the laird towards Bannatyne – he had given him a life-rent take of Chapeldonan, for example – convinced the authorities he was heavily involved.

After much time spent languishing in gaol, Auchendrane, his son James and Bannatyne were all tried at the Justiciary Court in July 1611 for their involvement in the murders of Sir Thomas Kennedy and the lad Dalrymple. All three were sentenced to death. They were beheaded at the 'mercat croce' in Edinburgh, and their estates were forfeited to the crown.

But there is, in fact, more to this story. Far from being a ruthless maniac, John Muir of Auchendrane was evidently a respected elderly gentleman and baillie (magistrate) for Carrick; when he was executed his predicament elicited a lot of sympathy. Many believed he had unfairly become a victim to the complicated system of allegiances that developed thanks to the endless feuding he had been embroiled in. Despite his own conspiracies and the violent skirmishing in which he occasionally indulged, he was not necessarily a man out of his time.

According to a widely-held belief, if a murder victim was touched by the killer then providence would allow the corpse to gush forth blood and reveal the culprit. The most famous example of this phenomenon concerns the strange death of Sir James Stansfield (or Standsfield), a former Cromwellian ally who had nonetheless received a knighthood under the Restoration after establishing a wool manufactory. When his body was discovered floating in a pond not far from his manor house, New Milns, near Haddington, East Lothian, in November 1687, evidence of this nature helped to condemn the knight's eldest son, Philip. Surgeons declared there was clear evidence the old man had been brutally throttled and when the corpse was being placed back into the coffin a remarkable thing happened.

Tradition dictated that the deceased's nearest relatives lifted the cadaver, after it had been clothed in clean linen, and when Philip placed his hands on the body 'it darted out blood through the linen, from the left side of the neck'. Philip let the body fall and ran from it, crying, 'Lord have mercy upon me!' By the time Philip went on trial in Edinburgh on 6 February 1688 accused of murder, material witnesses of a questionable nature had been procured against him. Others were also implicated in the crime by now, the suggestion being that Philip – reputedly a depraved young man – had plotted the assassination of his father in order to avoid disinheritance. From the conspirators' allegedly overheard discussions, it appeared Philip had guarded his father's bedchamber door at New Milns armed with a pistol while a tailor named Tomson strangled the old man. They had then deposited the victim's body in the pond, leaving the bank nearest to it 'beaten to mash with feet' although it was a frosty morning.

On 24 February 1688, Stansfield was executed at 'the cross of Edinburgh', where, according to Lord Fountainhall, some technical difficulty in the procedure resulted in the prisoner being manually strangled. His tongue was also pulled out, for cursing his father and his right hand was lopped off for parricide. Philip's head was also cut off and stuck up at the East Port of Haddington, while his headless carcass was hung in chains between Leith and Edinburgh. Several days later, some hooligans took it down and flung it in a ditch. It is unknown whether his alleged co-conspirators met the same fate; furthermore, it should be observed that the correctness of the verdict has been repeatedly called into question through the ages.

'WILL YE NOT SINK WITH SIN?' THE FRENDRAUGHT FIRE
A disastrous incident late in 1630 had its origins in another Scottish blood feud, between James Crichton, Laird of Frendraught in Aberdeenshire, and Gordon of Rothiemay, a near-neighbour of his.

Vendettas and disturbances between the two families culminated in Rothiemay's death following a violent skirmish near the River Deveron on 1 January that year. Several more were badly wounded on both sides, including one who died ten days later.

John Meldrum, of Reidhill, had assisted Frendraught in his quarrel. He received a wound during the trouble and although Frendraught granted him compensation for his injury, Meldrum thought it insufficient, so stole two horses from the park of Frendraught one night. A sub-feud thus having developed, Frendraught prosecuted Meldrum for livestock theft and the latter was forced to seek refuge with John Leslie of Pitcaple, whose sister he had married.

On 27 September 1630, Frendraught went with a group of followers to arrest Meldrum at Pitcaple for the horse theft. One of the Leslies, James, opened conciliatory negotiations with Frendraught, which at first appeared to be going well: Frendraught was prepared to be reasonable, because, after all, the Leslies had supported his previous feud with Rothiemay. However, one of the laird's party, Robert Crichton of Couland, grew incensed and, when punches were thrown, he produced a pistol and shot James Leslie through the arm, nearly killing him there and then.

Subsequently, and completely predictably, the Leslies began to raise an armed force against Frendraught, who they held responsible for the rash actions of his kinsman during the summit. Frendraught desired to limit the trouble, however, and so on 5 October he procured the assistance of George Gordon, Marquess of Huntly, to act as mediator.

Thus, the Laird of Frendraught met the Laird of Pitcaple at Huntly's castle, called the Bog-of-Gight. The reconciliation failed, since Pitcaple was simply too angry; after all, his wounded son James still hovered between life and death after being shot.

The Marquess of Huntly thereafter detained Frendraught and his followers at the Bog-of-Gight, largely for their own safety, before – two days later – sending them home accompanied by a strong armed guard that included his son John, Viscount of Aboyne. Bizarrely, this guarding party also included John, 2nd Laird of Rothiemay - son to he who Frendraught had killed at the River Deveron several months earlier. This young man's temper had been appeased by Frendraught's payment of £2,200 to his mother in damages.

This unlikely group travelled west for nineteen miles, under what must have been very tense conditions. However, they arrived at Frendraught Castle unmolested by any Leslie supporters and that evening, 8 October 1630, Frendraught felt compelled to feed his protectors and offer them apartments to sleep in overnight.

These chambers were in the castle's old tower, and the guests slept in small groups on three floors. Around midnight, the whole of the tower almost instantaneously took fire. So ferociously did the flames consume it that Viscount Aboyne, the Laird of Rothiemay, Colonel Ivat (one of Aboyne's friends), a man called English Will and two servants all perished. It was said that Aboyne might have saved himself, but he rushed from the bottommost chamber up a wooden staircase in an attempt to help Rothiemay, who was at the top; both died when they became trapped. Although a number of people escaped the conflagration, at least six people were killed, possibly more. Aboyne and Rothiemay are held to have been consumed by the flames while crying uselessly from an upper window, 'Help! Help! For God's cause!'

All the while Frendraught, his family and the household staff reputedly remained an unconcerned spectator in a detached part of the house. News of this terrible event spread throughout the kingdom, and while some suggested the conflagration had been an accident, most agreed it had been caused by a deliberate act of incendiarism.

But, if so, whose hand was behind the atrocity?

Many blamed Frendraught himself for burning the old tower and his guests, perhaps by setting a vault beneath the edifice ablaze, his intention being to kill young Rothiemay – perhaps in hope of recovering the money he had given him in reparations. But would the laird really have set part of his own home on fire, just to kill someone who he had only recently made peace with? Particularly when it is known that the fire consumed a great quantity of his own silver plate and coin, as well as the title deeds to his property and other important paperwork.

Some even went so far as to blame Frendraught's wife, Elizabeth (the eldest daughter of the Earl of Sutherland), who – it is said – took an active part in her husband's disputes. Perhaps she thought that by committing the atrocity it might be blamed on someone else – the Leslies, presumably, who had publicly vowed vengeance during the Bog-of-Gight summit. An anonymous ballad written a few months later certainly blamed the deaths on a conspiracy instigated by Lady Frendraught. In part, it read of Rothiemay, one of the victims:

'Mercy, mercy Lady Frendraught;
Will ye not sink with sin?
For first your husband kilt my father;
And now ye burn his son.'

But if Frendraught or his wife had planned the crime, then they must have decided upon it all but immediately, since Aboyne and Rothiemay had only accompanied Frendraught home by accident.

The Marquess of Huntly, whose son Aboyne had died in the disaster, firmly believed Frendraught to be behind it and took his case to the Privy Council in Edinburgh. This appointed a commission comprising the bishops of Aberdeen and Moray, Lord Carnegie and a coroner called Bruce to investigate; on 13 April 1631, they forensically inspected the burned tower to ascertain how it may have been destroyed. Afterwards, they wrote to the Council their firm belief that the fire had been deliberately started, most likely from within the vaults or chambers of the tower itself. Huntly never wavered in his belief that Frendraught had committed the crime himself, even going so far as to implore King Charles I for help during a royal visit in 1633.

Others, however, continued to blame adherents of the Leslie family for setting the castle tower on fire. It didn't help the Leslies' case when it became known that – in their passion – they had actually threatened to commit such an act, allegedly even entering into a conspiracy to do so. On this basis Frendraught thereafter managed to secure John Meldrum of Reidhill on suspicion of being the incendiary. Meldrum was carried to Edinburgh, where he was tried for murder following the king's departure from Scotland: this must have disappointed the Marquess of Huntly greatly, since he sincerely believed Frendraught himself was guilty.

Meldrum's conviction was helped by the arrest of two men at Inverness who claimed to be indirectly connected to the conspiracy. Both these men testified before the lords of the Privy Council; among their evidence against Meldrum was an accusation that he had been heard threatening to burn Frendraught the night before the fire. Meldrum was sentenced to be hanged and quartered at the cross of Edinburgh, although nothing was really proved against him beyond this. He died, denying the charges, in August 1633.

Despite this outcome, for some years afterwards the Laird of Frendraught suffered raids upon his property by parties of lawless horsemen who blamed him for the fire, during which attacks they burnt his corn and sometimes murdered his people. All the while, the Marquess of Huntly chose to look the other way. In the end, Frendraught journeyed to Edinburgh to seek help. This cycle of violence – still part of the communal way of life, it seems, in some areas of Scotland – rumbled on and the question of who started the fire was never really satisfactorily answered.

The stigma that she might have been a murderess stuck with Lady Frendraught for the rest of her life. In 1637, she applied to Father Gilbert

Blackhall, asking him to be her Confessor and spiritual advisor. He wrote:

'I refused absolutely to see her because she was suspected to be guilty of the death of my lord Aboyne... whether she be guilty or not, God knoweth...'

THE WELL OF SEVEN HEADS

The Keppoch murders occurred in early September 1663, when a party of men – variously said to be rival claimants, discontented followers and/or common freebooters – attacked the house of Alexander MacDonald Glas of Keppoch in the western Highlands. The wealthy young chief was brutally knifed to death alongside his younger brother Ranald.

The government issued a commission authorising Sir James MacDonald of Sleat to catch the culprits by whatever means necessary, and these instructions he carried out ruthlessly. Those accused of the murders were Archibald MacDonell in Keppoch, either cousin or uncle to the young victims; Donald Gormo in Inveroymore; Alexander MacDouald in Tulloch; Angus MacDonald in Murligan; Allister MacDonald in Bohuntine; Allister MacDonald in Crenachau; Donald MacDonald in Blairnahinven; and Angus MacDonald in Achluachrach, all in the Brae of Lochaber. Some of the gang were allegedly put to death by a vengeful kinsman called Iain Lom after being run to ground at Inverlair. The others dispersed entirely, to the relief of the whole region.

Sir James had managed to oversee this repression by the end of 1665, when he was promised a reward by the Earl of Rothes, then Lord High Treasurer and Keeper of the Great Seal of Scotland. Iain Lom later achieved fame as a Gaelic poet, telling the story of his kinsmen's murder in a work entitled *Murt na Ceapaich*.

According to a well-known tradition, the heads of seven of the executed murderers were presented at Invergarry Castle, having been washed in a spring at Loch Oich. This spring now goes by the name of the Well of Seven Heads and a remarkable stone obelisk there displays a hand holding a dirk and seven life-like decapitated heads. The monument was established in 1812.

SCOTLAND'S LAST 'PRIVATE WARS'

Although by the end of the seventeenth century clan chiefs and landowning gentry were increasingly apt to try and settle their differences via the courts, the occasional flare-up still occurred. In 1680, for example, John Campbell

The obelisk near Loch Oich, around 1910. (The Roseries Collection/Mary Evans Picture Library)

of Glen Orchy – who had purchased the lands and title of the earldom from the debt-ridden George Sinclair, 6th Earl of Caithness – invaded Caithness with an army of 700 Campbell allies to make good his claims. He was opposed by George Sinclair of Keiss, who claimed to be the next heir to the earldom, and on 13 July the two sides engaged each other at a place called Altimarlach ('thieves' burn') about a mile or two from Wick along the banks of the Wick River. The Sinclairs, partly by stratagem, were utterly annihilated. Around eighty of them are said to have been massacred along the riverbank; perhaps as many as 300 were killed altogether. Campbell's losses are believed to have been very low.

The matter was ultimately settled by the Privy Council in Edinburgh, however. John Campbell was forced to relinquish the earldom in 1681 to Sinclair of Keiss, but was created 1st Earl of Breadalbane by way of compensation. In many ways, the situation worked out well for both claimants, meaning the 'battle' that came to define the entire proceedings was quite an unnecessary bloodbath.

Although this is sometimes said to have been Scotland's last 'private war', this is not quite the case. On 4 August 1688, a feud between Coll MacDonald and the MacIintosh Clan, regarding lands occupied by the former, led to an attempted invasion of Lochaber by the MacIntoshes. The aggressors were heavily defeated on a height called Maol Ruadh.

Correspondence dated 15 September 1688 received by John Ellis, a civil servant based in Dublin, reveals:

> *'We are told from Scotland that the skirmishes which lately happened in the Highlands, between the two families, or clans, of the MacDonnels and the MacIntoshes, are now appeased by some forces of that kingdom, but that several have been killed on both sides. The first difference began about taking possession of certain lands which were decreed to the one in prejudice of the other.'*

Chapter 11

War Crimes

The very first blood of the nation's civil wars is thought to have been shed in July 1642 following a huge meeting organised on Preston Moor (now Moor Park, Fulwood) by Sir John Girlington. This convention followed his receipt at Thurland Castle, Lancashire, of a proclamation from the king dated 6 June requesting that Sir John promote the interests of the monarchy. Having read the petition aloud on the moor, Sir John proceeded to further announce a 'commission of array', which authorised the arming of loyal subjects in defence of the king and his prerogatives. Angry disagreements broke out between supporters of the king and those who favoured Parliament, which culminated in Girlington – then High Sheriff of the county – calling out, 'You that are for the king, follow us!' Those gathered upon the moor split into two factions, and Sir John Girlington immediately rode towards Preston itself where he took control of the military supplies with the assistance of Lord Molineux, Lord Strange and some 400 others.

Considerable quantities of gunpowder and match were, in fact, stored at Preston, Liverpool and Manchester, and Lord Strange (the 35-year-old James Stanley, later 7th Earl of Derby) next led a party of armed men from Bury into Manchester to contest ownership of the military stores there. However, they were opposed by the people of Manchester under Mr Assheton of Middleton, who had been training the citizens in the use of muskets and pikes. A stand-off developed, Strange's men crying, 'For the king!' while the Manchester citizens' subversive rallying cry was, 'For the king and Parliament!'

When Lord Strange was invited into the town to dine with an enclave of Royalist sympathisers, the situation began to degenerate – largely because he entered with a retinue that resembled a small army, including numerous nobles, gentlemen and a troop of horse 120-strong. The population of Manchester became alarmed that the Royalists had arrived to take over the town, so Parliamentary supporters – including Sir Thomas Stanley of Bickerstaffe – ordered the town's drums beaten to rouse the trained bands.

These then besieged the house of Alexander Green at the end of Market Street, where Strange was being entertained at a banquet.

It is unclear what triggered it, but a bloody melee later ensued during which Richard Percival, a weaver of Kirkmanshulme, was fatally wounded when a Royalist supporter discharged a pistol at him. The victim had apparently been heard to 'give out some words in favour of the Parliament', so Lord Strange immediately ordered his men to attack the trained bands that were thronging the streets of Manchester.

The Royalists, however, maintained the skirmish was commenced by Sir Thomas Stanley of Bickerstaffe, who, although a kinsman of Lord Strange, fired a pistol at him in a murder attempt. What seems reasonably clear is that Lord Strange was in the process of exiting Manchester for Ordsall when one of his entourage was knocked from his horse and badly injured. Percival was shot immediately afterwards; he was interred on 18 July.

This fatality occurred on 15 July 1642 and the unfortunate Percival is said to have been the first person in Lancashire, if not the whole of England, to die in the civil war, for although England was not yet officially at war, it would be within a matter of weeks. However, it is worth pointing out that the schism developing across the country in general must have produced other pockets of violence prior to the 'official' start of the war on 22 August 1642 – so the killing at Manchester may have been only one among many. Tumult had been brewing steadily since violent clashes in Westminster and Whitehall the previous December between riotous apprentices and the king's officers.

Two weeks later, Lord Strange was impeached in Parliament for levying war against Manchester, as well as being held accountable for the murder of 'Richard Percival, linen webster'. The person who actually shot Percival dead is believed to have been Richard Fleetwood of Rossall, who was caught when Preston fell to the Parliamentarians in February 1643. He does not appear to have suffered execution though, because records indicate he was still alive several years later.

A subsequent Parliamentary tract entitled *The Beginning of the Civil Wars in England (or, Terrible News from the North)* suggested that no less than twenty-seven people were killed in this violent collision between 'the Manchester people and the armed bands of Lord Strange'. The violence in Manchester did not resurrect itself immediately, however, so Lord Strange busied himself in strengthening his army across the county with the intention of taking full possession of the town in the name of the king.

Strange subsequently became a major Royalist figurehead in Lancashire

A violent street fight between Royalists and revolutionary Parliamentarians. (Courtesy of Pembroke Castle)

over the next few years. In 1644, having become 7th Earl of Derby, he participated in the besieging of Bolton in the north-west of England, before it was stormed on 28 May with such violence and plunder that the event became known as the 'Bolton Massacre'. During the carnage, Royalist soldiers ran amok, 'killing, stripping and spoiling all they could meet with'. Typical of those murdered was:

> *'Katherine Saddon, an aged woman of 72 years old, run with a sword to the very heart outright, because she had no money to give, and some others killed outright after they were mortally wounded, because they stirred or answered not greedy unjust desires.'*

During the general mayhem, the earl is reported to have treacherously murdered in cold blood Captain William Bootle, formerly one of his own servants, who he harboured a private vendetta against. This was in spite of a promise to give him quarter. The earl was captured seven years later near

Nantwich in the aftermath of the Battle of Worcester, by which time Parliament had all but defeated the Royalists. Following a trial by court-martial at Chester, James Stanley was returned to Bolton and executed there around noon on 15 October 1651 for precipitating the Storming of Bolton. After he was executed on a scaffold erected at 'the Cross' great disorder developed, the cause of which was uncertain, although in quelling it the soldiers killed a child. Apparently, Captain Bootle's murder was one of the great controversies of Stanley's trial, for he denied at all being 'a man of blood'.

Horrors of an equal magnitude occurred in Scotland. James Graham, 1st Marquess of Montrose, emerged as a brilliant military strategist during the early years of the civil wars, when his pro-Royalist forces took on the Covenanters, a Scottish Presbyterian movement initially allied loosely to England's Parliamentary forces. Among Montrose's various military successes, however, one episode in particular stands out, an incident which occurred on 13 September 1644 during his army's advance on Aberdeen, the main Scottish seaport supporting the Covenanters. His first act prior to besiegement was to send a drummer-boy to the provost and magistrates of Aberdeen, carrying a letter 'politely' ordering the city to surrender, or face the consequences. Contrary to the rules of war, the drummer-boy who delivered this message was murdered in cold blood by some troopers of the Fifeshire horse, who shot him with their pistols.

Montrose's fury at this killing swept through the ranks of his men and when they eventually cut their way into the city after driving off the Covenanter cavalry, what followed was a massacre. The remnants of the Fifeshire regiment were almost annihilated. Over 160 burgesses and dignitaries of the city were massacred, and the carnage in the streets was immense as Highland troops under Alasdair Mac Colla and Irish Royalists ran amok. It is said that the Irish soldiers, seeing men clad in half-decent clothes, stripped them before murdering them, while Aberdeen's shops and houses were thoroughly ransacked. The last piper of Aberdeen was among those murdered, possibly in symbolic revenge for the drummer boy. The streets became strewn with the naked corpses of the unburied dead; it is believed – realistically – that while Montrose's losses were in single figures, the Covenanters and Aberdeen townsfolk were massacred in their hundreds, possibly to the number of 1,000. In the end, Montrose ordered all his soldiers to return to their colours at the camp, under pain of instant death, so as to end their violence.

The Covenanters positively hated Montrose for what they saw as his betrayal of their cause; and it was these under General David Leslie, later 1st Lord Newark, who finally halted Montrose's seemingly invincible progress on the battlefields of Scotland. Following his eventual capture, just prior to being hanged from a 30-foot gallows in Edinburgh on 21 May 1650, the marquess combed his hair and famously joked, 'My head is yet my own.'

The Covenanters – whose government sentenced Montrose to death – have an important role in Scottish history. Broadly speaking, around the time of the dissatisfaction in England, they engineered a simultaneous revolt against Charles I over his refusal to reverse certain religious policies in Scotland. This led to the signing of an independently-minded 'National Covenant' in Greyfriars Kirkyard, Edinburgh, in 1638; Charles's government in the north next began to lose popular support, allowing the organised Presbyterian Covenanters to develop into Scotland's *de facto* government. Because of this schism, battles were fought with Scottish Royalists during Scotland's own civil conflict.

The Covenanter General David Leslie's own successes in the arena of conflict became indelibly tainted by an atrocity he committed against a Royalist enclave of 300 Highlanders defending the castle of Dunaverty, near the Mull of Kintyre in 1647. The besieged clansmen – chiefly MacDougalls – surrendered possession of the castle following a promise of mercy. However, Leslie's indecision over their punishment was swayed thanks to the machinations of his chaplain, the Reverend John Nave, who persuaded the general that all the captives had to die for atrocities *they* had committed during earlier campaigning. Three days later, all those who had surrendered were put to death in cold blood, in an episode of massacre that stands alongside the worst excesses of cruelty seen during the seventeenth century. The clan's young chief alone was spared, on condition he exile himself to France.

Quite apart from the great battlefield clashes – of which Marston Moor, Yorkshire, in 1644 and Naseby, Northamptonshire, in 1645 were so decisive for the Parliamentary forces in England – there occurred in the background some of the most horrendous atrocities imaginable. Acts of destruction that would not have been out of place in Viking times formed part of the wider conflict, and one can merely wonder at the staggering inhumanity the people of the time allowed themselves to succumb to. Murder in its basest form was committed by participants on all sides, be they Royalist, Parliamentarian, Covenanter or civilian.

As the nation disintegrated, brazen acts of violence became common. This helmet and sword allegedly belonged to Robert Philipson, of Belle Isle, Cumbria, who rode his horse into Kendal's church looking for a Parliamentarian enemy, Colonel Briggs, to assassinate. He murdered a Parliamentary sentinel during the incident in June 1645, before escaping the town.

THE BLURRED LINES OF WAR

Parishes, counties, towns and cities across England began to offer their allegiance to either King or Parliament and as the nation started to implode, acts of violence became commonplace. Many of these were of an unusual, even surreal, nature, as participants from either side illustrated their zeal on behalf of their chosen cause.

For example, illegal executions were practised, as at Bristol after the city was occupied by Parliamentary forces under Colonel Nathaniel Fiennes in February 1643. On 7 March, word was passed to Colonel Fiennes that certain respected Bristol citizens intended to facilitate a Royalist takeover. Dozens of arrests followed at addresses in Wine Street and Christmas Street. Among those apprehended were Robert Yeamans, an alderman and former sheriff, and George Boucher, a wealthy merchant, the owners of the two houses where the plotters had gathered. On 30 May 1643, both men were unceremoniously hanged in Wine Street by Fiennes's two executioners, called Langridge and Clifton. Yeamans was afterwards interred in St Mary le Port Church, while Boucher was buried in St Werburgh's Church.

It only remains to be said that in the summer Prince Rupert's forces battled their way bloodily into Bristol and re-took the city for the king. Fiennes and his remaining men were forced to retreat on 27 July and Charles later declared Yeamans and Boucher to have been murdered – adding that a general pardon would not extend to Nathaniel Fiennes and a number of others, including Herbert, the late provost-marshal of Bristol. Despite the king's wrath, Fiennes was never held to account for the killing of the two Royalist plotters, and he died in 1669, aged around 61.

Another bloody incident of a strange nature occurred in Hoghton Tower, an ancient fortified manor house standing on a Lancashire hillside beside the River Darwen, where the owners – the Hoghton family – remained staunchly Royalist. During Sir Gilbert Hoghton's absence the house was defended by a small garrison of thirty or forty musketeers. In mid-February 1643, these defenders are believed to have decoyed a much stronger Parliamentary force under Captain Nicholas Starkey onto the premises by falsely accepting an offer of quarter. They had, in fact, lured Starkey and his men into a trap; by treacherously firing a trail of gunpowder that led to Hoghton's munitions store, they caused a gigantic explosion that tore through the Parliamentary ranks. The explosion appears to have erupted from the building on its eastern side, although it may have occurred at the

The entrance to Hoghton Tower, which suffered a mysterious – and timely - explosion.

205

Gate House leading into the second court. Starkey and dozens of his men were massacred. Despite the setback, however, the Parliamentarians took the manor house. Many of the Royalist soldiers within managed to escape, although six who were not quick enough were apprehended upon suspicion – but whether they suffered punishment for the blast is unknown.

Summary executions also occurred with disturbing regularity. On 28 August 1648, for example, the Royalists surrendered Colchester, Essex, to Sir Thomas Fairfax and Henry Ireton. Fairfax, having inspected the town, held a council of war during which he proclaimed examples had to be made, so Sir Charles Lucas and Sir George Lisle, having honourably surrendered in the hope of mercy, were sentenced to be summarily executed. At seven o'clock that evening both men were shot by a platoon of musketeers, Lucas exclaiming, 'See, I am ready! Rebels, do your worst!' Lisle, for his part, bravely advised the platoon to draw nearer, whereupon one of them said, 'I warrant you, sir, we'll hit you!' Lisle retorted, 'I have been nearer when you have missed me. I'm ready, traitors, do your worst.'

The shooting of Lucas and Lisle amounted to an assassination. This illustration comes from a contemporary monarchist pamphlet, The Loyall Sacrifice.

WAR CRIMES

Implicated in this double homicide was 38-year-old Colonel Thomas Rainsborough, whose own death as a by-product of the war is particularly noteworthy. Having quartered his infantry in and around Doncaster, the colonel was stabbed to death outside an inn during a botched kidnapping attempt during the early hours of 2 November 1648. The crime was committed by a small party of Royalists from Pontefract under Captain William Paulden, who – in an act of breath-taking boldness – artfully infiltrated Doncaster before passing themselves off as Parliamentary messengers. They then forcibly abducted Rainsborough from his quarters at the inn. This place was a house occupied by Mr William Smith, which was located on the western side of the cross in Doncaster. The colonel is said to have been killed by one among the Royalists called Allen Austwick, who also murdered a lieutenant in the melee, before all those involved thundered off on their horses and escaped the town.

The group holed up in Pontefract Castle, which was then besieged with renewed urgency in the aftermath of Rainsborough's murder. Captain Paulden died a few days later, succumbing to a high fever. When the Parliamentarians finally took the castle, Colonel John Morrice and Coronet Blackburn were taken prisoner during an attempt to escape abroad. Morrice, aged 53, was the Governor of Pontefract Castle; Blackburn was aged 52. Both were implicated in Colonel Rainsborough's murder. While awaiting trial, the pair actually managed to escape York Castle by using a rope to slide down an exterior wall; however, Blackburn fell and broke his leg and Morrice would not leave him, meaning both were retaken.

After 22 weeks of imprisonment they were sentenced to death by two judges, Thorpe and Puleston, who were purposely sent to Parliament-controlled York to try them. On Saturday, 22 August 1649, the convicted soldiers were executed at the Tyburn outside Micklegate Bar, York, their corpses afterwards interred in the churchyard of St John's, Hungate.

According to Benjamin Boothroyd's 1807 history of Pontefract, Austwick – the man who physically killed Rainsborough – managed to slip through the net, and lived until after the Restoration. What is interesting is the suggestion that Rainsborough may have been deliberately targeted because of his role in the assassination of Lucas and Lisle in Colchester. As these examples illustrate, either side was willing to punish enemy fighters for crimes committed outside the 'rules' of war if it suited their purpose. However, this impartiality did not often extend so readily to those on their own side who might act in a likewise fashion.

207

View of Old York from Clifford's Tower, virtually all that remains of the city's castle, from where Rainsborough's assassins tried to escape.

THE MURDER OF THE DEAN OF WELLS

One case highlighting this double standard concerned Dr Walter Raleigh, a nephew of the famous explorer Sir Walter. He had been promoted to the Deanery of Wells, Somerset, in 1641, but on the outbreak of war he became persecuted for no other reason than his loyalty towards the king, whose chaplain he had been. It was while he was absent in this latter capacity that Parliamentarians looted his parsonage-house in Chedzoy, plundering his livestock and turning his family out into the cornfields. Dr Raleigh attempted to re-establish his old life at Chedzoy as the conflict in the west swung to-and-fro; but ultimately, he was arrested when nearby Bridgwater fell to Sir Thomas Fairfax and Oliver Cromwell.

After initially being kept under house arrest in Chedzoy, Dr Raleigh was moved from place to place – always as a captive – from Ilchester to Banwell-house and finally to the Deanery in Wells. Here he was committed to the custody of David Barrett, a shoemaker and constable of the town. Raleigh asked permission of his gaoler for leave, so that he might see his wife; this request was refused, so the dean next complained loudly that others were allowed this privilege. When news of Barrett's favours to some of his prisoners reached their ears, the Parliamentary representatives in the county threatened to sack him if it happened again. This made Barrett even angrier with Raleigh, who he already despised as though a personal enemy.

The following morning Barrett found Dr Raleigh writing a letter to his wife and tried to snatch the paper from him. The clergyman snatched it back

A local tradition says that the soldiers who took Raleigh sharpened their swords on St Mary's Church, Chedzoy, accounting for these grooves.

and Barrett – by now utterly incensed – drew his sword and rammed it into Dr Raleigh's stomach so forcefully that the tip of the blade reached his backbone. The victim was sitting down at the time, with no weapon to defend himself and after the assault he slumped from his chair as though dead. However, he lingered for around six weeks before dying of his wound on 10 October 1646, aged about 60.

Dr Raleigh's wife attempted to see to it that Barrett was prosecuted for murder, but when the killer took his place at the bar he was acquitted of any wrongdoing and returned to his former position. Barrett is believed to have been a Welshman who came to Somerset and made a living by plundering, before somehow earning an annuity of £16. He married a woman from Wells, although a second woman soon arrived from Wales claiming to be his legitimate wife and demanding the £16 annuity. It is further said that Barrett's sister-in-law thereafter suffered some kind of debilitating illness, declaring on her deathbed that she was damned for falsely claiming Dr Raleigh had provoked his own murder by striking Barrett first. She claimed that she had been coerced into making this accusation by the murderer.

Since many leading opponents of Charles I were drawn from the Puritan community, those fighting beneath the Parliamentarians in the wider conflict often felt compelled to assault local churches. Puritans advocated greater strictness in religious discipline, believing that the established church mirrored Catholicism too closely; therefore, established English clergymen were frequently treated inhumanly by Parliament's soldiers as a by-product of this doctrine. Following the re-taking of Bristol by Parliamentary forces, one high profile victim of the abuses was the Right Reverend Thomas Howell, the Bishop of Bristol. In November 1645, the Bishop's Palace was turned by the army into a malt house, with a mill being erected. The building's roof had already been plundered of its lead, exposing the bishop's heavily pregnant wife to the wind and rain; she died soon afterwards while giving birth. The bishop himself was dragged violently out of the Palace, and died within a fortnight in January 1646.

It would be possible to list many more examples like this. One need only glance at *Mercurius Rusticus*, a Royalist news-book first published in 1643 by Bruno Ryves, whose primary intention was to educate his readership upon the brutality of Parliamentary soldiers. Some of the stories within certainly paint the 'rebel' troops as little more than an organised gang of marauders. However, those on the king's side were not immune from committing similar crimes, and it should be noted that the poet George Wither started a Parliamentary *Mercurius Rusticus* as a counter to the Royalist allegations. In

Many English churches still bear the scars of desecration by Parliamentary soldiers. This is the mutilated effigy of Susannah Noel in North Luffenham's church, Rutland. She died in 1640, and three years later her husband Henry attempted to defend the hall there against Puritan 'Roundhead' troops. His small force killed one of the besiegers, but in the end the hall was taken. Noel himself died thereafter in a London gaol.

Somerset, for example, an appalling crime took place *c*.1644. On the road to Taunton, Sir Francis Dodington, a Royalist zealot and former county sheriff, is said to have met a minister, bellowing at him, 'Who art thou for, priest?' upon which the latter answered, 'For God and his gospel.' Dodington drew a pistol and shot the minister to death in cold blood there and then. Such were his excesses that following the war Sir Francis was forced to flee Dodington Hall to France.

Overall, perhaps typifying the precarious situation members of the common clergy were apt to find themselves in is the case of the Reverend William Losse. This man, formerly of King's College, Cambridge, had been the vicar of Weedon Lois, Northamptonshire, for some twenty-five years. On Sunday, 2 July 1643, twelve Parliamentary troopers under Captain Samuel

St Mary and St Peter's Church, where Reverend Losse was murderously attacked.

rode from Northampton into the village and attempted to arrest Reverend Losse while he was officiating at the reading desk in St Mary and St Peter's Church. The vicar was not even told why he was being taken into custody, and after declaring he would 'never be a slave to slaves' he ran into the church. The troopers pursued him into the belfry, where they shot and stabbed him. Finally leaving, they warned that if the vicar should live then they would return and finish the job properly.

It is unclear whether the wounded vicar died there and then or partially recovered, although the latter is perhaps more likely; at any rate, he was certainly deceased by August 1645, when his will was proved by his wife. A brass plaque to Mr Losse's memory in the church where he was attacked sums up the general level of martyrdom suffered by the clergy. In part, it reads:

> *'He [Reverend Losse] was one of 7,000 clergymen who, for the honour of God, and for witness of His truth as expressed in the tenets of the Church of England, were contented (in those evil and cruel times) to suffer murder, violence and insult, to be dragged from their benefices, and cast with their families upon the world, forbidden to earn their bread as scholars, or else sent to die upon the hulks, or in prison, or in foreign slavery. Of whom at the Restoration only 600 survived to resume their livings.'*

VIGILANTISM

As the war dragged on, it can be generally stated that Britain entered a period of utter free-for-all, where murder, atrocity and abuses of power became common. In 'Bristow' (Bridestowe), Devon, for example, a troop of horse was sent by the Parliamentarian Earl of Stamford to apprehend a husbandman who had lately declared for the king. Finding him away from home, they lynched the man's 10-year-old son. *Mercurius Rusticus* observed, 'Whether the child did ever recover, is more than my informer can assure me.' This alone indicates the terror that might visit even the smallest hamlet without warning; Bridestowe is to this day merely a small, inoffensive village hidden away on the edge of Dartmoor. Much of the civil wars were a far cry from the semi-legitimate battlefield contests with which they would become largely associated. War crimes became the norm; the most picturesque of English villages could become mere backdrops for appalling exercises in mass murder.

Parliamentary troops lynched a 10-year-old boy in the village of Bridestowe.

Particularly interesting are the accounts of violence perpetrated by civilians, which illustrate just how badly the law and order situation had degenerated during the war. Wellingborough, for example, was the scene of an anti-Parliament uprising following the detention of a clerk of the peace, Mr Gray, on 27 December 1642. In attempting to enforce order, Captain John Sawyer and eighty men were opposed on the Wilby road by a crowd of local people – 'who seldom love or hate moderately'. Someone in the mob fired at the captain as he rode his horse towards them, hitting him in the head and neck with goose-shot, before another rushed up and hit him with a club, knocking him to the ground. Sawyer was then attacked by several local women before he could be rescued from the melee. He died twenty-two hours later, and there next followed an organised Parliamentary assault upon Wellingborough which put the crowd to flight by sheer force of numbers. During this episode, Captain Francis Sawyer – brother to the assassinated man – rode up to Mr Flint, curate of Little Harrowden, on the road between Wilby and Wellingborough, and struck him on the head with an axe attached to a pole. *Mercurius Rusticus* tells us that such was the force of the strike it chopped open Mr Flint's head down to his eyes and killed him instantly.

In Barthomley, nine miles east of Nantwich, an even more heinous retaliation occurred on 22 December 1643. It began when someone fired from the top of the church steeple at a contingent of Royalist troops from Lord Byron's regiment, who happened to be passing through the parish. The sniper killed a soldier and in response, the Church of St Bertoline was besieged and a group of local men smoked out. The captives were forced to strip naked, then twelve of them were systematically murdered in cold blood, including one young man called John Fowler, described as a minor, who had his throat slit personally by Major Connought, the Royalist in charge. Fowler, the village rector's son, may have been the sniper who fired at the soldiers. According to the diary of Henry Newcombe, Connought was later executed for Fowler's murder following a trial at Chester on 13 October 1654 before a Parliamentary judge, John Bradshaw.

Certain rural areas in England saw the emergence of vigilante gangs called 'clubmen'. These were comprised of thousands of armed peasants, who initially held no particular political affiliation – all they wished for was to keep the ravages of war from their villages and fields. To this end, groups of clubmen launched assaults upon whoever they had reason to believe threatened their livelihoods, without caring which side they were for. Their motto was, 'If you offer to plunder our cattle; be assured we will give you battle.' Wearing white ribbons on their hats, and often armed with farming implements, they sometimes clashed violently with military deserters, stragglers and scouting parties. By March 1645, the clubmen had in the western counties become something akin to a permanent, organised force, sometimes being commanded by gentlemen. Typically illustrating their determination is an official report of 2 July 1645, stating that 'in this day's march was a soldier executed, being by the country apprehended and accused, for plundering of a gentleman passing on the way near Marlborough.' Perversely, however, what began as a grassroots peace movement had by this time become instrumental to the continuing degeneration of law and order. Like many vigilante groups, the clubmen's violence began to become disproportionate and they threatened to burn the houses of those who would not join their campaign, which in the west started to focus largely on the harassment of Royalists.

By degrees, as their power grew, they began to become drawn into the war itself. That was until 4 August 1645, when Cromwell's men engaged the clubmen in a ferocious battle at Hambledon Hill, an ancient, deeply trenched hillfort in Dorset's Blackmore Vale. Around 200 clubmen were killed or wounded; those who survived were imprisoned in Shroton's church and several ringleaders – arrested in Shaftesbury three days earlier – were

Hambledon Hill, location of the battle.

215

subsequently deported to London. Cromwell, who had engaged the militants because he considered their movement the start of a peasant's revolt, sustained fifteen losses during the battle, including a captain called Paltison.

One incident of mass murder by vigilantes occurred around 24 July 1645. At the time, the ferry across the River Severn on the Welsh side was owned by a respectable family called St Pierre. King Charles had recently ridden through Shirenewton and used the ferry to cross the Severn to Gloucestershire. The boat had only just returned to the Welsh side when a corps of about sixty republicans collared the ferrymen and ordered them – with drawn swords – to take them across the river in pursuit of the Royalist party.

The boatmen were staunch supporters of the king, but did as they were ordered. However, they took the republicans only as far as a wide reef called the English Stones, separated from the Gloucestershire side by a then-dry body of water called English Lake. When the republicans were dropped here, it was low water; to all intents and purposes their way looked clear. However, the tide had just turned and the English Lake began to rapidly swell with water; all sixty of the republican horsemen drowned, even as the ferry made its way back to the Welsh side.

When Cromwell was informed of this event – which amounted to an atrocity, since the boatmen would have known they had doomed their enemies infallibly – he abolished the ferry crossing lest a similar catastrophe occur. It was not renewed until 1748.

THE KILLING TIME
Thanks to their exclusion by, and suspicion of, the new English regime, the Covenanters in Scotland later took against the English Parliament and backed the cause of the heir-in-waiting, Charles II. However, after the Restoration, letters were brought to light suggesting the Covenanters' erstwhile leader, Archibald Campbell, 1st Marquess of Argyll, had co-operated nonetheless with the Protectorate regime during the Interregnum. Charles II immediately had Campbell arrested and imprisoned when he presented himself at Whitehall.

In the end, the great Highland chief and patriotic Scotsman was ignominiously decapitated by a guillotine-like contraption called 'the Maiden', before his head was stuck on a spike at Edinburgh's toll-booth on 28 May 1661. Fundamentally, Campbell – who was in his mid-fifties when he was executed – was considered untrustworthy and his death helped Charles II consolidate power in Scotland, much to the great expense of the

Covenanters, whose waning position now deteriorated catastrophically.

Although he was convicted of treason, it was also levelled at Campbell that he and certain named others were perfectly culpable of an atrocity carried out by Campbell clansmen upon the Lamonts in 1646, knowing it to be against the laws of war. The incident had developed out of the battles between Covenanters and Scottish Royalist forces, when the Lamont Clan took the opportunity to participate in raids upon Campbell lands in Argyllshire under the misapprehension that the Campbells were weakened through the national conflict. Hundreds of men under Sir James Lamont committed two appalling massacres at Strachur and Kilmun, being in these crimes assisted by the forces of the afore-mentioned Highland mercenary, Alasdair Mac Colla. Among *his* previous crimes, he had personally ignited a barn in Kilninver housing captured Campbells, including women and children, burning around 100 to death.

These acts earned the Lamonts the undying hatred of the Campbells, who were not as meek and depleted as their enemies supposed, and they launched an awesome war of extermination upon their aggravators. At some point in June 1646, men under the Clan Campbell besieged the castles of Toward and Escog, then the houses of Sir James Lamont, reneging upon terms of surrender, taking their victims prisoner and holding them in great torment and misery while they plundered the two properties. After several days keeping their captives bound hand and foot in Toward Castle, the Campbells set about the systematic butchery of great numbers among them. A great many captives were ferried by boats for nine miles to Dunoon, a coastal village on the shore of the Firth of Clyde. Here, thirty-six people, many of them gentlemen and vassals of the Lamont Clan, were lynched from one tree standing in the kirk-yard. Others were stabbed or shot to death with pistols, the killings apparently following a mock-trial performed by the Campbells. In all, around 200 Lamonts were murdered, many of them entirely innocent of anything.

Sir James Lamont himself and his immediate kin were spared by the Campbell chiefs – although this leniency was granted merely so that his signature might be obtained on certain legal deeds admitting he had been in the wrong, as well as on others which handed over the Lamont properties to the Campbells. The surrender complete, Sir James Lamont was subsequently incarcerated in the dungeon of Dunstaffnage Castle and later in Stirling Castle. He was only liberated when Cromwell took against the Covenanters and the Campbells, and overran the nation in 1651.

By the time the Stuart regime executed Archibald Campbell, 1st Marquess of Argyll, in 1661, the status quo had changed entirely in Scottish politics; the once-powerful Presbyterian Covenanters had become rebels and something of a persecuted minority in their own country. By 1666, militancy among the more extreme Covenanters was deemed so threatening to the new establishment in Scotland that it became necessary to engage them in combat. This clash occurred at Rullion Green in the Pentland Hills on 28 November. Here, dragoons commanded by a Royalist general, Thomas Dalyell, killed dozens of Covenanters, executed more and put the rest to flight.

On 11 July 1668, a preacher named James Mitchell, implicated in the Pentland insurrection, fired a pistol at James Sharp, the Archbishop of St Andrews, as he entered a carriage in Blackfriars' Wynd (Blackfriars Street), Edinburgh. He succeeded in wounding Andrew Honeyman, the Bishop of Orkney – who accompanied the archbishop – in the wrist instead. His actions had very injurious consequences for the Presbyterians; a general purge against them was implemented, based on the excuse that the plot to shoot Archbishop Sharp went wider than merely the person who had pulled the trigger. The assassin himself wandered the country for a long time before returning to Edinburgh to run a shop. Here, Archbishop Sharp spotted him one day and recognised him as the man who had fired at him. Early in 1674, Mitchell was apprehended. He endured years of brutal punishment before finally being hanged in Edinburgh's Grass-market on 18 January 1678, his death sentence having been aided and abetted by a good deal of outrageous perjury.

Archbishop Sharp is believed to have insisted upon Mitchell's execution so as to set an example to any future would-be assassins. The primate was by 1678 a deeply hated man among Covenanter circles, despite having been a former Covenanter himself. He had been a marked man since 1661, when he was entrusted with presenting the Presbyterian position to Charles II, only to change sides and accept the archbishopric instead. The move earned him the unyielding contempt of his former comrades, and the execution of Mitchell – which many agreed was indeed a judicial murder engineered by the primate himself – only strengthened their resolve against him.

On 3 May 1679, a party of militant Covenanters caught up with the archbishop's carriage as it carried him across a desolate heath called Magus Muir, about three or four miles from St Andrews, following a visit to Ceres. According to Bishop Gilbert Burnet:

'They seeing this concluded, according to their frantic enthusiastic notions, that God had now delivered up their greatest enemy into

their hands. Seven of them made up to the coach, while the rest were as scouts riding all about the moor. One of them fired a pistol at [Archbishop Sharp], which burnt his coat and gown, but did not go into his body. Upon this they fancied he had a magical secret to secure him against a shot; and they drew him out of his coach, and

Sharp's daughter Isabel tried in vain to protect her father. (© Terry Parker/ Mary Evans Picture Library)

*murdered him barbarously, repeating their strokes till they were quite
sure he was dead. And so they got clear off, no body happening to go
cross the moor all the while.'*

Sharp was aged about 61 when he was assassinated and his end was pitiful.
He pleaded with the ringleader, 'I know you are a gentleman... you will
protect me!' before he was struck so violently on the head that his skull was
broken and his brains spattered upon the ground. His daughter, who had been
travelling with him, witnessed his death.

Encouraged by Sharp's murder, the Covenanters decided to risk a full-
scale confrontation with the government. But although they met with initial
successes against government troops during the Battle of Drumclog, a
Royalist army from the south, under the king's illegitimate son, James, Duke
of Monmouth, crushed the rebel Covenanters at Bothwell Bridge on 22 June
1679. Five Covenanters captured during the fighting were later hanged for
allegedly protecting the murderers of Archbishop Sharp.

Monmouth's rout proved the undoing of the Covenanters as a warlike
threat to the government. During a subsequent violent skirmish at a place
called Airds Moss, southeast of Kilmarnock, on 22 July 1680, the extremist
Covenanter leader, Richard Cameron, was shot dead alongside numerous
others. The Royalist party are said to have suffered twenty-eight fatalities.
Captured during this clash was David Hackston of Rathillet, leader of those
who assassinated Archbishop Sharp. He is said to have been executed with
the utmost brutality, seeing his hands cut off before his heart was extracted
from his chest. Following this excruciating death, he was decapitated. His
head, along with that of Cameron, was fixed on the Netherbow port,
Edinburgh. His lopped-off hands were displayed before his cadaver, in a
gruesome parody of an act of prayer.

Four years after Archbishop Sharp's murder, another of the assassins,
Andrew Guillan, a Balmerino weaver, was tried, found guilty and executed
in Edinburgh. His head was fixed up at Cupar, and his body was hung in
chains on Magus Muir on 22 July 1683.

Around this time, repression of the Covenanters approached something
akin to a policy of deliberate extermination in Scotland; skirmishes were
fought, martyrs were created and the era came to be known as 'The Killing
Time'. One of the atrocities committed against them was of such spectacular
proportions that it defies belief. This concerned the deaths of around 200
prisoners taken after the Battle of Bothwell Bridge, who were simply allowed
to drown on a transportation vessel that sank during a storm in the Eynhallow

Sound, Orkney Islands, on 30 November 1679. The vessel's captain, William Paterson, forbade any of his men to open the hatches, although this simple act of mercy might have allowed most of the prisoners to save themselves. In March 1680, Captain Paterson was actually compensated by the Privy Council for the incidental losses he sustained in the shipwreck.

The Killing Time reached a dismal new low with the execution of two women on the mud and sand of Wigtown Bay, around fifty-five miles west of Dumfries on the remote western Scottish coast. Having refused to swear an oath of abjuration renouncing the Covenant, Margaret Lauchlane, aged about 63, and Margaret Wilson, perhaps aged about 18, were both condemned to death for noncompliance by the Laird of Lagg. Sir Robert Grierson, later known as 'Cruel Lagg', completely ignored a pardon recommended by Edinburgh's Privy Council. On 11 May 1685, the pair were forced onto their knees, tied to stakes on a slope within the sea-mark and then ordered to recant as the water level gradually rose over them.

The murderous execution of the two women was just one enormity among many and the cycle was aggravated by a low-level form of guerrilla warfare that developed among the Covenanters in reaction to their persecution. On 8 November 1684, James Renwick's *Apologetical Declaration* was affixed to a great many market crosses and kirk doors; this was a manifesto condemning government severities against the Presbyterians. Shortly after its publication, two soldiers of the Life Guard, Kennoway and Stuart, were murdered in the parish of Livingston, West Lothian, on 22 November. Although a Commission was appointed to terrorise the community and find the assassins, those who murdered the two soldiers were never identified. Both men were killed in cold blood exiting the door of a house in 'Swine-abbay' and bore reputations for abuses committed against innocent people during the Killing Time in the name of the government, according to Robert Wodrow's 1722 account in *History of the Sufferings of the Church of Scotland*.

In December 1684, the curate of Carsphairn, Mr Peter Peirson, was in his manse alone when it was besieged by at least six men intent on coercing him into renouncing Catholicism and protecting the Presbyterians. Peirson answered his door armed, so one among the group, James MacMichael, shot him dead with a pistol. Robert Wodrow wrote of the murderers:

'I only remark further, that, Mitchel, Herron, and MacMichael were all of them killed one way or other this year… this is the fullest account I can give of this matter.'

Lethal skirmishes, tit-for-tat abuses, murderous government repression and inhuman detention occurred continually throughout this period in Scottish history. In February 1688, James Renwick, the aforementioned agitator, was hanged in Edinburgh's Grassmarket. He is generally considered the last of the Covenanter martyrs but although James II proclaimed religious tolerance for Presbyterians in June 1687, Renwick's execution continued to portray the establishment – and the new monarch – as oppressive and tyrannical.

TUMULTS OF THE GLORIOUS REVOLUTION

England's so-called Glorious Revolution of 1688, which overthrew King James II and placed Prince William of Orange and his wife Mary – James's daughter – on the throne, is sometimes described as a bloodless coup, although this was not the case.

William of Orange landed at Brixham, Devon, on 5 November with 12,000 European infantry and 3,000 cavalry; once again England began to slide in the direction of civil conflict. One of the early supporters of the revolution against King James II was John, 3rd Lord Lovelace, whose ancestral home was Ladye Place at Hurley in Berkshire. During a march to join the prince, the 48-year-old Lord Lovelace and his party of around 100 horsemen were engaged on 14 November 1688 by a company under Captain Lorange. The clash occurred at Cirencester, a Gloucestershire market town, when Lovelace resolved to battle his way through Lorange's men. In all, around seven or eight people were killed, including the captain and his son, with others wounded. Another among those who died was Bulstrode Whitelocke, a neighbour of Lovelace's. The Cirencester parish register of burials says he was 'kil'd at the King's Head' in the Market Place. In the end, Lovelace was overpowered, and he and thirteen of his men were conducted to Cirencester gaol, somehow avoiding being summarily executed.

Occurring almost simultaneously with Lovelace's insurrection, revolutionary tumult against King James – still just about the ruling monarch at this point – began to develop in London among the people. Luttrell noted in his diary that a number of apprentices engaged in pulling down Catholic chapels in Lincoln's Inn Fields and St John's were killed by James's soldiers, highlighting the developing schism. A coroner's jury brought in 'murder' verdicts against the troops around 17 November, in direct opposition to the monarchy.

According to correspondence received by a civil servant in Ireland, John Ellis, there were other military engagements fought. On 24 November 1688, he understood that the king was intending to take command of his whole

Approximate site of the almost-forgotten Battle of Wincanton.

army on Salisbury Plain, Wiltshire and that, 'It is generally said, the advance guards of both armies have had some sharp encounters, and many men killed on both sides.' One particularly bloody collision occurred at Wincanton, Somerset, when Colonel Sarsefield, commanding a detached party of horse and dragoons, engaged an advance party of foot; the colonel, who was for King James, killed about thirty 'rebels' and had four more hanged. Of his own men, six died in the battle, including the son of a colonel called Webb. The exact location of the clash is in doubt, but in 1903 the Wincanton historian George Sweetman placed it in the eastern part of the town, at Coylton Terrace. This is near a steeply-sided rise at Bayford Hill; although somewhere along Lawrence Hill has also been suggested as the site.

In reaction to this, Charles Schombergh (later the 2nd Duke of Schombergh) annihilated a force of Royalists 'upon Doncaster road', killing fifty-three out of sixty-five combatants and refusing to give any quarter whatsoever to his opponents. Schombergh, a pro-William mercenary, was experienced in warfare; he is held to have acted so ruthlessly because Sarsefield had behaved likewise.

On 11 December 1688, Ellis learned that the Prince of Orange was expected to arrive in Oxford shortly, although his advance had been briefly halted by a bloody encounter with King James's forces 'about Reading on Saturday night or Sunday'. Around fifty of the king's dragoons under Colonel Butler were killed, and the colonel failed utterly to stop the prince's progress onwards.

It took just six weeks for William of Orange to become undisputed ruler of England. In the end, James II was deserted by his demoralised army, his court, the common people and even members of his own family, like his younger daughter Anne. The Catholic monarch became convinced he was to be assassinated, so first arranged for his wife and heir to escape safely before escaping the capital himself on 11 December. This he did in the early hours of the morning, in disguise and famously dropping the Great Seal into the dirty waters of the Thames as he escaped by boat at Vauxhall. When his flight became common knowledge, revolutionary rioting engulfed London and other towns, with the mob sacking embassies and Catholic properties.

Around this time, a great rumour swept the nation that Irish sections of James II's army were preparing to massacre as many people as they could in London and elsewhere. This, mercifully, proved to be false information, but on 14 December an Irish trooper fired a carbine while riding a horse at Henry Fitzroy, 1st Duke of Grafton – a nephew of the deposed king who had nonetheless helped the revolution. Grafton was at the head of his regiment in the Strand at the time, which was marching to Tilbury Fort in Essex. The shot missed the duke, the assassin being immediately killed in a melee that followed, one of his grace's soldiers shooting the man dead. Fearing this was the start of the Irish revenge, panic swept the city anew, amid general anti-Catholic rioting.

There were some incidents, but they were isolated. Following the king's flight, an Irish regiment was ejected from Tilbury Fort on the Essex side of the River Thames. These troops crossed the water and committed violent disorder at Gravesend, Kent, before seizing a richly laden ship in the river bound for Smyrna. In attempting to take off they ran the vessel aground, and so were stopped – although not without the loss of several lives in an ensuing violent skirmish with great numbers of people.

However, nothing was as titanic as the battles of the civil war - quite simply because the Prince of Orange's revolution was a popular one. William of Orange's forces entered London on 18 December 1688 and took the city. King James II was picked up by a large group of fishermen while attempting to leave England by sea. They attacked him, robbing him of jewels and guineas, then carried him to Faversham, Kent, after which he was returned as a prisoner to the capital. The desperate monarch is said to have been sick with grief and fear by this time, particularly so when he found the Prince of Orange installed at Windsor, as though already ruler of the three kingdoms.

William exiled James II, who immediately escaped to Rochester and took a ship to France. The throne of England was declared vacant by the House of Commons and jointly offered to the new arrivals, William and his wife Mary.

Chapter 12

Judicial Murder

In the second chapter, we looked at the threats that each royal and ruler faced throughout the seventeenth century. In this chapter, we look at the other side of the coin – the abuses they themselves committed to keep their positions secure.

It would be a fair assessment to say that no monarch or government of the seventeenth century escaped getting blood on their hands, either directly or by proxy. Queen Elizabeth I, as mentioned earlier, baulked at the judicial assassination of Mary, Queen of Scots, largely because she dreaded being seen in the eyes of Europe as someone who would sacrifice a fellow queen for her own safety. After much prevarication, the execution was carried out nonetheless at her instruction in 1587, although Elizabeth blamed everyone but herself. This almost-medieval practice of cold-bloodedly disposing of one's own political enemies was something carried into the Stuart era.

The threats the monarchs of the day faced were extreme; therefore, their retaliation was also extreme, often mirroring a lethal purge. Although such cases were processed through the courts and legal system, the necessity of a 'just' verdict often meant the law was frequently circumvented in an illegal or dictatorial manner. Quite often, in reality what it amounted to was murder in its purest form, although of a more subtle and protracted nature, carried out in such a way as to minimise the stain on the ruler's character.

That murder occurred in forms now difficult to appreciate is perhaps best illustrated by the case of the already-referenced Sir Walter Raleigh; his is a good example of how someone need not be overtly murdered when they could be manoeuvred from the political scene to their demise by enemies more cunning or powerful than they.

Following the death of Elizabeth, the rivalry that had sprung up between Robert Cecil, the Secretary of State, and Raleigh, Captain of the Guard, found a victor in Cecil – the man who had for some time been in secret negotiations with James in Scotland concerning the succession. With the new king's

The mound of Fotheringhay Castle, where Elizabeth had Mary, Queen of Scots killed.

backing, the wily Cecil was far too strong an opponent for Raleigh; the latter was soon deprived of his offices and implicated in a treasonous plot.

On 17 November 1603, a Special Commission was held at Winchester – London having been hit by an outbreak of plague – during which Raleigh was charged with having conspired with Lord Cobham to place Arabella Stuart, a near relation of the king, and descended equally from Henry VII, onto the English throne, dispossessing James. Raleigh's alleged involvement rested solely on the accusations of Lord Cobham himself, who had been persuaded to testify against him. Raleigh defended himself ably with a calm and noble demeanour, leading one contemporary letter writer to observe that the claims against him were 'no more to be weighed than the barking of a dog'. Despite Raleigh's accurate assertion that, by law, two witnesses were required against him for a conviction, Cecil nonetheless desired his removal from public life – and thus he was found guilty and sentenced to die.

Raleigh's eloquence found him support among the common people and in the end, he was reprieved, along with others, including Cobham. However, he was sentenced to a lengthy term of imprisonment in the Tower of London, which he endured until 1616. By that time, Arabella Stuart had died while herself a prisoner in the Tower; Cobham – still imprisoned – had meanwhile grown old and sick.

The plot Raleigh had been connected with became known as the 'Main', but there was another supposed conspiracy at the time too: the 'Bye Plot', otherwise known as 'the treason of the priests'. The object of this was to kidnap King James I, and several were executed or gaoled for their alleged involvement. But Raleigh's imprisonment was not too harsh, by the standards of the time; his wife was permitted to live with him and he had access to the Lieutenant of the Tower's garden. Interestingly, he would also have been one of the Tower's prisoners at the time a wicked and cold-blooded assassination occurred elsewhere within the walls of this mighty fortress – the killing of Sir Thomas Overbury (see Chapter 2).

After his release on 20 March 1616, Raleigh was yet fit and well enough to raise a fleet of vessels to search for the fabled gold-mine of El Dorado in South America. His release was mediated by the infamous courtier George Villiers and his expedition was given the approval of the king, both of whom desired a percentage of the profits if the enterprise was successful.

This was Raleigh's second attempt to locate El Dorado, but it fared worse than the first, suffering much violent confrontation with the Spanish on that far-away continent as it did. By the time Raleigh returned home to the British Isles almost a broken man, negotiations were in process to arrange a marriage between King James's second son Charles and the Infanta of Spain. To encourage this union, Raleigh was apprehended upon a charge of having fraudulently pretended he had gone to South America to discover a mine, when his (alleged) real object was to make piratical attacks upon the Spanish settlements. In the end, Raleigh was sacrificed by King James I for the dual motives of placating the Spanish royal house and failing to deliver any wealth following his mission to South America. Therefore, it was determined at length that Raleigh's former death sentence – questionable in itself – should be reinstated.

After a by-the-numbers show trial at Westminster, Raleigh was again sentenced to death on 28 October 1618; the following morning he was decapitated by the executioner in the Old Palace Yard. The end of this adventurous man is said to have been worthy of the last of Queen Elizabeth's great heroes.

More importantly, for our purposes his exit presents a good illustration of a 'judicial murder'. There is no doubt that Raleigh was callously and politically sacrificed, his death having been unjustly engineered via a corrupted legal process, as well as devious, ruthless political enemies – and a king who chose to look the other way.

The following is a chronology of just some of the legal travesties and dubious executions that besmirched each reign throughout the seventeenth century.

THE AFTERMATH OF THE GUNPOWDER PLOT

Following the failure of the Gunpowder Plot in the capital in November 1605, a number of prominent conspirators who had headed to the Midlands in anticipation of a planned uprising, took refuge in Holbeche, a house located between Stourbridge and Wombourne belonging to one of their friends, Stephen Littleton. Although depleted by desertions, those who remained at Holbeche prepared to defend the house against military assault, despite by now being tired, hungry and wet. While drying piles of plundered gunpowder out before the fire they suffered further misfortune when a spark jumped from the hearth and ignited the powder. This caused a small inferno that engulfed the ringleader, Robert Catesby and two others, John Grant and Ambrose Rockwood, seriously injuring them. Worse, Richard Walsh, the Sheriff of Worcestershire, who headed a company of some 200 men, was pursuing them with urgency. The hue and cry that had begun in London following Guy Fawkes's arrest had quickly spread throughout the country and the traitors' plundering as they made their way had naturally left a singular trail for Walsh to track, allowing him to follow the clues from Warwick Castle.

Holbeche House was surrounded on the morning of 8 November 1605. A shooting melee erupted, musket fire being poured into the house despite those within (it is believed) being primarily armed only with swords. Nonetheless, it appears they were resolved to die for their cause. Thomas Winter was the first casualty, felled by a shot to the shoulder while crossing the courtyard. He was not killed however, and nor was Rockwood, who – not yet having recovered from the gunpowder accident – was similarly injured.

Brothers John and Christopher Wright were fatally wounded, as were Robert Catesby and Thomas Percy (reportedly by the same musket ball) before the battle was over. Percy was a relation of the Earl of Northumberland, and constable of Alnwick Castle, who was married to the Wrights' sister. Members of the sheriff's party then stormed the property and, in an unseemly spectacle, are said to have stripped the bodies of those men who lay dead and dying from their injuries. A number of holes can still be pointed out on the façade of Holbeche to this day, from shots fired into the building.

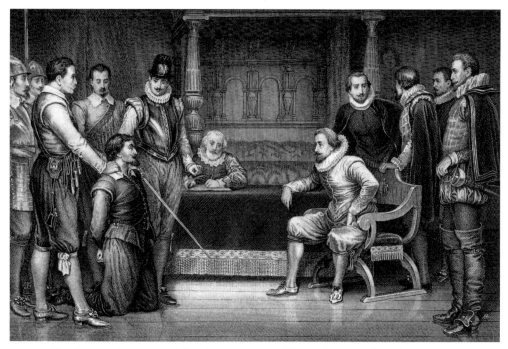

Fawkes was interrogated in the presence of James I: unattributed engraving after J M L Ralston. (© Terry Parker/Mary Evans Picture Library)

That Catesby and Percy were in fact assassinated during the incident on the orders of the Secretary of State, Robert Cecil, has long been suspected by historians. One circumstance not easy to explain is that John Streete, the man who killed the pair, received for his service a handsome pension of two shillings a day for life. This was a suspiciously large reward for killing two practically unarmed men from behind a tree in cold blood - an action that involved no personal risk on Streete's part, and denied the government an opportunity to interrogate two of the principal suspects.

Could it be possible that among the plotters there was a double-agent, acting as a decoy duck to lure the others to destruction? Numerous theories suggest that this traitor among the traitors may have been Thomas Percy himself, who was in fact assassinated, alongside Catesby, upon the specific orders of Sir Robert Cecil, the Secretary of State, in whose employ Percy had secretly been all along. It has long been rumoured that Cecil, wishing to eliminate dangerous witnesses in the form of the two men, gave the following urgent order: 'Let me never see them alive.'

Streete's annuity was a reward for committing the act, and helping avoid an embarrassing episode that might have brought to light testimony

230

suggesting the government was engaged in a deliberate policy of entrapment and subjugation.

It is interesting to note that something resembling a religious purge followed the deaths of those directly involved in the conspiracy. A number of characters peripheral to the plot began to feel the full force of the law and the executions spread beyond London. For instance, Stephen Littleton, the owner of Holbeche, who escaped the premises, was captured at Hagley in Worcestershire and eventually executed at Stafford. His uncle Humphrey Littleton was hanged, drawn and quartered on 7 April 1606 at Red Hill outside Worcester, primarily for attempting to harbour fugitives including his nephew. There were others, but by now the purge had taken on a purely religious dimension.

There were disturbing elements to the prolonged proceedings. A Jesuit priest named Henry Garnet was implicated by Thomas Bates, Catesby's arrested servant, and discovered in concealment at Hindlip House, near Worcester. He was examined before the Privy Council on 13 February 1606, and the examinations were often repeated, but no amount of persuasion or threats could induce Garnet to confess his involvement in the plot. Evidence of some nature was therefore obtained by devious means, Garnet at length acknowledging that an intention to blow up the Parliament House had been revealed to him by an absconded Jesuit called Tesmond, who had learnt of it during confession from Catesby and another plotter. He maintained, however, that he had attempted to dissuade Catesby from his treasonous purpose. Garnet's trial occurred on 28 March and he defended himself with ability and courage; however, he was convicted on the very same day, although further interrogation postponed his execution in London until 3 May 1606.

Nicholas Owen, another Jesuit lay-brother, little taller than a dwarf and credited with designing numerous secretive priest-holes, was also apprehended at Hindlip House. He was subsequently tortured to death in the Tower of London while being interrogated. The wholly questionable aspect of executions like these can be gleaned from the fate of a Jesuit called Hall, Garnet's companion at Hindlip and in the Tower, who was executed at Worcester. Hall was not shown to have been privy to the plot previous to its discovery, being condemned merely by association and – seemingly – for his reluctance to condemn the plotters' aspirations in strong-enough terms.

Of delayed fallout from the Gunpowder Plot, it is worth observing the case of Peter Heywood, whose family originated from Heywood, near Rochdale. Heywood was a justice of the peace and a lawyer, who was instrumental in searching the Westminster cellars and discovering the gunpowder during Baron Thomas Knyvet's famous raid of 1605. In fact, it was he who actually apprehended Guy Fawkes in the act of leaving the vault, taking from him a lantern in the process, which can now be seen in Oxford's Ashmolean Museum. Heywood continued to be a prominent persecutor of Catholics until one day in November 1640, when he was stabbed in the side with a rusty dagger by a man during a visit to the Court of Requests, Westminster Hall. The attacker reproached Heywood during the incident for persecuting innocent Catholics, and turned out to be a Brussels-educated Dominican friar from Kent, John James. When James's lodgings were searched, and his landlord interrogated, it emerged that he had travelled deliberately to Westminster on the day 'to do that mischief'. It also became apparent he was aware of his victim's minor role in suppressing the Gunpowder Plot thirty-five years earlier. Justice Heywood did not die immediately of his wound, although the injury is likely to have contributed greatly to his death some fourteen months later.

As for the assassin, on 2 August 1641 there was:

> 'a great debate upon the Bill read against Mr James, a Papist, for stabbing Justice Heywood; the purport of the Bill being, that his right hand be cut off, his lands be disposed of, and [he be sentenced to] imprisonment during [his majesty's] Pleasure.'

LEFT TO ROT IN THE TOWER

When ministers fell out of favour it was often catastrophic for them, with imprisonment and financial ruin sometimes the result. Such a victim was the English statesman Sir John Eliot, whose death – like Raleigh with his father – left an indelible stain on Charles I's character.

Although Sir John was a monarchist, believing the king had a role in constitutional government, he was still fiercely opposed to King Charles's authoritarian style. His leading role in the House of Commons' violent disruption of 1629, which led to the dissolving of Parliament, infuriated Charles and earned Sir John a term of imprisonment in the Tower.

Correspondence written by an intimate acquaintance, John Pory, on 15 November 1632 reads:

> 'The same night, Monday, having met with Sir John Eliot's attorney in St Paul's churchyard, he told me he had been that morning with Sir John in the Tower, and found him so far spent with his consumption as not like to live a week longer.'

When Sir John fell ill, he begged to be allowed to leave the Tower so as to recuperate, promising to return when his health was stronger to finish his sentence. However, King Charles felt the request was not sufficiently humble, largely on account of Sir John's refusal to acknowledge any guilt for his pro-Parliament, pro-people stance during the disorder of 1629.

On 27 November 1632 Sir John Eliot died aged 40. Immediately after the event, his son petitioned the king, requesting permission to remove the body to Cornwall for burial at the family estate. However, this the king refused, stating coldly: 'Lett Sir John Eliot's body be buried in the church of that parishe where he dyed.' The great statesman's body was afterwards thrust in some obscure corner of the Tower church.

This petty act of vindictiveness, designed to wreak a final indignity on Sir John's remains, nonetheless had the effect in Parliamentary circles of elevating the dead man's status to that of a martyr.

PARLIAMENTARY ABUSES

One incident in particular highlighting the burgeoning power struggle between Charles I and Parliament concerns the fate of Thomas Wentworth, 1st Earl of Strafford. Strafford, one of the king's most unpopular advisors, having been denounced in the House of Commons as 'that grand apostate to the common-wealth', was impeached and imprisoned at the end of 1640, with any diplomatic attempt by the king to save him being conspicuously absent. Strafford, a former Lord Deputy of Ireland, was tyrannical, unpopular and arrogant, yet brave and well-versed in legal matters. John Pym, a Parliamentarian who led the anti-monarchist factions, was determined to remove Strafford from the outset; he viewed him as Charles's ablest minister and therefore Parliament's greatest threat. In compiling a case for treason against Strafford, much useful data came from the Irish Catholic gentry, who were united with the English politicians in their hatred of him. One of the main charges against the earl was that he was preparing to bring an army from Ireland to enforce an absolute monarchy and by this tyranny subvert the fundamental laws of the kingdom.

Howsoever this may have been, Strafford's continual denial of treasonable practices was emphatic; how could anyone be guilty of treason if they were following their sovereign's wishes? The fact that said policies were anti-Parliament was academic, he argued. The earl's trial collapsed in disarray on 10 April 1641, so the Commons next drafted, and passed, a Bill of Attainder which declared Strafford 'guilty' without a need for the formalities of a trial. The bill, however, still needed to be passed through the House of Lords, and finally, signed by the king himself.

Therefore, the earl's life hung in the balance. Ironically, his fate was sealed by a plot designed to help him. A force of around 100 Royalists, under a mercenary named Captain Billingsley, sought to occupy the Tower of London, where Strafford was imprisoned, but failed to gain access. Their intention had been to release the earl and escort him to Ireland so that he might raise an army; when news of the abortive attempt swept London, it developed into wild rumours of a grand Royalist coup backed by 1,500 armed men in Lancashire under the Catholic Earl of Worcester. On 5 May 1641, John Pym told the Commons an exaggerated story that suggested troops from France were sailing towards Portsmouth to assist in a monarchist coup. The Bill of Attainder was passed by the House of Lords on 10 May, it perhaps being the case that they saw no possible way of bringing the entire matter to an end other than to agree to Strafford's execution. King Charles – hopelessly outmanoeuvred and with public opinion in London on Parliament's side – was forced to sign Strafford's death warrant. On 12 May 1641, the earl – known as 'Black Tom Tyrant' to his many enemies – was decapitated by an executioner who brought an axe down onto his neck. His death took place on Tower Hill, and when the executioner held up Strafford's head a roar of approval swept through the ranks of the crowd.

In many ways, the Earl of Strafford's execution is the classic example of a judicial murder. The case against him was not strong, yet his death was the only outcome that would have satisfied both the English public and Parliamentary ambitions. Revenge must also have been scented by the House of Commons, as in his earlier days Strafford had been a Parliamentarian who had originally opposed royal policies, before switching sides. It is also clear the actions of the House of Commons were every bit as underhand and dictatorial as the accusations they levelled at Strafford. In direct opposition to the king, the House of Commons had demonstrated that they possessed an awesome power to manoeuvre the assassination of a political opponent legally without fear of reprisals from their sovereign. What is most apparent, however, is Charles I's weakening position; the case of Strafford was creating a schism throughout the nation, drawing in the Irish and also the Scottish Covenanters, who similarly despised the earl. The king recognised that Strafford had to die in order to rein in a situation that was sliding out of control, so to this end he sacrificed his most competent advisor to forestall a national civil war.

Of course, it merely delayed one. Four years later, in the midst of a constitutional struggle that had turned into armed conflict, Parliament passed another dubious, high-profile death sentence upon William Laud, the 71-year-

Portrait of Strafford, after an original by Sir Anthony van Dyck. (courtesy of Warwick Castle)

old Archbishop of Canterbury. Laud, another of King Charles's most unpopular advisors, having been denounced in the House of Commons as 'the centre from whence our miseries flow', was imprisoned in the Tower in February 1641, following his impeachment the previous December. As with Strafford, the king did next to nothing to save him.

By the time moves were made to bring the archbishop to trial on treason charges, it was October 1643 and the House of Commons' power had grown immensely, to the detriment of the House of Lords, whose power had waned significantly during the interim. Nonetheless, when the archbishop's trial began it was before the House of Lords. Following months of legal to-ing and fro-ing, the prisoner ultimately presented a very eloquent defence of himself on 11 November 1644. In fact, so weak did the case against him gradually become that a schism between the upper and lower Houses threatened to see him set free. However, it is clear the House of Commons was determined to seek Laud's death, and they attempted to secure the matter by passing a Bill of Attainder that very same day among themselves before next manoeuvring a weakened House of Lords into giving the bill their legal backing. Both Houses sentenced the archbishop to be executed on 10 January 1645. A pardon by the king being completely over-ruled, the clergyman was beheaded on Tower Hill, the executioner severing his head with one almighty stroke. Archbishop Laud's friends were permitted to take his body to All Hallows Barking Church nearby for burial.

Much of this, in fact, stemmed from a form of revenge. Many supporters of Parliament were Puritans, a kind of extreme Protestantism. Bitterly opposed to the Catholic Church, and also the established English religion, the Puritans believed churches and services should be simpler, or purified. Bishops and archbishops were despised, since the Puritans equated these positions with Catholicism; Laud was a natural enemy because he had overseen the pillorying and mutilation of three Puritan opponents in 1637 in the name of King Charles. Therefore, once in the hands of the Parliamentarians, Laud stood no chance of a reprieve. The fact that his trial bore the façade of a legitimate exercise (the prisoner being allowed a legal team, etc.) meant little. Whatever his politics, Laud was in effect assassinated via the judicial system by a group of people who desired nothing but his death.

THE MAN WHO KILLED THE KING
By 1646, King Charles I's waning circumstances on the battlefields of England had forced him to attempt reconciliation with the Scottish Presbyterian Covenanters. After escaping Oxford in disguise, he presented himself to the Scottish Commissioners at Southwell, Nottinghamshire, who 'escorted' him north in what was semi-captivity, but still the lesser of two evils. However, the *de facto* Scottish Parliament saw Charles as a bargaining chip, and demanded he convert to Presbyterianism – the root of their battle with the Scottish Royalists. They also demanded the imposition of the Covenant, confirming the Presbyterian national church.

The Naseby battlefield, where the tide of war is generally considered to have turned against the king in 1645.

At the same time, the English Parliamentarians put the 'Propositions of Newcastle' to Charles, in an effort to define the terms that would end the conflict. Despite his situation, the monarch remained aloof, instead making a masterful attempt to exploit the differences between the Scottish and English politicians' aspirations, while agreeing to neither.

In the end, the Scots simply lost patience with Charles, and handed him over to the Parliamentarians at Newcastle in January 1647. For a while, he was kept under house arrest at Holdenby (Holmby) House, seven miles from Northampton. Although the wider conflict dragged on in the background and violent schisms began to develop among the Parliamentarians themselves, for Charles, the military campaigning was all but over.

An escape from house arrest in November 1647 and a noble self-exile on the Isle of Wight followed, from where he attempted a second treaty with the Scots. But Charles's end was ultimately set in motion by General Henry Ireton; this man was Oliver Cromwell's son-in-law, and it was he who

King Charles I spent his last night as a free man at the Saracen's Head Inn in Southwell, Nottinghamshire.

presented the English Parliament with the *Remonstrance of the Army*, a manifesto demanding that the king be put on trial for having been instrumental in starting the entire war.

Towards the end of 1648 a motion was passed to allow Charles to return to London, but this journey from the Isle of Wight he undertook as a Parliamentary prisoner. By this point, Charles's campaign was on the back foot militarily and all his negotiations had been conducted from a weakened position. Oliver Cromwell had also by now joined Ireton in the clamour for Charles to be held accountable as a bloody tyrant who had torn the nation apart.

On 27 January 1649, Parliament concluded a trial in Westminster Hall that condemned the king to death for treason; while Cromwell and Ireton collected the requisite signatures for his majesty's death warrant, the king all the time refused to recognise the legitimacy of the proceedings in any manner. He declared it was 'the freedom and liberty of the people of England' that were in effect being tried, and General Sir Thomas Fairfax – so instrumental in the Royalist downfall – refused to participate in signing the warrant. But it meant nothing; like others before him, King Charles stood no chance from the moment his trial ensued.

King Charles's execution occurred at about two o'clock on the afternoon of 30 January 1649. The previous evening, he slept at St James's and the following day he was led to a scaffold erected in front of the Banqueting House, in the street now Whitehall, London. There was a tense delay when it was pointed out to Cromwell that the law demanded the Prince of Wales must be proclaimed king once his father was dead, so Charles was ushered into an ante-room to wait while Parliament rushed through three readings of a Bill that made the succession an illegal act.

According to one account of 1666, the king 'was conveyed thorow the Banquetting-house, and a way being made through the great window he came upon the scaffold.' The executioner and an assistant, both of them disguised with hoods, awaited him. The day was bitterly cold and huge numbers of soldiers separated the scaffold from the rank and file common people; so much so that Charles's final speech – in which he famously declared he was transcending from 'a corruptible to an incorruptible crown' – went largely unheard by most except those in the immediate vicinity. He also forgave 'even those in particular that have been the chief causers of my death.' The chopping block was unusually low, and when the time came Charles was forced to lie on his front, rather than kneel, to be beheaded. His last words instructed the executioner to 'Stay for the sign'. The executioner replied, 'Yes I will, and please your majesty. 'Following a short pause, the executioner in one blow severed the king's head from his body, before holding it up for the crowd to see and shouting, 'Behold the head of a traitor!' At the moment the blow was struck, a universal groan issued from the crowd. As soon as the execution was over, two troops of horse assisted in the dispersal of the multitude, many of whom were pressing forward to obtain some memorial of Charles's blood.

The groan that swept through the ranks of the people present was not necessarily in sympathy with Charles. It was more to do with the realisation that the country had reached such a dismal low point it had become necessary to commit the unbelievable crime of regicide. After the execution, the king's body was embalmed on the orders of Sir Thomas Herbert and William Juxon, Bishop of London, and subsequently removed to St James's. Thereafter the remains were conveyed to Windsor, where they were silently interred, without ceremony, on 7 February in a vault about the middle of the choir of St George's Chapel.

This portrait is believed to depict the executed king – after his head was sewn back on prior to interment. (Courtesy of Chetham's Library)

Although the men instrumental in arranging the king's death are known to history, the man who physically committed the regicide was masked and his identity is not known with any conclusiveness. That said, the single-stroke decapitation was carried out professionally, so it is highly likely the executioner was experienced. This has led to the supposition that it was Richard Brandon, 'headsman and hang-man to the pretended Parliament', and the same man who had decapitated the Earl of Strafford in 1641, who committed the deed.

Curiously, Brandon died himself a few months later, on 20 June 1649. Following his death, a pamphlet was published entitled *The Confession of Richard Brandon*, which alleged he had admitted he was the man who had killed the king; this revelation was supposedly made while Brandon lay on his deathbed in Rosemary Lane. It is said that his health took an immediate downturn following the act because the king never forgave the executioner, although he forgave Cromwell and the others for his death. Thus, guilt, visions and depression plagued Brandon until his death. It is also said that when Brandon was being interred in Whitechapel, the mob threatened to grab his corpse and bury it in a dunghill, or else chop it to pieces – suggesting they, at least, believed him to be the one responsible for physically killing Charles I.

If this is indeed the case, then the executioner's masked assistant would very likely have been Ralph Jones, a Rosemary Lane ragman who acted as Brandon's second.

'CRUEL NECESSITY'

The night after King Charles was beheaded, Lord Southampton and a friend of his got leave to sit up by the body in the Banqueting House at Whitehall. As they were sitting there, very melancholy, about two in the morning, they heard the tread of somebody coming very slowly up the stairs. Next, the door opened and a man entered whose face was hidden by a cloak. This mysterious man approached the body, which he considered very attentively for some time, before shaking his head, sighing, and murmuring, 'Cruel necessity!' He then departed in the same slow, deliberate manner he had come in. Lord Southampton could not distinguish anything of his face, but from the voice and gait he easily guessed the mysterious visitor had been Oliver Cromwell himself.

Even before his elevation to the dictatorial position of Lord Protector of England in 1653, Cromwell's many enemies never missed an opportunity to lay secret murders at his door. When Robert Devereux, 3rd Earl of Essex, died on 14 September 1646, without any indication he had been ill, it was widely put about that Cromwell, or one of his inner circle, had poisoned him. The supposed reason for this was that, although the earl was a Parliamentarian and thus an ally of Cromwell and Fairfax, both men envied and feared him as the greatest threat to their burgeoning military powerbase because of his singular ability.

Devereux had died unexpectedly following a stag-hunt in Windsor Forest, and although Cromwell is said to have been 'wonderfully exalted' by his death, one of the latter's distant descendants, also Oliver, observed realistically in 1822:

> 'Whatever might be the imperfections of Cromwell's character, a disposition to rid himself of his enemies by assassination was not one of them.'

It is possible that allegations of this nature haunted Cromwell because of his cousin, Robert Cromwell. During Whitsun 1632, Robert, aged about 18, was tried for poisoning to death his master, a London attorney called Mr Joseph Lane. An inquisition interrogated an apothecary, four doctors and a servant, and decided on 29 May that 'Lane died a violent death by poison.' However, there remained a suspicion that the medicine had become accidentally contaminated before Robert Cromwell ever took receipt of it. The report was presented to the king himself, and a lack of data beyond this suggests an acquittal was forthcoming. By 1649, however, Royalist pamphleteers were happy to report that the youth had been executed, despite the questionability of the case against him. Sixteen years after this, the historian James Heath agreed in his *Flagellum* (1665) that Robert Cromwell had, in fact, been hanged.

It is true that the new order, in eliminating powerful opposition, did refrain from a full scale and bloody extermination, in England at least. The shift in the balance of power dictated that all those militarily opposed to Parliament were now considered traitors and prosecutions for treason were preferred to secret assassination or public massacre. But what passed for mercy under these circumstances could often be extremely cruel too, even whilst being lenient. John Poyer, the Mayor of Pembroke in south-west Wales, had formerly been an advocate of Parliament; but during the progression of the conflict in that part of the country he took against his former side. Learning that Cromwell himself was smashing his way through Wales to quell a Royalist insurrection in May 1648, Poyer declared he would be the first man to charge against the 'Ironsides' cavalry; that even if Cromwell wore a back of steel and a breast of iron he would still violently oppose him. However, Pembroke Castle surrendered on 31 May and Poyer – together with two other defenders, Laugharne and Powell – was conducted to London and imprisoned in the Tower.

There they remained prisoner until after the king's execution. They were then tried by Court Martial and sentenced to death. However, the new government was anxious to illustrate a degree of leniency, so a perverse lottery was organised. Cromwell consented to carry out the death sentence in only one instance, and therefore the prisoners were allowed to draw lots for their lives. On two of the lots was written 'Life given by God' whereas the third was blank. A young boy drew the lots, the fatal one being given to Colonel Poyer, who, on 21 April 1649, was shot in the Piazza, Covent Garden. He met his fate calmly and died like a soldier. Laugharne and Powell were ordered by the new government out of the country and into exile.

REVENGE OF THE 'MERRY MONARCH'
Following the restoring of the monarchy in 1660 there was a general clamour for stability, reconciliation and amnesty. Nonetheless, one of the first matters

Poyer was sentenced to death by a perverse lottery. (Courtesy of Pembroke Castle)

that occupied Charles II and his Parliament was the judicial punishment of those principally involved in the execution of his father.

This appears to have been a course of action Charles was determined upon, for he had declared as much just after his father's death eleven years earlier, during a speech in Jersey which hinted at nothing so much as pure revenge. He had stated at the time:

> *'Out of a bitter sense and indignation of those horrid proceedings against our dear father, we are, according to the laws of nature and justice, firmly resolved, by the assistance of Almighty God, though we perish alone in the enterprise, to be a severe avenger of his innocent blood, which was so barbarously spilt, and which calls aloud to Heaven for vengeance.'*

Subsequently, an Act of Free Pardon, Indemnity and Oblivion was issued by the two Houses and the new monarch, as to all treasons and political crimes committed between 1 January 1637 and 24 June 1660. However, this did not extend to those who participated in 'sentencing to death, or signing the instrument for the horrid murder, or being instrumental in taking away the precious life of our late sovereign Charles the First.' A lengthy list of the regicides was drawn up, and nineteen who surrendered in the hope of mercy were granted their lives, suffering various harsh terms of imprisonment instead, although others who were implicated escaped the country. Although some were subsequently pardoned, ten regicides were nonetheless executed throughout October 1660 during what might be described as a revengeful, tyrannical exercise in judicial murder.

Typical of the grim public scenes that ensued was the execution of Thomas Harrison, son of a Newcastle-under-Lyme butcher, who had been appointed by Cromwell to transport Charles I from Windsor to his trial, afterwards sitting as one of his judges. Pepys observed on 13 October 1660:

> *'I went out to Charing Cross, to see Major-general Harrison hanged, drawn and quartered; which was done there, he looking as cheerful as any man could do in that condition. He was presently cut down, and his head and heart shewn to the people, at which there was great shouts of joy. It is said, that he said that he was sure to come shortly at the right hand of Christ to judge them that now had judged him; and that his wife do expect his coming again. Thus it was my chance to see the King beheaded at White Hall, and to see the first blood shed in revenge for the King at Charing Cross.'*

In 1662, three self-exiled men implicated in the king's death were executed, having been taken into custody by the alert English ambassador in the Netherlands and extradited to London. Pepys recorded on 19 April that year:

> *'This morning before we sat, I went to Aldgate; and at the corner shop, a draper's, I stood, and did see Barkestead, Okey, and Corbet, drawne towards the gallows at Tiburne; and there they were hanged and quartered. They all looked very cheerful; but I hear they all die defending what they did to the King to be just; which is very strange.'*

Throughout the prolonged proceedings numerous others were jailed for life, whilst some died languishing in gaol.

Perhaps even worse was the ritualistic posthumous execution of Oliver Cromwell and his late companions in regicide, Henry Ireton and John Bradshaw. On 29 January 1661, the corpses of these three were taken up out

After 300 years of being passed around, Cromwell's head ended up here at a secret location somewhere near the antechapel of Sidney Sussex College, Cambridge.

of their graves inside Westminster Abbey. When Cromwell's vault was opened, there was a particular clamour among the people to see his cadaver lifted out. There was a plan to treat a fourth regicide, Thomas Pride, in the same fashion, but this appears to have been aborted, probably because his corpse was too badly decayed for what the authorities had in mind. The bodies of the other three were taken to the Red Lion, Holborn, then drawn to Tyburn upon a sledge the following day – which was not only a day of fasting, but also the twelfth anniversary of King Charles I's own execution. All three cadavers were ritualistically hanged while still in their corpse-shrouds and left there until daylight began to fade. Cromwell, who had been excellently embalmed, in particular must have presented a disturbingly lifelike spectacle to Londoners, hanging in a 'green seare cloth' as he did. They were then cut down and buried in a pit beneath the gallows, but not before each corpse had been decapitated. Pepys later observed how their

One republican, Theophilus Brome, was so worried he would share Cromwell's fate that his will stated his head should be hidden within the walls of Higher Chilton Farm, to safeguard it against monarchists. He died in 1670, and his skull still resides in the house in Somerset.

heads had been 'set up at the further end of [Westminster] Hall.' He also noted:

> *'[It] do trouble me that a man of so great courage as he was should have that dishonour, though otherwise he might deserve it enough.'*

THE PUBLIC'S SCAPEGOAT

One especially controversial and unjust execution during Charles II's reign has been all but forgotten, despite occurring in the aftermath of a very famous event – London's 'Great Fire' of September 1666.

The devastating conflagration is famously believed to have started in Pudding Lane, off Eastcheap in central London, and by the end of it all thousands of houses and almost 100 churches had burnt down, including the

Norman Cathedral of St Paul, which collapsed inwards spectacularly. The number of people who died is said to have been miraculously low, however, in single figures in fact, although common sense would suggest it was a lot higher than promoted. Some bodies must have been simply vaporised; while in the aftermath scapegoats became persecuted, looting commenced and one can imagine that refugees began to starve, grow ill and freeze.

Pepys's diary makes it clear that, even while the conflagration tore through the city, there was a common belief that 'there is some kind of plot in this'. Many were arrested on suspicion and it soon became dangerous for any stranger to walk in the streets, as they risked being attacked by mobs looking for someone to blame. For example, spectators in Moorfields witnessed a Frenchman attacked by a crowd and almost dismembered, because he carried 'balls of fire' in a chest. They were afterwards found to be tennis balls, but only after the damage to the man had been done. A woman who was seen walking in Moorfields, carrying some young chicks in her apron, was likewise grabbed by a crowd who declared that she was carrying fireballs; she was violently abused and beaten with sticks before her breasts were cut off. Many people blamed the Dutch, as at the time a trade war had developed between the Netherlands and Britain and a significant English victory had lately occurred at sea off the Suffolk coast. Very quickly, any foreign accent became enough to provoke violence, the situation only reined in when the king ordered his officers to pacify the crowds; otherwise, it is possible a wholesale massacre of all foreign nationals might have occurred. Typically, Sir John Southcote was forced to bribe a constable and watchman for the release of a French servant, whose crime had been to be heard talking in broken English.

Before long the public had their scapegoat in the form of 26-year-old Robert Hubert, a French Catholic watchmaker from Rouen in Normandy. He was seized in Essex during an apparent attempt to get out of the country, and thrown into Newgate along with many other foreign nationals. Here, he confessed that he had been hired in France to come to England and commit the arson. Having lately arrived on a Swedish ship called the *Skipper*, Hubert claimed to be personally responsible for setting the first houses on fire along with a mysterious acquaintance called 'Stephen Piedelou'. Piedelou, who had come over with him, apparently headed a force of around twenty-three arsonists. Upon his own confession, Hubert was tried and convicted of arson, although even at the time there appears to have been a growing suspicion among the authorities that he was unbalanced. However, since he persisted in declaring his guilt, and even independently confirmed the seat of the fire to be a bakery in Pudding Lane, he was sentenced to death in October 1666.

Hubert was hanged at Tyburn; afterwards a furious mob of Londoners is said to have obtained possession of his corpse and torn it limb from limb.

An investigative report, which was presented to the House of Commons on 22 January 1667, heard allegations that, 'Notwithstanding the confession of the said Hubert, it was confidently reported the fire in the aforementioned Farryners house began by accident.'

There were enough contradictions in the whole affair for it later to be judged that Hubert might have been an innocent man hanged, although a great deal remains unexplained to this day. He was, apparently, the only one to suffer the penalties of the law as an incendiary; it is unclear whether he sought notoriety, or had lost his mind; or even whether his confession was enforced to provide Londoners with a scapegoat. Pepys investigated the matter himself in February 1667, noting of Hubert's suggestion that he placed an improvised combustible in the bakery window:

> 'The master of the house, who is the King's baker, and his son, and daughter, do all swear there was no such window, and that the fire did not begin thereabouts.'

However, he goes on to add:

> 'The fellow [Hubert], who, though a mopish besotted fellow, did not speak like a madman, [and] did swear that he did fire it.'

Pepys concludes with the observation that 'so horrid an effect should have so mean and uncertain a beginning.'

'I CANNOT PARDON HIM, BECAUSE I DARE NOT'

There were other bloody indictments levelled at the country's so-called 'Merry Monarch'. His controversial execution of the great Scottish statesman, Archibald Campbell, has already been observed. Another terrible stain on Charles II's reputation was the judicial murder of Oliver Plunket, the Catholic Primate of all Ireland, who lost his life due to the intrigues of the era. Arrested in Ireland in connection with an alleged conspiracy against the crown in the wake of the so-called Popish Plot in London, it was Plunket's misfortune to have as an enemy Arthur Capell, the new 1st Earl of Essex, who agitated for Plunket's prosecution in England. One reason for Essex's move was that he wished to regain the position of Lord Lieutenant of Ireland; he hoped that if

Plunket were compromised it would have the knock-on effect of discrediting one of the primate's allies, the current Lord Lieutenant of Ireland, the Duke of Ormond. The anti-Catholic hysteria exhibited in London at this time ensured that Plunket was sentenced to death on suspicion of treason; by the time Essex realised his plotting was going to lead a man to his death, it was too late. Oliver Plunket suffered a traditional traitor's death at Tyburn on 1 July 1681, with the king stating harshly to Essex at the time, 'Then, my lord, be his blood on your own conscience; you might have spared him, if you would; I cannot pardon him, because I dare not.' Charles knew the martyred primate was innocent of the charges against him and had hoped he would be tried in Ireland, subsequently being acquitted. However, once the wheels were set in motion and England's excitable, anti-Catholic Whig politicians had extradited him to London, Plunket was a doomed man. The fact that he was canonised in 1975 stands in evidence of his martyrdom: his head is preserved at Drogheda, and his relics at Downside Abbey in Somerset.

Capell himself did not die a natural death. Having been implicated in the Whig-led 'Rye House Plot' to assassinate the king and his brother James, the earl was two years later imprisoned in the Tower. On the morning of 13 July 1683, a serving-maid poked her head into Capell's cell – known as 'Major Hawley's house' – and discovered his body lying in a small closet room, face down, with one elbow bent near the face, while his legs extended through the doorway. Her screams of 'Murder!' rang through the fortification; the earl's throat was later discovered to have been cut from ear to ear so violently that he had almost been beheaded. His body was drenched in blood and a razor, notched and dripping, was found on the chamber floor, three feet away from the bed. He was aged about 52 at the time of his death.

The coroner's verdict considered Capell's death a suicide, deciding he was suffering from fits of deep melancholy. The decision did not satisfy everyone, particularly when it came to be known that King Charles and his brother the Duke of York had shortly beforehand left the Tower, having arrived at eight o'clock that morning – probably to observe Lord Russell, the principal plotter, leave there on his way to Newgate gaol prior to his trial. The two royals were in fact in the act of sauntering to their barge when a great clamour arose above the wall of the fortification they had just quitted.

The circumstances were questionable enough to provide fodder for those who wished to believe that Capell was murdered by his keeper in the Tower, while the king and duke were present. Indeed, there were several suspicious and contradictory details; the incredible violence done to Capell's neck, the assertion that the razor was too small and ineffectual to have committed the damage, reports of the *actual* murder weapon being thrown out of a different window by a mysterious hand, muddled witnesses who appeared to have been primed, and so on. The balance of probability, however, suggests Capell almost certainly killed himself, despite the rumours. What is missing most is a motive. Charles is said to have been deeply saddened by Capell's death, saying, 'My Lord Essex need not have despaired of mercy, for I owed him a life.' This was a reference to Capell's father, a Royalist who had been executed alongside two other noblemen by Parliament in 1649.

THE HANGING JUDGE
When Algernon Sidney – the republican son of the Earl of Leicester – was tried for his part in the 'Rye House Plot', only one witness appeared against him. The law required two witnesses, so this problem was circumvented by producing some of Sidney's papers, in which he maintained the lawfulness of resisting tyrants. An infamously ruthless judge, Sir George Jeffries, had by now been elevated to the position of Lord Chief Justice and he chose to equate Sidney's writing with the testimony of a living witness. Algernon Sidney was accordingly executed on 7 December 1683, glorying in his own 'martyrdom' for causes he had defended and supported since his earliest youth.

Under Charles's successor, James II, Jeffries became even more notorious; his zeal bordered on murderous. Following the rebellious Duke of Monmouth's crushing at the Battle of Sedgemoor in 1685, Jeffries was sent to the West Country to try captured rebels in the name of King James. His cruelty earned the proceedings the name of the 'Bloody Western Assizes', and the cadavers of executed 'traitors' soon festooned the landscape of western England. Some participants are said to have been summarily executed after the battle, while those sentenced to death by Jeffries numbered in the multiple hundreds. After being discovered hiding in a ditch with only a few peas in his pocket for sustenance, Monmouth himself was conducted to London and beheaded on Tower Hill after being convicted of treason. His execution was notoriously badly botched, the overwhelmed executioner, Ketch, taking multiple blows to decapitate the duke. He allegedly completed the beheading using a knife to saw through the last sinews.

The 'Bloody Assizes' also spread beyond the west. They further commenced at Winchester, where Alice Lisle, a widow of one of the regicides, was condemned for harbouring two rebels named Hicks and Nelthorp, both fugitives from Sedgemoor. Jeffries was determined to sacrifice this innocent, pious and charitable lady, who was upwards of 70 years of age;

Sedgemoor, Somerset, where Monmouth's insurrection was crushed.

he is said to have worked himself up into such a lunatic pitch of frenzy against Nonconformists during the trial that he could hardly have been in a rational state of mind. Alice Lisle became symbolic of the 'Bloody Assizes' and the travesty may be summed up by observing simply that the tribunal was one where the greater crime was committed by Jeffries himself. The widow was denied a trial in London, where many could have appeared in her favour, and solicitations on her behalf to King James II for a pardon fell on deaf ears – his only act of 'mercy' being to change her sentence from one of burning to one of beheading. Alice Lisle was decapitated with an axe in Winchester's market square that September, mourned by many as a martyr who had been judicially murdered.

Among all the trials he oversaw, perhaps Jeffries's single worst abuse of his position concerned the punishment he imposed upon Elizabeth Gaunt. This woman, a London Anabaptist, spent a great part of her life in acts of charity, visiting jails and looking after the poor whatever their religious or political persuasion. She had the misfortune to be sought out by one of the Rye House rebels, called Burton, whom she took into her home. There is, however, a gigantic question mark over how much she knew concerning the treason her new 'lodger' was implicated in. Although she was apparently engaged in sending him out of the kingdom, it is generally agreed she was not privy to any traitorous conspiracy.

Around two years after the Rye House plot, Burton came to hear that King James II had passed a comment to the effect that people who concealed rebels were 'the worst sort of traitors, who endeavoured to preserve such persons to a better time'. To this end, James declared 'he would sooner pardon the rebels'. Burton – in an unbelievable act of two-facedness – handed himself over to the authorities and directed them to Elizabeth Gaunt, naming her as his protector!

Poor Elizabeth was seized and tried for high treason before Judge Jeffries. She was convicted upon the single testimony of her one accuser, the outlawed Burton. Contrary to every principle of justice or humanity, she was condemned to be burnt to death – the traditional punishment for women convicted of this offence.

On 23 October 1685, Mrs Gaunt was tied to a post at Tyburn. Straw was heaped around her body, before this was set afire by the executioner and she was left to burn alive. In her last speech, written and delivered to the keeper of Newgate gaol, Mrs Gaunt observed, 'I am clearly murdered.'

The turmoil of the era would ensure that Jeffries did not die a natural death and that the king in whose name he acted would not have a long reign. When James II and Prince William of Orange joined battle for the throne in 1688, with revolutionary fervour engulfing London, the detested Jeffries disguised himself in the garb of a common seaman, dreading public resentment as he did. His intention was to leave the capital, and it was while he was drinking in a cellar in Wapping on 12 December that he had the misfortune to be recognised by a scrivener. This person had been tried by Jeffries some time before and the experience had so terrified him that it had emblazoned the judge's features upon his mind.

Jeffries, fearing he was recognised, feigned a cough and turned to the wall with a pot of beer in his hand. But the scrivener went out into the street and shouted he had found the 'Hanging Judge'. The mob surged into the alehouse, seizing Jeffries, beating him ferociously and spitting into his face, before carrying him to the Lord Mayor, no doubt in the expectation he would be tried and executed. The Lords of the Council had Jeffries committed to the Tower, where he died of disease at about nine in the morning on 18 April 1689, aged 43. A Jacobite pamphlet would later allege that the Prince of Orange had had Jeffries assassinated by poison, but there is not any great foundation for this, although it is possible the rough treatment he received at the hands of the mob aggravated his death.

The mob violently assaulted the hated judge: engraving by Wade, in Russell's History of England. (Mary Evans Picture Library)

A LINGUISTIC MISUNDERSTANDING?

Following Sir George Barclay's abortive attempt upon the life of King William III in 1696 (see Chapter 2), it emerged that some of the conspirators had early on been in contact with Sir John Fenwick, a prominent opponent of the new Protestant monarch. Fenwick had preferred a Jacobite counter-revolution to assassination – under a French force commanded by the Duke of Berwick, illegitimate son of the exiled James II. But despite his revolutionary tendencies, Fenwick, of Wallington, Northumberland, was a worthy man; he was an MP, responsible for building the Great Hall in Christ's Hospital.

Having been informed upon, Fenwick was caught because he was recognised on the high road while attempting to escape in June 1696. His face had by then become exceedingly well-known, and although he spurred his horse on to the Kentish coast, managing to make it to a safe-house, the authorities were not content to let the most wanted man in England slip away. An enormous search party guarded the lanes of Romney Marsh, beating the thickets and barging into houses until in the end Fenwick was located underneath a bed. His approximate location was accidentally betrayed by a French privateer that sailed close to the shore to rescue him, which was spotted by Kentish fishermen.

In treason cases, more than one witness was required. One of the two proposed witnesses against Fenwick was lured to the Dog tavern in Drury Lane, London, by a cunning and daring adventurer named O'Brien, who had been employed by relatives of several imprisoned conspirators. When the witness – an ex-actor and rumoured highwayman named Cardel Goodman – turned up at the inn, he found O'Brien and another Jacobite waiting for him. They told Goodman he must exile himself – or else they would cut his throat immediately. Goodman consented, and he was thereafter allegedly conducted from London to Saint Germain, France, by O'Brien, who never left his side.

On the afternoon of the day on which Fenwick was examined by the king at Kensington, rumours began to circulate that Goodman – integral to a conviction – had gone missing from his house. He was not to be found at any of his usual haunts and shortly afterwards a decapitated human head was found in a frightfully mangled, unidentifiable state. A great clamour swept London declaring that Goodman had been treacherously murdered by his own former comrades, but it is unclear whether this was the case. Although a proclamation in the *London Gazette* on 9 November 1696 offered £1,000 for the recapture of Cardel Goodman, this went unclaimed; the matter was confused three years later by a claim from the Earl of Manchester, then the

English ambassador in Paris, that Goodman had successfully exiled himself there. Therefore, it is unclear if the beheaded man had been the state's missing witness.

Fenwick was nontheless attainted of high treason and beheaded on Tower Hill on 28 January 1697. Aged 53 when he was executed, he was in effect sentenced by a law made on purpose to stain the scaffold with his blood. After his death, he was interred in St Martin's Church. One informant, George Porter, had illegally sufficed as the principal evidence against him.

It was not this execution, however, that tarnished the usurper's reputation but rather the infamous affair at Glencoe, a scattering of hamlets located in a bleak part of the Scottish Highlands surrounded dramatically by wild and precipitous mountains.

The valley was the seat of the Clan MacDonald, headed by the elderly Alastair Mac Iain. What precipitated the matter was Alastair's failure to swear loyalty to the crown by 1 January 1692. He had in fact attempted this at Fort William, but was there told he should be in Inveraray, some sixty miles to the south, where he eventually swore on 6 January – five days too late. Traditional enemies of the chieftain, such as John Campbell, 1st Earl of Breadalbane and Holland, and John Dalrymple, the Master of Stair and Secretary of State over Scotland, immediately saw an opportunity for revenge against the Clan MacDonald. Alastair Mac Iain was represented to the royal court as an incorrigible Jacobite rebel and a ruffian desensitised to bloodshed who would never adhere to the laws of his country or live peaceably under any sovereign.

An order – signed and countersigned by the king's own hand in London – was issued authorising the subjugation of the Clan MacDonald. Dalrymple next gave out particular and urgent directions to put the inhabitants of Glencoe to the sword for disloyalty. This order charged that no prisoners were to be taken, so that the example might be all the more terrible. Dalrymple was a pro-union Lowlander, who despised many of the Highland clans, considering their way of life backward and detrimental to Scotland's image in Europe. It is also clear that the threat of punishment alone was considered not forceful enough, for the Master of Stair is recorded as having written: 'Better not meddle with them than meddle to no purpose. When the thing is resolved, let it be secret and sudden.'

The horrific outcome of this instruction has entered Scottish folklore, earning Glencoe the names 'the Glen of Sorrow' and 'Glen of Weeping'. Lieutenant Colonel Hamilton, stationed at Fort William, organised a regiment of 120 men headed by Captain Robert Campbell of Glenlyon – himself a sworn enemy of the MacDonalds. However, this man was reportedly a convincing liar who would be somewhat more readily trusted since his niece was married to Alastair's second son Alexander.

On 1 February 1692, the soldiers – who amounted to little more than an assassination squad – marched to Glencoe. Perversely, for twelve days Campbell's contingent of soldiers quartered themselves peaceably among the people of the glen, being fed and looked after, explaining their mission was elsewhere and they were merely passing through. Then, at the prearranged time of five o'clock on the morning of 13 February 1692, the business of repression began.

Captain Robert Campbell began the execution of his duty by seeing to it that his host, a man named Inverriggen, was dragged out of his bed, bound hand and foot and cold-bloodedly murdered. Nine other MacDonalds in the immediate vicinity met the same fate, including a 12-year-old boy who clung to the captain's legs and begged for mercy. Campbell, it is said, ruthless as he was, showed signs of wavering, so a member of the common soldiery named Drummond stepped in and shot the child dead in cold blood.

At the hamlet of 'Auchnaion' (Achnacon) a tacksman named Auchintriator was sitting with eight of his family around a fire, having risen early, when a volley of musket fire was poured into their number, fatally wounding all of them but one – Auchintriator's brother, who caught the soldiers off guard by running at, and then through, their ranks to escape.

Meanwhile, a lieutenant named Lindsay knocked upon the door of old Alastair, and, using friendly language, managed to obtain entry to the chief's house. As the clan leader pulled on his clothes, calling upon his servants to bring refreshments for Lindsay and his men, someone shot him through the head, killing him instantly. Two of his attendants were murdered alongside him. His wife was at the time already up and dressed; the assassins next turned on her, tearing off her clothes and stealing her jewellery. They even stooped to biting her fingers so they could remove her rings; so rough was their treatment of the woman that she died the following day.

However, the assassins made a critical error in using firearms for their first kills, rather than swords, since the crash of gunfire gave notice, from three different parts of the valley at once, that murder was being committed. From dozens of cottages the half-naked peasantry of Glencoe slipped away under the cover of a pre-dawn snowfall into the recesses of the glen, including the sons of Alastair, who were especially marked for assassination. John, in particular, had a close escape after slipping from his dwelling as a detachment of twenty soldiers arrived outside to kill him.

Even today, echoes of the long-ago slaughter at Glencoe can sometimes seem hauntingly close.

Apart from the members of the clan who had been cold-bloodedly murdered, huge numbers of the fugitives are believed to have perished in the snowy conditions through hunger, cold and lack of shelter. All in all, between seventy and eighty people are thought to have died in the 'Glencoe Massacre', with approximately the same number having survived through good fortune rather than any strategic planning. Even then, the survivors might have wished they had perished, for they scratched a miserable living for years afterwards in an attempt to survive as a clan.

News of this atrocity took some time to filter out, and even then, there were differing versions. However, by slow degrees the grim truth began to emerge. Since the atrocity had been all the more shocking for its treacherous and almost unprecedented breach of hospitality, a 1695 Commission, led by privy councillors in Edinburgh, found little hesitation in pointing the finger of blame squarely at the Master of Stair, John Dalrymple. However, there was little punishment it could inflict, despite the culpable parties being clearly evident.

This was for the most part due to King William having originally authorised the execution order that precipitated the massacre, although it is generally agreed he was entirely ignorant of the finer details in the document he signed. Although the wording had been quite clear – the cause would be a 'vindication of public justice to extirpate that set of thieves' – it is possible that the king, whose English was imperfect, was unaware of the awesome ramifications of what he was signing. He certainly appeared as shocked as anyone later on when it emerged how violently 'his' orders had been carried out.

For his part, Captain Robert Campbell is said to have become a man deeply troubled by guilt, perpetually haunted by his conscience. Of particular interest is the account of Charles Leslie, an Irishman living in London, who encountered Lord Argyle's regiment when they were quartered in Brentford on 30 June 1692. Leslie spoke with a Highlander who had been at the massacre, who told him, 'Glencoe hangs about [Campbell] night and day, and you may see *him* in his face.' Robert Campbell was apparently present during part of this interview. Leslie later published an account of the atrocity, called *Gallienus Redivivus, or murder will out*.

The Master of Stair, John Dalrymple, felt neither fear nor remorse, however. One of his letters declares, 'Do right, and fear nobody; can there be a more sacred duty than to rid the country of thieving? *The only thing that I regret is that any got away.*'

Afterword

There is so much that has had to be left unexplored. Certain *cause celebres*, for example, gripped the public imagination and were never quite resolved to everyone's satisfaction, as in the case of Captain Spencer Cowper, a barrister-at-law whose trial at Hertford in 1699 for the murder of Sarah Stout polarised opinion. Some cases attracted no controversy, however, and merely reflect the violent impulses that overtook people, such as the fatal shooting in Edinburgh in 1689 of Scotland's foremost civil affairs judge, Sir George Lockhart, by a disgruntled claimant in one of his cases. Some abuses reinforce how intolerant society was, such as the brutal, violent persecutions of the early Quakers; while many instances highlight the sad losses sustained by the political or artistic sphere thanks to London's perpetual state of disorder. Typically, the violent killing of a promising young actor called Hildebrand Horden in Covent Garden's Rose Tavern saddened not only the stage but also mortified female theatre-goers, many of whom turned up wearing masks to tearfully view his shrouded corpse in 1696. Some cases retain fascinating elements of mystery, such as the chance discovery of a dying, fatally shot man called William Brearcliffe out on remote Gunnerton Fell, Northumberland, in 1689. But while Brearcliffe's murder has almost slipped from the pages of history, numerous other cases have entered regional folklore. The decline of John Fitz, of Fitzford House, Tavistock, into murder and insanity, for example, features in many Devon guidebooks to this day; while the notorious T-shaped double gibbet standing on Inkpen Hill, West Berkshire, serves as an ever-present reminder of the execution of two murderous lovers, George Bromman and Dorothy Newman, in 1676. Finally, some cases were simply strange. Consider the cold-blooded murder of Anne Walker, whose repeated appearances from beyond the grave forced the trial and execution of her two killers at Durham in 1631.

Hopefully what we have looked at, however, has illustrated the struggling state of law and order in Britain throughout the seventeenth century. What is truly astonishing about the century we have just explored, and to understand some context, is that in the case of England, her population is believed to have been between four and five million – less than one tenth of what it is today. With this in mind, the murder rate suddenly seems that much greater.

Particularly so when we learn that, of this figure, around 200,000, or one in every 25, died during the civil wars, or of effects directly related to the conflict. This doesn't even take into account Scotland, where the losses were also immense – and aggravated by the prolonged Killing Times that outstripped the conclusion of the wars. At the very least, it illustrates how far the nation has come since those turbulent times, for it must be remembered that a police force as we would understand the term was still generations away.

Inkpen's double gibbet in the 1920s. (Mary Evans/ Grenville Collins Postcard Collection)

Index